Praise for *The Financial Times Guide to Starting a Business*

"A must read for anyone starting a business. Mike's straight-talking approach is refreshing – and so bloody useful. He has so much experience to share..."

Nigel Botterill, Founder, Entrepreneurs Circle

His knowledge is broad, unfailing and generously shared, in fact I've found working with him so helpful that I take him with me when I move from job to job!

For those of you who can't access Mike in person then get this book and have a little bit (or quite a lot) of his business wisdom right there on your shelf. It really will prove invaluable as you navigate your start up journey.

Elizabeth J. Cameron – Senior Enterprise Advisor, University of Bristol

The UK remains a great place to start a business and all start-ups need a bit of help as they embark on their entrepreneurial journey. This guide is a great addition to a founder's support suitcase.

Emma Jones CBE, Founder, Enterprise Nation and Small Business Commissioner for the UK government

Mike covers all the essential considerations (even the ones entrepreneurs often find dull!) in a way that's both insightful and thoroughly enjoyable. He presents the reality of starting a business without ever losing the excitement that comes with it.

Andy Pringle, Start Your Own Business (syob.net)

I've been working closely with Mike for over a year in supporting business owners looking to grow through our Masterplan programme. Mike brings a wealth of experience which means he's able to look at the bigger picture and ask the right questions of the owner, so that they can clearly understand their strategic direction, as well as the actionable steps they need to undertake to get there. I've read thousands of business books, but what makes this Guide so valuable and unique is how Mike balances the importance of you as the Owner and Leader from Mindset, Vision and Purpose, with the practical how-to advice on all aspects of setting up a business from insurance and taxation through to legal considerations and premises. Mike openly shares all his experience and knowledge so that the reader comes away with complete confidence, inspiration and invigoration.

Martin Norbury, Scale Expert & Author of *I don't work Fridays*

THE FINANCIAL TIMES GUIDE TO STARTING A BUSINESS

THE COMPREHENSIVE GUIDE FOR ENTREPRENEURS

MIKE FOSTER

Harlow, England • London • New York • Boston • San Francisco • Toronto • Sydney
Dubai • Singapore • Hong Kong • Tokyo • Seoul • Taipei • New Delhi
Cape Town • São Paulo • Mexico City • Madrid • Amsterdam • Munich • Paris • Milan

PEARSON EDUCATION LIMITED
KAO Two
KAO Park
Harlow CM17 9NA
United Kingdom
Tel: +44 (0)1279 623623
Web: www.pearson.com

First edition published 2026 (print and electronic)

© Pearson Education Limited 2026 (print and electronic)

The right of Mike Foster to be identified as author of this work has been asserted by him in accordance with the Copyright, Designs and Patents Act 1988.

The print publication is protected by copyright. Prior to any prohibited reproduction, storage in a retrieval system, distribution or transmission in any form or by any means, electronic, mechanical, recording or otherwise, permission should be obtained from the publisher or, where applicable, a licence permitting restricted copying in the United Kingdom should be obtained from the Copyright Licensing Agency Ltd, Barnard's Inn, 86 Fetter Lane, London EC4A1EN.

The ePublication is protected by copyright and must not be copied, reproduced, transferred, distributed, leased, licensed or publicly performed or used in any way except as specifically permitted in writing by the publishers, as allowed under the terms and conditions under which it was purchased, or as strictly permitted by applicable copyright law. Any unauthorised distribution or use of this text may be a direct infringement of the authors' and the publisher's rights and those responsible may be liable in law accordingly.

All trademarks used herein are the property of their respective owners. The use of any trademark in this text does not vest in the author or publisher any trademark ownership rights in such trademarks, nor does the use of such trademarks imply any affiliation with or endorsement of this book by such owners.

Pearson Education is not responsible for the content of third-party internet sites.

ISBN: 978-1-292-48376-4 (print)
        978-1-292-75161-0 (ePub)

British Library Cataloguing-in-Publication Data
A catalogue record for the print edition is available from the British Library

Library of Congress Cataloging-in-Publication Data
A catalog record for the print edition is available from the Library of Congress

10 9 8 7 6 5 4 3 2 1
30 29 28 27 26

Cover design by Michelle Morgan

Print edition typeset in 9.5/14pt Stone Serif ITC Pro by Straive
Printed in the UK by Bell and Bain Ltd, Glasgow

NOTE THAT ANY PAGE CROSS REFERENCES REFER TO THE PRINT EDITION

THE FINANCIAL TIMES GUIDE TO STARTING A BUSINESS

Pearson

At Pearson, we believe in learning – all kinds of learning for all kinds of people. Whether it's at home, in the classroom or in the workplace, learning is the key to improving our life chances.

That's why we're working with leading authors to bring you the latest thinking and best practices, so you can get better at the things that are important to you. You can learn on the page or on the move, and with content that's always crafted to help you understand quickly and apply what you've learned.

If you want to upgrade your personal skills or accelerate your career, become a more effective leader or more powerful communicator, discover new opportunities or simply find more inspiration, we can help you make progress in your work and life.

Every day our work helps learning flourish, and wherever learning flourishes, so do people.

To learn more, please visit us at **www.pearson.com**

The Financial Times

With a worldwide network of highly respected journalists, *The Financial Times* provides global business news, insightful opinion and expert analysis of business, finance and politics. With over 500 journalists reporting from 50 countries worldwide, our in-depth coverage of international news is objectively reported and analysed from an independent, global perspective.

To find out more, visit **www.ft.com**

CONTENTS

Author's acknowledgements	viii
About the author	ix
Introduction	x

1	How to build your entrepreneurial mindset	1
2	Are *you* ready to start up?	35
3	Planning your business	65
4	How to understand your numbers	125
5	How to market your business	159
6	How to boost sales	219
7	How to maximise profit and price right	237
8	How to build the right team	253
9	How to exceed your customers' expectations	283
10	Scaling your start-up for growth	311
11	What to do next	333

Index	335

AUTHOR'S ACKNOWLEDGEMENTS

Thank you to everyone I've worked with and those in my network who have supported my journey. This book is a combination of our interactions and conversations that each day has built my knowledge, experience and expertise.

ABOUT THE AUTHOR

Mike Foster is an experienced, strategic business coach and mentor who has supported hundreds of business owners to start, develop, scale and grow.

Having managed a team of business start-up managers for a high-street bank, he went on to help a start-up leisure business spinning out of the district council.

Mike has started and developed six of his own businesses and sold three, before moving into a mentoring role in 2013.

INTRODUCTION

Welcome to the exciting journey of starting your own business!

This book is designed to be your comprehensive guide, filled with practical advice, proven strategies and inspirational insights to help you transform your idea into a successful business.

Starting a business is an exhilarating journey filled with opportunities, challenges and the promise of personal and financial growth. In today's rapidly evolving marketplace, aspiring entrepreneurs are more empowered than ever to turn their ideas into reality. It is one of the most rewarding yet challenging endeavours you can undertake. Some say it is simple but it's not easy. Of course, if it was the easy answer, then everyone would be doing it and doing it well! It requires a blend of vision, perseverance and practical know-how. Throughout this book, I will share my experiences and the lessons I've learned from over a decade of running my own businesses and supporting or mentoring hundreds of clients. My aim is to provide you with the tools and confidence you need to navigate the complexities of entrepreneurship, whilst providing the content to fuel or spark your thoughts and ideas or cover the questions you did not know how to answer.

We will cover everything from refining your business idea and developing a solid plan, to marketing your services effectively, managing finances and building a team that exceeds your customers' expectations. Each chapter is practical, based on proven models and structured to guide you step-by-step, ensuring you build a strong foundation and avoid those common pitfalls experienced by many start-up business owners.

This book will develop your thinking, help you understand what it takes to start a business and survive those statistically difficult initial years. The content is a balance of guiding material and thought-provoking examples of what has worked for other early stage entrepreneurs. You will learn models, be challenged and develop a solid foundation from which to develop the business you want. This is a book to support your lifelong learning skills, to develop your critical thinking, independence, sustainability and entrepreneurialism.

The entrepreneurial spirit

At the heart of every successful start-up lies the entrepreneurial spirit – a blend of creativity, resilience, and a willingness to take calculated risks. Whether you're a seasoned professional looking to pivot into entrepreneurship or a passionate newcomer with a groundbreaking idea, this book will help you harness that spirit and channel it into actionable steps. We will explore the mindset required to thrive in the start-up ecosystem, emphasising the importance of adaptability, continuous learning and networking.

Practical frameworks and strategies

Throughout this book, you will find practical frameworks and strategies that can be applied at every stage of your start-up journey – from ideation to launch and beyond. Each chapter is designed to provide you with actionable insights and proven models, ensuring that you can implement what you learn immediately.

Your journey begins here

As you embark on this journey, remember that every successful entrepreneur started with a single step. This book aims to demystify the start-up process, providing you with the confidence and knowledge to take that step. The principles outlined in this book will serve as your roadmap as we explore the exciting world of business start-ups.

Let's unlock the potential of your ideas and transform them into a successful business.

The table of contents provides a natural flow of considerations to help you build the strategic and tactical business plan for your business:

Introduction

1. How to build your entrepreneurial mindset
2. Are *you* ready to start up?

3   Planning your business
4   How to understand your numbers
5   How to market your business
6   How to boost sales
7   How to maximise profit and price right
8   How to build the right team
9   How to exceed your customers' expectations
10 Scaling your start-up for growth
11 What to do next

This book will reference laws, rules, best practice and tax regulations, but as an international guide we recommend that you always seek guidance from local professional advisers to understand your local laws and policies wherever you are located.

> **Remember this**
>
> **Have belief and persevere**
>
> 'If you do not believe in yourself then nobody will.'
>
> We will all experience a situation that could rock our self-belief, but it is one thing as an entrepreneur that has to be core to your personality.
>
> The world of business is not a smooth path towards your goals. There will be times you need to pick yourself up, dust yourself down and move forward again, which of course your self-belief can hugely influence.
>
> Our attitude impacts our actions, our actions impact our results and our results impact our belief. Then our belief impacts our attitude, and the cycle repeats itself.
>
> I encourage you to persevere with the right activities to achieve the success you strive for.
>
> So, never give up but do review regularly as it is pointless persevering in the wrong direction.

Action planner			
Action	Person responsible	Deadline	Completed

Complete this planner as you work through the chapters.

What action needs to be executed, by who and by when?

CHAPTER 1
HOW TO BUILD YOUR ENTREPRENEURIAL MINDSET

In this chapter, we will be exploring the importance of having a mindset that keeps you focused on the right things, on the future as much as the present, and how resilience will play a big role during your entrepreneurial journey.

This will check in and reflect on your purpose, your motivation, your thoughts and your thinking.

Ten reasons to run your own business

Deciding to start your own business is normally the result of several triggers that have made you finally say – 'that's it, I need to do something myself!'

You may be approaching that point now, or you may have taken the leap a year or so ago. Here are 10 top reasons for starting your own business. Do you resonate with any? Such reasons often provide the motivation to go for it or remind you why you did it in the first place.

1 **An opportunity to make a change for the better**
    Trigger points ... It could be a slow burning feeling that you can provide a better or more ethical service in the same industry as your employer, or it might be a sudden realisation that you're spending time away from family and missing out on important personal goals.

    Whatever it is, you know you can make a change for the better by becoming your own boss and starting your business.

2 **Gain control over your career and job security**
   Running a business and gaining customers isn't risk free, but it is exciting. You choose your hours, days and customers. You choose your networking opportunities, the social media you use and when to take time off.

   Because you're in control of your own career and no longer beholden to someone else's 'why', you will always be motivated to maintain that job security. That means every day will be motivating!

3 **Pursue your passion, your way**
   That niggling feeling of 'can I really make a career out of this?' will always be with you unless you give it a chance. Your passion will never leave you; you have the chance to make it a bigger part of your life. How does the saying go? If you love your work, you never work a single day, or something like that.

4 **Support non-profits, get involved in social issues or help solve community problems**
   One of the most fulfilling things about running your own business is that you can choose where to direct your profits. You can do this by spending time in a volunteer role that your previous employment wouldn't have allowed for, or by pledging to donate a percentage of profits each year. This is another example of taking control.

5 **Give your clients or customers the practical help they're looking for**
   Untie your hands and help who you want, when you want! You have a wealth of knowledge and understanding that is highly valuable to your network. You can choose what to charge and what to give away for free. It's really quite liberating.

6 **Achieve financial independence**
   This doesn't necessarily happen quickly, but it does happen if you work at it, lay clear plans and stay focused on the numbers to achieve your goals.

   If you aspire to build wealth, you can. As you grow your business, the more valuable it becomes as an asset. You could plan to sell the business down the line, retire from it whilst still taking a wage, or pass it on to a family member. Either way, it's valuable.

7 **The tax benefits**
You'll need to ask an accountant or financial planner to help you make sure you set your business up in the right way to be rewarded with certain tax breaks.

Before your business turns a profit, you can take advantage of tax incentives from the early days. Ask your expert adviser about the best way to take your income. It is often a mindset barrier for many leaving a corporate role until you establish how much less income you could take from a business compared to being in an employed role with a salary but have the same net cash to spend!

8 **Develop your expertise in a broad range of roles**
Your current job may not be what you excel at. Running your own business allows you to explore your skillset more freely and identify where you add most value to your own business. You don't need to do everything all the time but, certainly in the early days, you will quickly gain insight into all aspects of business. Later, you'll know which jobs to delegate or outsource to specialist businesses and which ones you want to continue doing yourself.

9 **Let your creativity flow**
It's your decision what products and services to offer, how to develop them, who to bring into the business alongside you and how to market them.

You could become a social media wizard or an expert blog writer. You may have a talent for graphic design that was never really used before because it wasn't in your job description.

Enjoy the opportunity to make something your own, be innovative and get creative with your business.

10 **Set your own culture**
The culture of work environments can be finely balanced. Some are outright toxic whilst some are far too informal. Did you embrace the culture of your last employer? Did the tone of voice align with your own? Was there enough support, leadership, guidance, encouragement, communication? All these things come into play with business culture, and you get to set the tone. What kind of business owner do you want to be?

Take a moment to reflect on *why* you are starting a business.

The entrepreneur mindset

Entrepreneur *(noun, by definition)*: 'A person who sets up a business or businesses, taking on financial risks in the hope of profit.' An entrepreneur is not just someone who is cavalier with their approach or owning multiple businesses, they are someone who has taken a risk. A calculated risk or just the risk of starting a business. Very soon, that could be *you*!

Let's start with mindset. Life often does not play out as we expect, and your entrepreneurial journey will have ups and downs along the way. The Entrepreneur Mindset is a way of thinking that enables you to be resilient, overcome challenges, be decisive and accept responsibility for your outcomes. It is a constant need to improve skills, learn from mistakes and take consistent action on ideas.

How many of these key characteristics of an entrepreneur mindset do you currently have?

- **Visionary thinking**: the ability to see opportunities where others see obstacles and to envision the future potential of an idea or business.
- **Resilience**: maintaining a positive attitude and perseverance through setbacks and failures.
- **Innovative and creative thinking**: continuously looking for new solutions, improvements and ways to differentiate in the marketplace.

- **Risk tolerance**: being comfortable with taking calculated risks and making decisions without always having all the answers.
- **Adaptability**: the ability to pivot and adapt to changing circumstances and market conditions.
- **Proactiveness**: taking the initiative and being action-oriented, rather than waiting for opportunities to come and reacting.
- **Learning orientation**: a commitment to continuous learning and personal development, viewing challenges as opportunities to grow.
- **Focus and discipline**: staying focused on goals and maintaining discipline to follow through on plans and tasks.
- **Resourcefulness**: efficiently using the various resources available and finding ways to overcome limitations or constraints.
- **Network and collaborative**: building strong relationships and leveraging networks for support, advice and partnership opportunities.

Cultivating an entrepreneur mindset involves nurturing these traits and applying them to daily decision making and problem solving in the pursuit of business goals.

From my experience and from working with or observing entrepreneurs for over 30 years, here are some mindset tips:

- **Success can only be defined by you** – unlike others, this book will not define success for you. It may be having a business with one million of revenue but, more importantly, you have to define what success means to you. For many entrepreneurs that I have worked with, it often influences your time, money and choices in life, but do you have clarity for yourself?
- **Don't wait for perfection, just get started with your activity** – a common trait is the desire to get it 'right' (perfect) before releasing it. For example, the website, the direct mail letter, the offer. It will 'never' be perfect, and this mindset often results in things never happening and fuelling procrastination.
- **Every outcome presents us with a lesson** – embrace failure as a learning opportunity. Understand that setbacks and failures are a natural part of the entrepreneurial journey. Instead of viewing them as defeats, see them as valuable learning experiences that provide insights and lessons to improve and grow. This mindset shift helps build resilience and encourages continuous improvement.

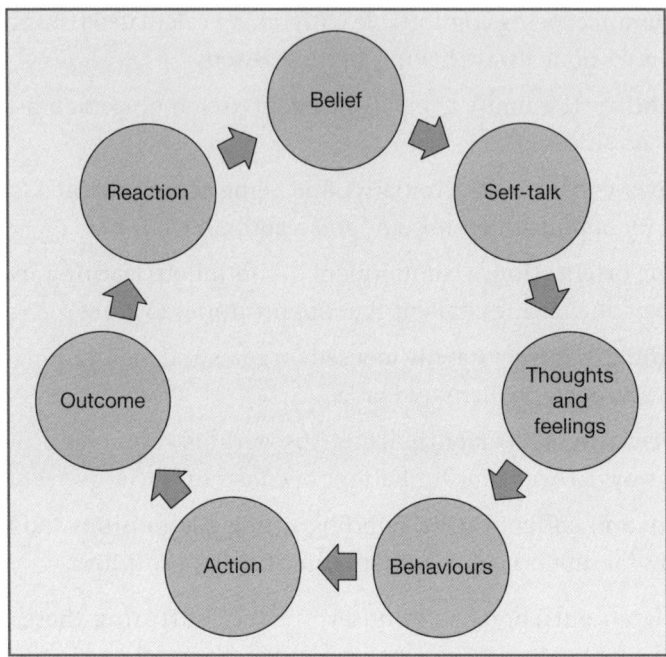

- **Many things in business often come back to a number** – for many entrepreneurs, the word 'numbers' presents a moment of fear or discomfort. The book will later cover some of the key considerations around your numbers but, from a mindset perspective, reflect to see how often an activity comes back to a number.

- **Sell emotions not the product or service** – engage with your prospects at an emotional level. Many businesses convert their features to benefits but then fail to relate these to their prospect or audience. Here are some examples where brands sell with emotion. Nike don't sell trainers, they sell motivation. Amazon don't sell packages or logistics but convenience. Disney is not about what is at each park but selling memories. Apple is not tech or gadgets but trends. Whilst Ferrari is not just a car it's the status.

- **Surround yourself with good people that fuel your energy and mindset** – most things in life are easier with the right support and that is the same when you run a business. For those moments when you need support, motivation and encouragement, then it helps to have the right people around you. This is likely to be a combination of your friends, family, partner and advisers.

- **Stay focused on your high pay-off activities (HPAs)** – keep your long-term goals and vision at the forefront of your mind. This focus will guide your decision making and help you stay motivated, even when faced with challenges. Regularly remind yourself why you started and what you aim to achieve and use this vision as a driving force to overcome obstacles and keep your diary dedicated to those HPAs, those things that move you forward and need your focus without distraction.
- **Be adaptable and open to change** – the business landscape constantly evolves, and being adaptable is crucial for success. Stay open to new ideas, be willing to pivot your strategies when necessary, and continuously seek innovative solutions to stay ahead of the curve. Your flexibility and a willingness to change can help you navigate uncertainties and seize new opportunities.

> ## Remember this
> ### Understand the personalities around you
>
> It is so important to know the personalities around you and the impact they can have on you and your business.
>
> Many successful entrepreneurs will comment on how important it is to have good people around you. However, this is much more than ensuring you have the skills around you to ensure the tasks you need doing are effectively completed.
>
> You should truly understand the behavioural style and personality of those individuals. Does their personality interact with yours? How does their personality suit you and your business? What do you have to do or change to ensure you get the best from other personalities? Who is likely to stab you in the back or who is likely to go over the fence into battle with you and not leave you wounded?
>
> An individual's behavioural style will impact on how they like to work, the pace at which they like to work, how they like to receive the information, how they interact with others and how they deliver the work.
>
> Truly understanding the behavioural style of individuals will help you lead, manage and drive the best results from your people.

Your strong reason why

Are you familiar with Simon Sinek's business theory, 'Start with why'?

If you're not someone who is familiar with this, I would recommend joining the multi-million-strong audience who have made his TED Talk one of the most popular ever produced! Start With Why on TED.com.[1]

If you are familiar with it, I encourage you to get laser focused on your 'why'.

The reason we are exploring your strong reason why is to bring it to the forefront of your thinking, to make sure you hold it in your vision and refer back to it as an aid to making decisions in your business.

How your why affects your business

> 'Fulfilment comes when we live our lives on purpose …'
>
> – Simon Sinek[2]

Do you have a strong reason why you do what you do? Why you work the hours you do, why you stay late, or why you sometimes compromise on other things you'd like to be doing?

As an example, one 'why' is to earn enough money to afford a mortgage on a larger house. Why do you need a bigger house? *So a home office can be set up.* Why do you need a home office? *So I can run a business from home.* Why are you running a business from home? *So I can be available for family needs/so I have more control over my work life.*

When you answer the question on your 'why', go deeper until you get to the root of your purpose. In this example, the reason why is not getting a bigger house, it's actually achieving a better work life. And incidentally, we can now identify other things that can be done to improve that work life which all drive you closer to your reason why.

It demonstrates that for many of us our business goals and personal goals have to be aligned. In this example, we want a better work life as the outcome, and the bigger house is part of the equation. However, our business goals now have

---

[1] Sinek, S. (2009) 'Start with why: How great leaders inspire action'. TEDxPugetSound, Puget Sound, WA, 18 September. Available at: https://www.ted.com/talks/simon_sinek_how_great_leaders_inspire_action?language=en.

[2] Sinek, S. Facebook. See: https://www.facebook.com/simonsinek/posts/most-of-us-live-our-lives-by-accident-we-live-it-as-it-happens-fulfillment-comes/10151791723221499/.

to align in order that the profits are generated and the business creates the available cash for you to buy and maintain that bigger house. Thus, the business goals for delivering this become purposeful and fuel your motivation.

Got it?

Keeping your reason why in focus helps you shape your business in many ways. It influences strategies, culture, decision making, growth plans, relationships and many more factors.

Using your why to help you stay on track

The next shiny thing can easily distract you from your original purpose. It might look like a shortcut or be something else you're passionate about. But can it help get you closer to your why? If the answer is no, let it go.

Stay focused on that why, and it will influence everything you do and how you do it.

Imagine you've been asked to shoot a clay pigeon down from the sky, but you can't clearly see the clay, and you don't know when it will be passing. You'd be tempted to start firing into the sky without judgement or precision. However, if you can see it clearly, focus on it well and you know when it will appear, you're more likely to hit it, and hit it sooner, saving ammunition too!

What is your motivation?

What are your motives? What drives you?

Some motives that may help your thoughts:

I want/need to:

- earn enough money to support my desired lifestyle
- provide for a family
- a sense of achievement
- exploit a gap in the market
- have freedom and flexibility during my working day
- be seen as successful and respected by my family and friends
- influence the environment.

There are a number of personal reasons why people start their own business. Some see an opportunity, some suffer a personal situation such as redundancy or unemployment, whilst others have a family history of self-employment or consider it as a way of earning their living.

Considering your true motivations can help you think about the goals you may set yourself and provides a measurement for success as defined by you and not as defined by others looking at your business externally.

Success means different things to different people. You need to define what success means for you and this will certainly help you to find the ways to achieve it. If you do not know what you are aiming for it is unlikely you will ever achieve it.

Understanding your motivations will help you identify the real purpose of your business and its aims and objectives. Motivations such as 'I simply do not want to work for someone else any more' are not strong enough on their own. If you are struggling, add that question 'Why?' and keep drilling to the detail.

You should also consider planning your exit from day one. It will have to happen to all of us at some point and I seriously hope that is not on your death bed. You need to have a vision of your exit from the business, so that you get the timing right for you. Too often business owners say my business is my retirement nest egg but, in reality, when they come to retire it may not be the right time to sell, or the value may not be as expected. Consider the need to groom successors and how to exit at your chosen time, not when other pressures may dictate. Then plan your business to build towards that exit plan. If you want to sell for a price of £250,000 in 25 years' time, what do you have to achieve in the meantime to get there? Possible exit options include: your family succession, selling the business, flotation of the business, a merger or simply closing down the business.

Thinking about your motivations can help you think about the goals you are setting yourself and provides a measurement for success as defined by you. Success means different things to different people. You need to define it for you to help find the ways to achieve it.

Knowing your true motivation can also help you make key business decisions in the future.

You may also find it useful to create a vision board. A pin board with pictures or references that remind you of your why, what you want to gain and your motivators.

Take a moment to think about your motivators, your why, your purpose, the reasons you get out of bed each day to do your thing …

> ### Remember this
> **Truly understand your motivation**
>
> Know your true motivation for running your business and keep that motivation in mind when presented with situations that require a decision.
>
> Entrepreneurs spend time considering their vision and objectives and planning the direction they want to take. They then have to be given a very good reason to be deflected from that route.

The human brain

Of course, your mindset is fuelled by your thoughts, so it's not you it's your brain!

Did you know that:

The human brain can process 11 million bits of information every second. But our conscious minds can handle only 50 bits of information a second. The distance between 50 and 11 million is where unconscious bias resides.

Our subconscious influences our behaviour even though we don't realise it!

But of course you are still in control.

The control of your mindset is just one reason why planning, action lists, scorecards and accountability work so well. These activities or tools place all your business-critical information on your subconscious mind and that's where those great ideas come from! Hence, why those best ideas often come in the shower, on a drive, during exercise or whilst on holiday.

The human brain plays a crucial role in business by influencing decision making, problem solving, creativity and interpersonal interactions. Allow your subconscious mind time to work. Fuel it with the right things such as your environment, your key data, the people you hang out with and what you watch, read or listen to.

The human brain is a complex and powerful organ that controls all aspects of our thoughts, behaviours and bodily functions.

The four key functional parts of the brain are:

1. Frontal lobe: involved in decision making, problem solving, planning, emotional regulation and voluntary movement.
2. Parietal lobe: processes sensory information such as touch, temperature and pain, and is involved in spatial orientation and body awareness.
3. Temporal lobe: responsible for processing auditory information, memory and language comprehension.
4. Occipital lobe: primarily involved in visual processing.

You only have one brain, so use it well and for the 'right things' for your responsibilities. We know that the brain can hold an incredible amount of information, but often it's not the place for everything. Get things out of your head, into the business system and maximise its power to solve your challenges and find your improvements.

Understanding how your brain works will help you optimise mental processes, improve decision making, be creative and enhance your emotional intelligence, ultimately leading to better business outcomes.

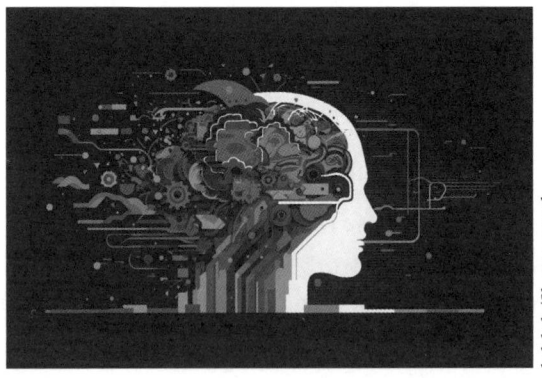

Identify your high pay-off activities (HPAs)

HPAs are those things that move you forward and need your focus without distraction. They are tasks or actions that directly contribute to achieving significant results and moving the business closer to its goals. These activities typically yield the highest return on investment in terms of time, effort and resources. They often need your leadership if not your involvement.

HPAs typically follow the Pareto Principle, where roughly 80 per cent of outcomes come from 20 per cent of efforts. For example, the common focus areas for HPAs are strategic planning, customer acquisition and retention, product development, innovation, relationships (internal and external), your talent development, market awareness, data management and process improvement. Focusing on these high pay-off activities helps ensure that your efforts are directed towards the most impactful areas, leading to sustainable business growth and success.

To maximise the impact of your HPAs, look to:

1 **Identify and prioritise:** focus on critical tasks and determine which activities contribute most to your business goals, deliver the most value or have the greatest impact on your business success.
2 **Delegate or automate low-value tasks:** free up time to focus on HPAs by outsourcing or finding efficient ways to handle less critical tasks.
3 **Protect your time for HPAs:** as they are often not seen as the day to day, it is easy to prioritise those things that grab your attention today. Create focused time blocks for your HPAs (e.g. x mins per day, per week), minimise distractions and reduce your interruptions.
4 **Regularly review and adjust:** continuously assess which activities are producing the best results and adapt your focus accordingly.

By concentrating on HPAs, you can increase productivity, efficiency and overall success, ensuring that time and resources are invested in the areas that yield the greatest returns.

Additionally, when you are focused on your HPAs and what needs your true time and attention, then it is much easier to identify the interruptions and distractions. Those moments when you are sucked back into the 'weeds' of your business or firefighting with the mindset that I'll do it now as I'll be better, quicker, right!

As you identify interruptions and distractions that are suffocating your time for HPAs then stop, reflect and identify what should be automated, delegated or outsourced and therefore reduce or avoid the repetition in the future.

What do you need to focus on next without distraction?

Beat imposter syndrome in your business

Many entrepreneurial business owners have an imposter in their shadow, on their shoulder, in the background. It may be something you've lived with for a very long time and not even realised it constituted imposter syndrome.

How do you know if it's imposter syndrome, and not self-preservation?

Self-preservation is about assessing risks and choosing to take the ones that you believe are achievable. You may take risks you feel are further from your grasp and go for it anyway or you may decide it's too risky. The difference between this and imposter syndrome is the way you speak to yourself, and why you make that decision. In the case of self-preservation, you take calculated risks and make your decision in favour of your wellbeing.

If you suffer imposter syndrome, you may be familiar with sentiments like these:

> 'When something bad happens, it's all I can focus on.'
>
> 'I dwell on mistakes I've made and find it hard to move on.'
>
> 'I always seem to assume the worst could happen.'

'I'm not doing as well as I could.'

'For sure it's not going to work, so why start.'

'I don't think people would listen anyway.'

Are you serving your imposter, or your wellbeing?

Often, we choose unhelpful behaviour because we're responding to a situation based on how it is making us feel. We often act to avoid unpleasant or difficult emotions by purposely avoiding a situation.

However, emotions do not necessarily reflect reality or fact.

We may blow things out of proportion, focus on the negative, jump to conclusions, label ourselves or react to certain words (e.g. what we 'should', 'must' or 'have to' do.)

Tactics for beating imposter syndrome

Here are some thoughts that may help you challenge or reposition the way you're thinking or reacting to circumstances, situations or certain people:

- Be realistic. Does anybody go through life without making mistakes or poor decisions?
- You can get a bad review occasionally yet still be successful.
- Get a little perspective. Ask yourself if you're exaggerating. Is it really always true?
- Get balance in your assumptions. Be fair and realistic.
- Challenge your thinking immediately by asking yourself what else could be happening and are you letting the negative unbalance the reality?
- Consider what evidence there is to support or contradict your negative thought. Test your predictions or assumptions.
- The past doesn't determine the future. Just because you had a negative experience last time doesn't mean it will happen again.
- Be flexible in your thinking. Replace 'should', 'must' and 'have to' with alternatives such as 'could', 'prefer', 'wish' or 'would like to'.
- Embrace imperfection.
- Try not to let one bad moment spoil a whole day of good work. Look at what else you've achieved!

If you still feel your unsettling thoughts are fair and accurate, consider ways to cope or other possible outcomes to protect your wellbeing.

Here are some useful questions to ask yourself:

- If it is true, what's the worst outcome to overcome?
- What is the most realistic?
- If this does turn out to be true, what can I do to cope or manage the situation?
- How have I coped in the past with similar things?
- How would I advise a friend, if they were in the same situation?

Remember this

Become immune to criticism

Entrepreneurs rarely let someone else's disapproval get them down or keep them from moving towards their goals.

As you are seen to be successful or are doing things better than others, you are likely to face criticism. Unfortunately, it is human nature.

You could listen, allow the criticism to impact on your outlook and even change your previously clear direction. Alternatively, hear any detail in the words, but importantly do not engage with the emotion.

Ask yourself if there is something to learn from the words or just something to ignore and continue your journey.

In his book, *No B.S. Business Success in the New Economy*, the respected Dan Kennedy says: 'To succeed as an entrepreneur, you must set aside your neediness for acceptance of others. Immunity to criticism is a "secret" shared by all highly successful entrepreneurs that I know.'[3]

It is not easy, because any entrepreneur is passionate about their business, product or service and is therefore likely to take such criticism personally.

---

[3] Kennedy, D. S. (2010). *No B.S. Business Success in the New Economy*. Entrepreneur Press.

Understanding and overcoming fear and trauma

Fear and trauma are powerful forces that can, and often, shape our lives and influence our actions, often subconsciously.

We might find ourselves bending over backwards to please others, avoiding conflict at all costs, or fearing rejection so strongly that it prevents us from executing required or desired activities. These reactions, though rooted in survival, can become barriers that hold many of us back. Trauma, too, can impact us deeply, both personally and professionally, influencing the way we see ourselves and the world around us. How we act and how we react.

Fear: false expectations appearing real

Fear often manifests itself as a reaction to perceived threats. The fight-or-flight response is an automatic physiological and hormonal change that occurs when the body considers itself to be at risk or threat. We tend to imagine the worst-case scenarios and we anticipate rejection or failure before they even happen or become a reality. There's a powerful acronym that resonates with many: FEAR is those False Expectations Appearing Real. This is the tendency to let our imaginations fill our thoughts with the negative scenarios that aren't necessarily true or real.

There are common responses to fear:

- **We often look to please people.** Many people strive with all their internal drive to keep everyone around them happy, but this often comes at the expense of their own needs. This is usually a defence mechanism, rooted in the desire to avoid conflict or rejection.
- **We seek to avoid conflict.** The fear of what we believe comes as a result of conflict which can lead to avoiding tough, difficult conversations or suppressing our true feelings, creating more tension, stress and resentment in the long term.
- **We will do anything to avoid rejection.** This is a powerful motivator that so often stops people from even considering the taking of risks or trying new things. The fear of rejection, which the majority of us have, can prevent someone from applying for a job, approaching an opportunity, starting a relationship, leaving a relationship or sharing their ideas.

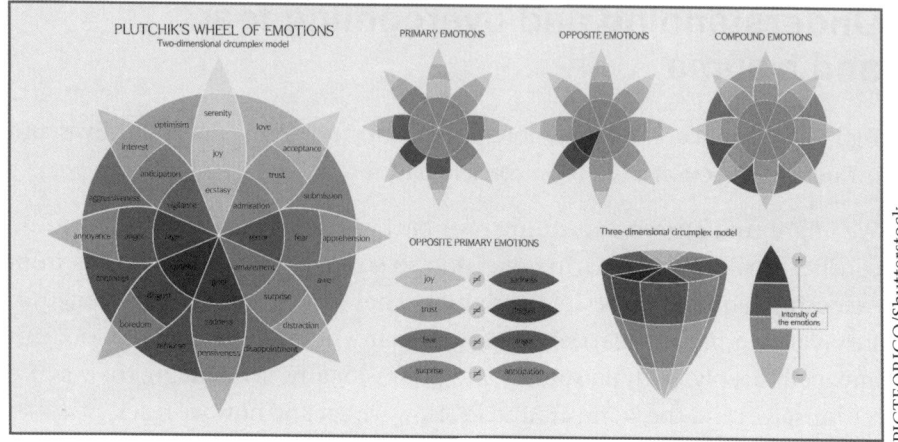

These common responses are often based on fears that may never materialise. They even stop us from finding the ways that can help us begin to challenge them. Fear can often paralyse our action and suppress any alternative emotion or considerations.

Recognising and understanding trauma

As often considered, trauma isn't always tied to catastrophic events. Many life experiences, both in personal and professional contexts, can leave a lasting impact that we later identify as trauma. Trauma can be anything from a childhood event that affected our self-worth to repeated professional rejections that created self-doubt.

Workplace incidents, failures or criticisms will contribute to your professional trauma and will leave a lasting impact on your confidence and build on the fear of future failure.

Recognising these experiences as trauma can be super powerful, as it gives context to the resulting feelings, actions and behaviours that stem from them. It allows us to understand that these reactions aren't personal weaknesses; they're natural responses to difficult experiences that need to be recognised and managed.

Once we recognise the impact of fear and trauma, we can begin to address and manage these feelings. Here are some tips for dealing with fear and trauma.

Keep your eyes wide open and challenge those false expectations. If you start to feel the fear, then ask yourself: 'What evidence do I have that this fear will come true?' Are there any facts or is the first reaction one that is based on assumptions? Challenge any assumptions and look for the facts that will reduce the anxiety and self-doubt. Visualise a positive outcome instead of focusing on what could go wrong and reframe those expectations to help boost your confidence in a given situation.

Many people who struggle with fear and trauma are often their own harshest critics. A long-standing mentor always said to me that there would always be one person that I'd never please – myself! Be kind to yourself and practise self-compassion. You will build your resilience by treating yourself with the same kindness you would offer a friend. It is OK to feel fear or pain as these are natural human responses, not signs of weakness.

I encourage you to seek support when needed, which will often be before you feel it is needed!

Sharing your experiences with your advisers, trusted friends or family members can provide an important external view that will create a sense of validation and understanding, thereby reducing any feelings of isolation.

It is also not a weakness to ask for therapy, counselling or support from specialist groups if needed, as they can be invaluable in processing trauma and managing fear. By speaking to a professional you can uncover subconscious patterns, and they could offer you new tools for coping.

Consider mindfulness practices, such as meditation, yoga or journaling. They can help you reconnect with the present moment, bring the balance and reduce the mental strain of fear and worry.

Additionally, keep in mind your 'why'. Moments of self-care activities, such as exercise, hobbies and spending time with loved ones will create balance and provide a sense of fulfilment that helps counter fear-driven behaviours.

If you find yourself struggling with people-pleasing or conflict avoidance, a powerful step is to set boundaries, and by practising assertiveness you will gradually reduce the fear of conflict and rejection. Small actions, that often feel huge, like saying 'no' to things that don't serve you well, can help build confidence and respect for your own needs.

Overcoming fear and trauma is about erasing past experiences or never feeling afraid again. It's about understanding the roots of your feelings and building resilience to live more freely and authentically. By recognising the impact of trauma and fear, whether from personal or professional experiences, you will feel more empowered to take control over your responses.

By challenging those false expectations, practising self-compassion, seeking support and setting those boundaries, you will more often than not transform fear and trauma into opportunities that empower you.

> **Remember this**
>
> **Follow your perception or gut feeling**
>
> Your perception is your ability to make an observation and decide how you plan to proceed.
>
> Many decisions of an entrepreneur are made using a gut feeling, and they make quick calculated decisions with the acceptance that all decisions have an outcome from which we can learn something.
>
> We can procrastinate and never make a decision, or we make a decision and then be prepared to make an honest review of the outcome and gain a lesson for the future. The situation we face at any time could possibly have a positive or a negative result and our initial approach to the task in hand could perhaps be taken with excitement or with fear depending on what we perceive could potentially happen.

Creating new habits for a better outcome

Habit creation is a process that takes time and effort. But if you are willing to put in the work and understand the influences, then you can create new habits that will help you achieve your goals and live a better life.

- **Plan:** take some time to think about what you want to achieve. Once you know you can start making a plan for how to get there.
- **Start small:** rather than trying to make a drastic change all at once, start by making small, incremental changes that are more manageable. Starting with small changes makes it easier to stick to the habit and builds momentum for larger changes. Then build momentum and confidence.
- **Be clear, have specific goals:** to create a new habit, it's important to have a clear understanding of what you're trying to achieve and why it matters. Define the habit you want to create and be specific about the steps needed to achieve it.
- **Make it easy:** when you're trying to create a new habit, it's important to make it as easy as possible for yourself to do.

- **Make it a routine:** incorporate the new habit into your daily routine and make it a non-negotiable part of your day. In his book *Atomic Habits*, James Clear talks about the power of 'Habit stacking' as an example of making things easier for yourself.[4] Identify specific times or triggers that will help remind you to practise your new habit.
- **Be consistent:** do the same thing each day, even if you don't feel like it. At first, it might be difficult to be consistent, but as you stick with it, it becomes easier.
- **Reward yourself:** when you achieve a step, be sure to reward yourself and stay motivated. This is a habit to break, as business owners are poor at self-recognition and reward.
- **Don't give up:** there will be times when you slip up and don't stick to your new habit. Don't beat yourself up about it. Just get back on track and keep going. Be patient but persistent.
- **Track your progress:** keep track of your progress towards your new habit and this will help to build momentum and keep you motivated.
- **Get support:** gain the support of friends, family, a mentor or coach to help keep you accountable and provide encouragement.

You can become better at creating new habits and achieving better outcomes in life with a few changes. Creating new habits takes time and effort but the benefits are worth it.

Small changes help to create your new habits

Any habit change is not easy, so you may have identified that some intentions either slipped or did not transpire at all. The reason this could happen is because your well-intentioned habits did not fully form. You may have become bored, not seen the success you'd hoped for, or simply couldn't fit them into your usually busy timetable.

Most people are naturally resistant to change. Change takes you out of your comfort zone, feels uncomfortable or risky and so, no matter how good your intentions are, you just can't replace old habits. Well, here are some small changes you can make to help you stick with your intentions to create healthy new habits.

---

[4] Clear, J. (2018) *Atomic Habits*. Penguin Random House.

1. Believe in yourself and your ability to change; tell yourself you can change.
2. Fuel your motivation for change by visualising what you want to do or to be.
3. Set yourself specific, measurable and achievable goals for the habit you want to create.
4. Break the change down into manageable activity steps.
5. Start a new behaviour with something small and easy (for example 'Put on my running shoes', the first step in creating a habit for fitness or weight loss).
6. Consider your environment and ask if it supports the desired habit or creates friction.
7. Trigger your new habit activity by tagging it immediately after something you already do. Therefore, when X happens, you also do Y.
8. When you start a new habit, focus your behaviour on the repetition. Repeat it often rather than focusing on the time it takes in total.
9. Stay persistent and be kind to yourself. Remember that change is a process, and setbacks are normal. Every outcome has a lesson!
10. Reinforce your new behaviour with something satisfying, a sense, a reward to fuel repetition.
11. Measure and track your progress towards creating your habit to maintain a streak of positive action and celebrate small wins – give yourself a tick!
12. Remember that change takes time, be patient and persistent.

Whether it's in business or the rest of your life, you *can* create healthy new habits and stick to them. Remember – one small change is easy to make ...

The 21/90 rule

A popular method for building habits and making lasting lifestyle changes:

- **Commit**: choose a goal, either personal or professional, and commit to doing it every day for 21 days.
- **Habit**: after three weeks, the goal should become a habit.
- **Lifestyle**: continue the goal for another 90 days to make it a permanent part of your lifestyle.

What habits do you want to change or *stop*?

What new habits do you want to create?

> **Remember this**
>
> **Push your comfort zone**
>
> Most of the population remain in their comfort zone, being like everyone else, surviving, getting by, playing it safe and often procrastinating. At times they feel insecure, doubtful and fearful, so they play it safe and often settle for less than what may be possible.
>
> A small percentage have the mindset to go for their dreams, to embrace the unknown and live with confidence, without limits and like change that helps them explore new things.
>
> It is such a mindset that differentiates many entrepreneurs.
>
> It's been said that 'successful entrepreneurs have a positive mental attitude'. Yes, they do, but it is much more than just having a positive outlook. They are open to opportunities, excited by change and make things happen.
>
> What are you doing to push your comfort zone? How often have you perhaps stopped yourself doing something because it was outside your comfort zone? Picking up the phone? Walking into a room of people? Making a direct request for the business to close the sale? Firing someone who needed to leave the business?

On reflection is it a disappointment or a lesson?

'It didn't go my way again.' Was it bad luck, a disappointment, a lack of planning or an outcome that has presented a point of learning?

It's a good habit to visualise what you want to achieve and document it as a vision and then plan the steps that move you towards it every day. That may be a plan in outline, or in more specific detail that covers periods such as 3+ years, in a year's time, in 90 days, within 30 days or for today!

If you like a plan then you have to be prepared for when things don't go the way you thought they may or how you had hoped.

Some business owners can take many days to recover from such experiences. First, there is the disappointment that the goal or objective was not achieved but then there's also the reflection on what or how it was executed. This can then lead to you questioning your ability to model your business, plan the growth, identify what to do next and ultimately thrive rather than just survive.

There will be many ups and downs along the way and not everything will be 100 per cent perfect (despite what you read on social media!). However, it's how you react to the disappointment that defines the efficiency of your journey and the impact on so many other activities or resources within the business.

It is a growth mindset that allows us to accept that we can't change the past decisions or actions. It is now looking forward to consider what needs to be undertaken next.

When you look to execute those best considered activities, which I'm sure were carefully decided, you will experience an outcome. It may not be what you aimed for. Consider what you can learn from the outcome. What should be repeated? What can be tweaked? What should never be tried again?

For example, as a business owner, we look to convert as many of our prospect opportunities to paying customers as we can. The sales process that we implement is done so to the best of our knowledge, with the steps and journey that we consider would maximise conversion. However, it's unlikely it will convert 100 per cent of your enquiries, so this presents an outcome that can be reviewed. A lesson that can guide an improvement that may only be one small change.

How are you reacting to such situations?

Remember, *you* are the master of your actions and your reactions.

How to combat perfectionism in business

Being a perfectionist, especially in business, can be a huge drawback! That's a strong statement, I know, but my experience and observations have shown that perfection does not exist. The harder you reach for it, the further away from your true goal you are led. You can even be paralysed into inaction through fear of not achieving a perfect result.

How can you combat your inner perfectionist, so that you can focus on excellence and move your business forward?

The characteristics of having a strong attention to detail and wanting excellent performance or results are not perfectionism. Anything can always be improved upon to the point of excellence, but the point of perfection is infinitely further away.

Combat perfectionism by setting realistic goals and expectations. Be realistic with yourself and manage your own expectations. Having a realistic expectation to begin with lessens the likelihood that you'll be disappointed in yourself at the end.

Refer to the mean value of your work

When you question the quality of your work and feel it isn't good enough then many of us tend to fall into a slump. Use the mean value of your work over a period of time. Every piece of work lands on a scale of excellence and the idea is that every piece produced aims to move that mean average up the scale. It's a great way to view the 'big picture' of your standards and stop fixating on one imperfection.

Look back at your last project or piece of work. Where did it land on the scale of excellence? Why?

If you can view your output and productivity with an analytical mind, you will see the areas of excellence. If you really weren't happy with what you produced, even though your customer was, can you ask yourself how realistic your expectations were to begin with, and then get a plan in place for the next time?

Be critical of yourself, but be fair

Herein lies a lesson in learning from failure, or in this case imperfections. Beating yourself up and berating yourself for missing the chance to be perfect will only cloud your judgement and perception of your own value. Your customers value you, so yes, view your performance with a healthy critical eye on behalf of those customers and in the pursuit of excellence, but be fair and honest with yourself.

Eight tips for managing your mental health in business

Business can be an emotionally turbulent pastime; it can be tough striving for better outcomes each day and it really can take a toll on your mental health. Be mindful to show yourself some love and manage your mental health as an entrepreneur.

Here are some tips to help you be mindful of your wellbeing:

1 **Unplug**
As someone in my network recently commented, we spend so much time plugged in to our email, phones, the news and social sites that it's sometimes nice to just unplug and spend some quiet time away from it all. The world won't end if you turn off your emails, your business won't collapse if you take a holiday. But even just a short walk outside (no headphones of course) can do a world of good for your mental health.

2 **Practise mindfulness**
Speaking of not thinking about work while you're unplugged, mindfulness can be tricky to perfect, but what it means when you practise it is that you actually increase your effectiveness whilst encouraging healthy benefits such as detachment from unhealthy habits.

Try to train your mind to focus with meditation – just for a moment, empty your mind of any thoughts. Just recognise them and accept that you'll address those thoughts later, and bat them away until then. You can do this at your desk, or even better, while taking a lunchtime walking break.

3 **Detach from distractions**
Controlling your own internal distractions might prove easier in the long term than controlling external distractions – those that come from colleagues, employees, family and the digital devices we rely so much upon. A clear policy of 'my door is always open – within certain times' helps you become mindful and less fraught.

4 **Daily journal**
For example, write yourself a short note at the start and then end of the day, a journal, answering three questions: What went well? How did I celebrate? What could be different/better tomorrow? This is an opportunity to connect with your actions via a reflection at the end of the day against your intentions at the start of it.

5 **Make a plan and stick to it**
This is not a reference to the business plan overall, but rather taking 20 minutes every day to highlight the activities that will result in the highest pay-off that day. This will help you to organise your thoughts around the day ahead and keep yourself organised. The alternative often sees us wasting hours each week.

6 **Automate, delegate or outsource**

   In business, there are always tasks that need to be done that just make you sink inside a little. Do you really need to do them? Can they be automated, delegated or outsourced?

Morning mindset	My top 3 goals for today	End of day reflection
What am I looking forward to today?	1. 2. 3. **Tasks to complete today** & committed to the diary **People to speak to today** Check in, follow up, lead, gift,	Score out of 10 the following: • My why was front of mind ____ • I was always productive ____ • My energy pot is high ____ • My stress pot is managed ____ • I have been proactive ____ • I've committed to my high pay off activities and habits ____ • I celebrated today ____ Looking in the mirror, how would I summarise my day? Journal prompts • 3 things I'm grateful for • 3 things I like about myself • What went well? • What could have gone better? • What would make me a better person tomorrow?
How will I turn up as my best today?		
How can I control any obstacles that could arise during the day? Obstacle Solution		
Looking in the mirror, what am I telling myself today?		
What would need to happen today to make the day a great day?		
What's my theme for today?		

   You are the business owner; the business exists because of you. Make it run the way that makes you happy. If the task really does need to be done by you and you alone, perhaps there is a way that focusing on it, reducing distractions and giving yourself a reward afterwards will make it less onerous.

7 **Talk, ask, share**

   It can be especially difficult in business to admit you're having a hard time in case it damages your reputation or changes public opinion of you. That being said, no matter who you are, it's important to find someone you can trust to talk over your problems with. Ask for help and it will come. If there is no one you're willing to open up to in your circle, there is help in the form of professionals who are equipped to help with entrepreneurial stress.

8 **Accept mistakes**

One of the hardest things to do is to stand upright, hold your hand up and say openly – I made a mistake. But it's one of the most freeing phrases you can say! If anyone in business tells you they haven't made a mistake, they're either lying or aren't really in business, it's that simple.

The tip here is to stop dwelling on it, don't beat yourself up about it, just find a way to make it right or better and take the lesson so you don't repeat it.

Ten ways to cope with entrepreneurial stress

First, we need to be aware of what stress is and where it's coming from.

Is it a bad day perhaps where everything didn't go your own way or when someone didn't hear you? Entrepreneurial stress is often linked to our business objectives and our personal aspirations as well as our expectations of ourselves and others.

Here are some coping strategies to maintain a healthy level of stress:

1 **Interruption and distraction log**

This is simply a piece of paper or a notebook into which you can enter the time, source and reason for a distraction or interruption. At the end of the day, you can take time to review your entries and work on how to reduce them. For example, if your team interrupts you at random times of the day, ask them to collaborate and collate concerns or needs, and come to you between designated hours. The same tactic can work for emails, phone notifications and booking meetings.

2 **Daily and weekly planning**

Twenty minutes of planning at the beginning of each week can save hours! Use the time to get the little things done, like setting notifications to silent. Have a solid plan for each day so that it prevents your time being dictated to you and allows you to stay in control of your activity.

3 **Connect your daily plan with your high pay-off activities**

Ensure your day focuses on those things that are most important to and for you. Using a daily planner will ensure you commit time to those activities that give you the pay-off you desire.

4 **Talk**

Speaking to a colleague, friend, partner or trusted connection can be immensely helpful. You could have your thoughts verified, challenged or just simply heard. You may be able to help someone else with their fears, concerns or challenges. Talking things out really does alleviate entrepreneurial stress.

5 **Exercise**

Have an element of physical activity in your life. Whatever you choose to do, it's a proven fact that physical activity lowers stress and aids sleep.

6 **Control the controllable**

This is a useful mantra as a reminder that some things are just out of your control. For example, you can't control political decisions or the economic outlook, you can only control how you react to them and the action you take. Implement time management tools, continue to educate yourself in your industry, and use your network for support to maintain that control. If watching the news or reading certain social channels drains your energy, as the content is out of your control, then stop it!

7 **Get away from your desk**

Stopping work can seem impossible at times, but if you don't take a moment to step away you could find yourself slowly becoming overwhelmed. There are micro-moments throughout the day you can often miss; stand up, breathe deeply, change your focal length, and then get back to it.

8 **Be in the moment**

Whatever you're doing, do that and think of nothing else, which can be easier said than done for many! However, if you're going for a walk, enjoy your surroundings, really listen to what's going on around you, talk to the dog or do whatever you need to, to make sure you're truly present in that moment and not churning over the events of the past or the day ahead. If you're working on a task, try not to let your mind wander or be distracted by another 'shiny object'.

9 **Delegate or outsource**

Is the source of your stress that you have too much to do in too little time? Is it because you are doing something you don't enjoy, that takes you too long or is not within your skillset? This may be an indication that your business has reached the point when you need to bite the bullet and expand your team, or otherwise delegate.

10 **Find a professional who helps with stress**
    You might do well to find someone who is professionally qualified to teach you the coping methods and skills to recognise your trigger points. Ask someone you trust if they can recommend someone, ask social media groups or check in with Mind, the mental health charity.

> **Remember this**
>
> **Build the ability to say no**
>
> How easy do you find it to say no?
>
> An entrepreneur has the ability to know or sense what is not right and simply say no.
>
> For example, can you say no to prospects that do not fit your ideal customer profile? Can you say no to prospects that do not value your offering and are not prepared to pay your desired fee? Can you say no to those who show you no respect? Can you say no to the idea of a colleague? Can you say no to the volunteer request that will help someone else?
>
> This is not a natural instinct for many of us but, if we cannot master this, then we will find it difficult to build the business we desire as we will continually be taking three steps forward and too many back.

Is there a difference between the best and the rest?

You will know that many high-performing sportspersons still have a coach, in fact more than one! There is of course a level of natural talent and, once they've won a major award, title, etc, then you'd have thought they now know what to do on their own. What differentiates the best from the rest?

It's much like in business. Some are successful and achieve so much, but the vast majority may struggle to hit those levels.

There are a host of differences, but they can effectively be boiled down to mindset and execution.

Here are some of the differences:

- Many give up at the first barrier, whilst others expect hurdles and look to master their journey.
- Many think they're good at everything, but the best understand their competence as their skill or expertise.
- The best consistently show up every day.
- Many run with their first idea because they think it's the best one, whereas the best recognise that it may not be the best idea and contemplate other options efficiently.
- The best don't focus on weaknesses, they focus on their strengths and get people around them who are strong in the areas where they are weak.
- Many believe that the world should work the way they want it to, whereas the best know that they have to work with the world as they find it.
- Many see feedback and coaching as criticism, whilst the best know they have areas to develop and seek such reflection.
- Many celebrate the isolated performance, which may be down to luck, whilst the best strive for consistency.
- The best invest in themselves, their process and their behaviour as they know how they train shows up in their performance.
- Too many run day-to-day or by the short term, whilst the best focus on the long-term plan.
- The best make decisions and accept responsibility rather than seeking a reason to blame something or someone.
- The best have a process, whilst the rest end at a goal.
- Some finish when they achieve something, but others see it as just the beginning.

Are you thinking like the best? Are you behaving in a way that keeps you ahead of the rest?

Things I wish I knew before I started

Starting a business is an incredible but emotional roller coaster. One minute it can give us the highest enjoyment and thrill, but the next moment can be unbelievably challenging, throwing curveballs in our direction and producing the unexpected at any moment.

The life of an entrepreneur is not straightforward but many of us wouldn't want it any other way ... although, perhaps, ideally with fewer obstacles and dips!

Looking back to when I started my first business, there are a few things I wish I had known in more detail. I was lucky that I'd been well trained during my time with Barclays Business Banking but at that time of actually starting my own business ... I didn't know what I didn't know. Luckily, I had good people around me to help answer my ever evolving questions.

In my role as a business coach and mentor today, I often hear people saying that they didn't even know the questions to ask when they started.

What I do know is that I *now* know a few things that could have saved me and will also save you ... time, money and stress. If I could go back in time to meet myself, there are a few things I'd share with myself and I'd like to share these with you:

1. You don't need to know everything before you start.
2. You are always marketing, and it starts from day one or from today.
3. Cash is king.
4. Perfectionism can paralyse progress.
5. Time is your most valuable asset.
6. Ideas are easy, shiny things are attractive, but the right execution is what it's all about.
7. Expect failure ... it is part of the journey.
8. Balance the hustle with your self-care.
9. Know your real numbers.
10. Know what you 'really do' and how you solve your prospects pain, problem, fear, want, need or desire.

I'll expand on each of these at the end of the following chapters.

> **I wish I knew this before I started my first business**
>
> ### Perfectionism can paralyse progress
>
> Perfection is a common trait in many entrepreneurs. We often want to please everyone, we don't like conflict and we do what we need to do to avoid rejection. I encourage you to realign your thinking. Instead of aiming for perfection, focus on continuous improvement. Remember your product or service is always developing, as the understanding of your market evolves. This may mean a pre-launch, a soft launch, a market test or something similar to learn as you build out your offering and before you feel it is 'perfect'.

Key points

- Acknowledge that your entrepreneurial journey won't be smooth.
- Hold your motivation with a clear purpose and a strong reason why.
- Celebrate your wins.
- Every activity has an outcome from which you can learn.
- Be self-aware, knowing your strengths and your areas for development.
- Don't wait for perfect, as it may never arrive.
- Create positive habits in the way you work and use your time.
- Push your comfort zone.

Additional resources

Books
Jeffers, S. (2023) *Feel the Fear and Do It Anyway*. Eugene, Harvest.
Humphrey, J. and Hughes, D. (2021) *High Performance*. New York, Random House.
Covey, S. R. (2004) *7 Habits of Highly Effective People*. Free Press.

Podcasts
The Diary of a CEO with Steven Bartlett

CHAPTER 2
ARE *YOU* READY TO START UP?

Starting a business is one of the biggest decisions you may make considering the options, responsibilities and lifestyle you have.

In this chapter, we will explore if you are ready to start the entrepreneurial journey and start your own business.

Are you?

Starting a new business is both exciting and rewarding, but it is also full of challenges. The level of commitment that you will need should not be underestimated.

The success of your business will depend partly on your attitude and skills. This means being honest about a range of issues – your knowledge, your financial status and the personal qualities that you can bring to your new business.

Dedication, drive, perseverance and support from family and friends will go a long way towards transforming your business idea into reality and will be especially important during the early days.

Do you have what it takes to set up a new business? Let's look at the day-to-day reality of starting a business and outline the skills and qualities that you will need.

Setting up your own business requires your full commitment. The physical and emotional demands of starting up in business should not be underestimated. Starting a business is a life-changing event and will require hard work and long hours, especially in the early stages. There can be times of financial uncertainty, and this may have a knock-on effect for both you and your family. Setting up your own business means that you will no longer be able to take advantage of the usual benefits associated with a permanent job. Your family and friends should be aware from the outset of the effect starting up a business will have on your life, and it is crucial that they are right behind you.

As a business owner you need core skills to execute your ideas to ensure that your new business survives in the long term. You should start by assessing your own skills and knowledge. This will help you decide whether you need to learn new skills or draw on outside help by delegating, recruiting or outsourcing.

There are certain qualities commonly found amongst successful businesspeople. Take a look at this checklist to reflect on some of the key considerations when deciding whether you are ready to start your own business.

- ☐ I am willing to make a personal sacrifice to start my business (time, money, interests ...).
- ☐ I have reserves and personal finances to support my initial months if there is a delay in winning new customers.
- ☐ I am prepared to lose my company benefits (e.g. holiday or sick pay, car, pension, healthcare ...).
- ☐ I am aware that without mindful management, this will put pressure on my close relationships.
- ☐ I am ready to manage periods of isolation when running my own business.
- ☐ I am confident in my business idea.
- ☐ I am determined and committed to do what it takes.
- ☐ I am a self-starter and won't be waiting for someone to tell me what to do.
- ☐ I will persist despite times when it may be difficult.
- ☐ I will show my initiative and creativity.
- ☐ I know how to manage my business finances.
- ☐ I will be a good people manager when needed.
- ☐ I have a business plan.
- ☐ I know how to market my business.
- ☐ I have the sales skills to convert my prospects.
- ☐ I am confident about how I will build my relationships with my customers, suppliers and team.

If you have not ticked all these boxes, then fear not. This is what this book is preparing you for with the knowledge and framework to consider these factors.

What's in your lifestyle plan?

Before embarking on any kind of journey, especially when starting a business, you need to get your plan together. The whole point of going into business is often to build yourself a better life, with more money, more time and more control.

In the last chapter we explored your 'why' but what is the lifestyle you want as a return on investment for all your hard work?

Once you have considered your desired lifestyle, there are three considerations in setting your plan:

1 Understand what it will take and your commitment.
2 Know your numbers in order to create your lifestyle plan.
3 Manage your time with focus on what needs to happen.

And we'll look at each of these individually.

Understand what it will take and your commitment

This is different for every business owner because it depends on you and you alone. However, you should reflect and understand this from day one; otherwise you may find yourself resenting the business as it may detract you from doing other things.

Why do you want to start a business? What factors would mean you are still in business in a year's time? What do you want from the business in the long term?

This is the moment to look in the mirror and appreciate, understand and commit to what you are prepared to do in order to have the business you want in the future. Such clarity will determine your high pay-off activities for each day and give you focus when you might get distracted by the next shiny thing. These considerations will also help you determine how far you are really willing to go to get what you desire.

You should consider your work/life balance and how much time you have or are willing to give to the new business. In addition, what time does the business need to give you back for the things you want to do (e.g. school plays, hobbies, social time …).

Establish if you can run the business doing what you enjoy or what needs to happen. What will fuel your energy tank rather than filling your stress pot? How much effort are you prepared to give the business, or will you just be hopeful? How much hassle or impact on your sleep are you prepared to take?

What support do you need in those early months or years such as working capital, people, assets or similar resources?

How much money do you need from your business now and in the future? To immediately fund your current lifestyle, then the lifestyle you desire, and then in later life (e.g. retirement).

Know your numbers in order to create your lifestyle plan

You can choose what success looks like to you. What do you want to be, have or do as a result of running your own business? What is the ideal lifestyle you want as a return on your investment in the business?

We're talking vision boards, goal setting and aligning your life plan with your business goals. After all, for many of us the business goals and personal goals are very much linked. Many people don't have clarity on these things and therefore they never align their business goals to what they really want in life, so therefore just drift along.

With clarity of what you want, you can then create the numbers side of this plan. This can be worked out by putting a cost to all those things in your desired life plan that you have identified. For example, how much does your mortgage cost, private school, club membership, holidays, cleaner, and so on. This is how much money your business needs to generate to reach what you defined as success.

Manage your time with focus on what needs to happen

You've heard the saying, 'You can always make more money, but you can't make more time.' Time is a limited resource so let's make sure you're using it to the best advantage.

If we can't make time, our next best option is to control it. Ask yourself:

1   Are you in control of your time, or are you distracted, procrastinating or unmotivated?

2   Are your working conditions conducive to a productive or creative day?

3   Can you stop interruptions – from family, co-workers, delivery people or employees?

4   Have you put enough time aside for high pay-off activities?

5   Can you carve out a routine – daily, weekly or monthly to work on those things that will bring you closer to your definition of success, instead of doing the day-to-day client work?

Start now or do it later?

Nothing changes unless you change first ...

If you're honest with yourself, you'd agree that if you continue doing what you've always done, nothing is likely to change. So, what step change do you need to make, as an individual, to get you where you want to be in 12 months' time?

You may also consider it is not the right time to start your business now.

There is no one-size-fits-all answer to whether you should start now or later. Carefully evaluate your readiness, market conditions and resources. Look to have a solid plan and the necessary support to navigate the journey successfully.

When deciding whether to start a business now or wait, consider the following factors:

Reasons to start now

Market opportunity: if there is a clear market need or gap that your business can fill, acting quickly can help you establish a foothold before competitors do.

Passion and motivation: high enthusiasm and motivation can drive the hard work required to launch a business. If you feel ready and inspired, it's a good sign to start.

Economic conditions: sometimes, economic downturns or changes create unique opportunities for new businesses. Assess if current conditions favour your business idea.

Resource availability: if you have access to necessary resources such as funding, a strong network or expertise, it might be advantageous to start now.

Learning and adaptation: starting sooner allows you to learn from real-world experiences, adapt quickly, and refine your business model over time.

Reasons to wait

Preparation and research: ensure you have a thorough business plan, market research and a clear understanding of your target audience. Starting without adequate preparation can lead to failure.

Financial stability: having a secure financial foundation and access to funding can be crucial. If your personal or business finances are not stable, waiting might be prudent.

Skills and knowledge: acquiring additional skills, experience or knowledge relevant to your business can increase your chances of success. Consider further education or gaining industry experience.

Market conditions: if the market is currently saturated or experiencing instability, it might be wise to wait for more favourable conditions.

Personal readiness: starting a business requires significant time and energy. Ensure you are personally ready to commit fully to the endeavour.

Balanced approach

Set clear goals: define your short-term and long-term objectives. Determine what you need to achieve before launching and what can be developed post-launch.

Pilot testing: consider a soft launch or pilot programme to test your concept with minimal risk. This allows you to gather feedback and make necessary adjustments.

Start part-time: can you start on a part-time basis whilst you have the security of other income to test the market and the buy-in to your solution?

Build a support network: surround yourself with mentors, advisors and a supportive network. Their guidance can be invaluable in deciding the right timing.

Work/life balance

What will it be like starting my own business?

Setting up your own business can be very rewarding, but there are pressures involved.

One of the main reasons why people start their own business, or even consider it in the first place, is to obtain a better work/life balance that they desire. Perhaps that is less commuting, having control, less stress, seeing more of the family, spending time doing your hobbies ...

However, in the early days, you should expect that an 'ideal' work/life balance is unlikely to be achieved without some very good planning and laser focus.

As you strive to structure the business to provide the stable foundations for your future success, it is likely that you will be working longer hours than perhaps you are working now! This is because there is lots to do, or business owners find lots to do.

Roles and responsibilities

If you start the business alone, you are usually wearing all the business hats at some point. One minute you are the business leader, then the salesperson, then the operations manager, then the finance manager and possibly the HR manager. It is usual, even with the prioritisation of responsibilities, to be working longer hours and most days of the week, just to fit it all in during the initial start-up period. However, for most it feels OK, as you know you are building something for the future gain and in the belief that you are now doing what you want to be doing.

Yes, short-term pain for long-term gain, but you have to be aware of the influencing factors and reasons you may be working the hours, or you will look back on your first anniversary, still working those long days, as it is far too easy to do so, as there is always something to do.

The important consideration here is to be aware of this fact, so as to avoid frustration, but more critically you know what you have to do to build the business that is less reliant on you.

One way is recruiting or outsourcing, but for what? Know when you are the finance manager or the salesperson, etc. and consider what you are good at, what you enjoy and what adds the most value in the initial years. This will help you understand what you can later delegate to an employee or even outsource to a business service provider.

Another recommendation is to hold onto your 'reason why'. Is that being achieved? If not, why not and what needs to change?

Be mindful of your time

It is often related to the better use of your time. It is far too easy to find something to do, but is it the right thing? Remember those 'high pay-off activities', which are those activities you have to do without distraction for the development of your business. These activities should be dominating your diary.

It is good to have the support of your family and friends. They may not have been through the process of starting a business, so ensure that those close to you are aware of the commitment needed to get the business started. But don't make excuses not to spend time with them because you have to work 'on' the business. That is an easy excuse when you are not working effectively and efficiently on your start-up business.

Very few businesses are overnight successes, and it will take time to build a business for the return you desire, the time and or money. So be prepared for long hours with low reward. This, together with responsibilities, of running the business and making decisions, may cause stress if not acknowledged, appreciated and then controlled.

Of course, as an entrepreneurial business owner at start up, the buck stops with you. The successes and failures will be from your decisions or perhaps the direction given to others. For some that is a great feeling, but for others, it is not and one that creates worry and procrastination in the home life.

You should also be prepared for the feeling of isolation. Some business owners struggle with this. In the past they have always worked in a team of people and now they are working alone, making decisions alone and not seeing people. That in itself is difficult but avoid just going to meetings for the opportunity to meet someone or recruiting someone because you want someone with you.

Use your time and energy to develop the business, with a plan that is most efficient for you and ensures you gain the work/life balance that you desire, as quickly as possible.

Additionally, understand what work/life balance really means for you. For some it will be working between the school run and spending as much time as possible with the family, but for others it will be very different and in fact working for yourself may just be the work/life balance you desire.

Capture here what work/life balance means for you:

Keep this in mind when building your business.

> **Remember this**
>
> **Know the value of your work/life balance**
>
> Yes, the journey of an entrepreneur is hard work, sometimes lonely and can involve some longer hours than desired at times. However, this is generally accepted as the entrepreneur knows that the action supports the goals and objectives that they have set themselves. If it does not support them then this could be the start of a problem.
>
> Personally, I remind myself daily of the quote, 'You work to live, not live to work.'
>
> If work/life balance is important to you, then know the real reason why you want one. Is it for your family time? Is it for your health? If you just hope you had a weekend off or no late nights in the office, but with no reason to stop, then experience shows that you do strive to make it happen.
>
> A simple exercise, to help you identify what you want from work/life balance, is to envisage that the business is operating well, you have every weekend off, never work beyond 6 pm and have half a day off each week. What are you doing? What would you like to be doing?

Can you afford to start your own business?

There are many factors to consider here including any existing resources, the ability to raise investment or debt finance, your attitude to risk and whether you can or are prepared to give up something of your lifestyle that you have today.

To determine if you can afford to start your own business, you should consider the following key questions:

1. How much start-up capital do I need? Calculate the total costs required to launch your business, including equipment, inventory, licences, legals, permits, marketing, etc.
2. What are my ongoing operating expenses? Estimate monthly costs like rent, utilities, payroll, supplies, insurance, etc.
3. How long until my business becomes profitable? Determine how many months of expenses you need to cover before generating positive cash flow.
4. What are my personal financial needs? Calculate how much money you need to cover your living expenses whilst the business gets off the ground.

5   What funding sources are available to me? Assess options like personal savings, loans, investors, grants, etc.

6   Do I have an emergency fund? Ensure you have savings to cover unexpected costs or slow periods.

7   What assets can I leverage? If needed, consider using personal assets as collateral for loans or selling items to raise capital.

8   Can I start the business part-time whilst keeping my current job? This allows you to test the concept with less financial risk.

9   What is my credit score? A good credit score provides more financing options.

10 Have I created detailed financial projections? Develop realistic revenue and expense forecasts to understand capital requirements.

11 Am I willing to invest my own money? Determine how much of your personal funds you're comfortable risking.

12 What return do I need now, shortly and in the future? Complete a forecast and establish if the business is likely to be able to pay you what you need each month to maintain a lifestyle, to soon pay for the lifestyle you desire and later provide for your later life in retirement.

By thoroughly evaluating these financial considerations, you can better assess if you're in a position to afford starting your own business at this time. It's crucial to be realistic about the costs involved and have adequate resources to sustain the business until it becomes profitable.

Testing the water

Before you start any business, or later consider a new product or service, it is recommended to undertake your market research. Don't just ask your friends and family, who are most likely to give you the response of resounding support, but actually speak with your prospective customers and market influencers to establish if there is a real want or need for your idea.

Any product development should always be aligned with your market development; otherwise you are in danger of taking a solution to market that nobody wants and are likely to fail.

Testing the water before fully launching a business is a smart strategy to minimise risk and gather valuable insights.

Undertake your market research using surveys and interviews to engage feedback. Complete a competitor analysis to identify what they do well, or what weaknesses you may exploit, and keep an eye on industry trends to ensure your idea aligns with current market demands.

Can you start the business on a part-time basis as a test? Can you kickstart your marketing campaigns with split testing strategies to identify how your audience engage?

Consider a soft launch or pilot programme to test your concept with minimal risk. You may offer a limited release to test your operations and gather initial feedback or promotional events to showcase your product and engage with potential customers in a controlled setting.

By testing the water, you can validate your business idea, refine your approach and build a solid foundation for a successful full-scale launch. This careful, data-driven approach helps mitigate risks and sets you up for long-term success.

After all, you don't want to invest your time and money to take a product or service to market that is not fit for purpose or what the market wants. Testing the water enables you to gain confidence in your investment.

The common reasons why start-ups fail and what to avoid!

Research has indicated that there are some common reasons for businesses failing. It is important that you are aware of the common reasons for business failure, which primarily impacts on your cash position, so that you can plan to avoid them.

- **No demand for your product or service** – taking to market an offering that no one wants and therefore sales are difficult or limited.
- **Not enough working capital** – you should forecast your financial requirements and ensure you have the finance to support the growth of your business.
- **Growing too fast** – plan your growth steps. Do you have the cash to fund the work for new customers whilst you wait to get paid?
- **Hiring the wrong people** – it is important to have good people around you and it is a mistake investing and then persisting with the wrong people. Identify and take action to remove them from your business as soon as possible.

- **Lack of experience** – have a plan to identify your experience or skill gaps and plan to build a team that complements you and brings other experience or more experience to your team.
- **Too few customers** – this could be a result of overestimated sales figures; know how you are going to win clients. But too few could make you too reliant on those clients.
- **Setting prices too low** – you may get known for being the cheap and cheerful supplier or later find it difficult to increase the prices.
- **Poor financial controls** – you should know your numbers and how your business operates at all financial levels. How many sales make up my income? What is the direct cost of delivering the product or service? What are my overheads and what trends am I experiencing? Make sure you are not taking out more than the business can afford to pay you.
- **Bad debts** – have a proactive way of collecting your money for work completed. How can you ensure your customers pay on time? What is your credit control procedure? Will you send statement reminders, letters or make calls to collect the money?
- **Poor control of your overheads** – continually review your overheads to understand the spend, identify the unnecessary expenditure and consider ways of reducing the overheads and improving your profit margins.
- **Competition** – be aware of what your competition are doing and how they are reacting to change or even reacting to you entering the marketplace.
- **Poor communication with staff** – how will your staff know what is expected of them? How will you communicate with them? Perhaps face to face or by email circulation?
- **Health issues of the key people** – what provision will you make to ensure your key people stay in the best possible health? Will you have healthcare plans? A stress policy? How will you know of any issues that may impact on your business?
- **Bad management and poor supervision** – how will you manage your people to get the best results?
- **Poor communication with suppliers** – how will your suppliers know your expectations to be met? How often will you review your terms, etc? If you have cashflow problems, how will you communicate these, as putting your head in the sand is never the long-term solution?

- **Poor communication with customers** – how will you know you are continuing to meet the expectations of your clients? How will you know your business with them is under pressure from a competitor?
- **Bad luck** – yes, suffering bad luck is a contribution.
- **Poor planning** – fail to plan, then plan to fail.

Pushing your business comfort zone

Challenge the fear, don't fear the challenge.

Are you sitting comfortably? Then it's time to begin pushing that comfort zone …

As an entrepreneur you'll recognise your 'positive mental attitude' as a vital tool for motivating you to take action. But what happens when that positivity takes leave and you're left feeling fearful?

Challenging the fear

Fear can be referenced as 'False Expectations Appearing Real', so the place to start is looking at your expectations vs reality.

Let's use referral networking as an example. You may be holding back from visiting networking groups because of a fear of speaking in public and delivering your 60 seconds every week.

There is the real possibility of words getting muddled, forgetting what to say, your voice cracking from nerves and getting the timing wrong. If all these things happened, then I am sure you would be devastated. You may believe that you could not convey confidence in your business and fear you will come across as a novice and lose the respect from the business owners in the room. Even worse, you've been talking yourself out of attending.

The reality is that when someone stumbles over words or confuses their point, no one really minds! Everyone has been adversely affected by nerves at some point in their lives and business owners understand that. However, there are tactics you can implement to avoid the common pitfalls, and they're based in planning and preparing.

Planning for success

With the example of delivering a 60-second presentation, you could plan with a script. You may therefore be more comfortable with the idea of reading than remembering, so you'd include all the points you want to get across to the room and then practise with a timer running. As a result, the fear is eroded.

Tip: when you lay out all the fears and consequences of something going wrong, it's far easier to plan tactics that help you work around them.

Some fears will be identified as appearing more real than they are, some will be real and carry a certain level of risk. Starting from a point of understanding, the reality of the situation will help you challenge your fears and achieve success.

How to start a business in six steps

Let's take a look at six steps to establishing a successful start-up business of your own.

Step one: initial considerations

Are you ready for this? The success of your business depends largely on your skill set and commitment. You will need to be honest with yourself on a range of issues such as your business acumen, financial status and personal qualities of entrepreneurship.

There is a good chance that you will need to dig deep to find the drive and dedication that got you started on this journey, and calling on family and friends to get you through the early days may be necessary. The next few months are likely to be physically and mentally challenging, with long hours, hard work and financial uncertainty, which means those closest to you will need to be behind you 100 per cent.

Some good advice here would be to make sure you remember your 'why' and remind others! Perhaps a graphic representation of your motivations where you can see it would be of help.

Reality check time. So, you've got the entrepreneurial qualities, the financial and emotional backup, but do you have the skills required, or do you need more training? Product development, people management, businesses planning, marketing, customer/supplier relations, sales, human resources and bookkeeping skills are all on you. Can you manage them, do you want to manage them, do you want to learn how to, or outsource them to professionals?

Step two: what sort of business are you?

The legal form of your business can have an impact on your personal risk in the business as well as make a difference to your financial returns. Consider whether your business is to be:

Sole trader

If you operate as a sole trader, you and your business are legally inseparable.

- Advantages: sole control therefore straightforward decision making, fewer restrictions over withdrawal of monies.
- Disadvantages: personally bear risks and liabilities of the business.

For taxation purposes, as a sole trader in the UK, your business profits will be taxed alongside any other personal income. You will be required to pay National Insurance, at a percentage on the taxable profits of the business. In terms of accounting, you will need to submit an annual self-assessment return to HM Revenue & Customs (HMRC) and will need to keep accurate and up-to-date records of all business transactions and accounts.

You must register with HMRC and it is recommended to open a separate business bank account. It is important to note that the liabilities of the business also fall to you as an individual. You will need awareness around your finances to ensure that, if you exceed the annual VAT turnover threshold in any 12-month period, you complete a VAT registration form.

Partnership

This is where two or more persons act as co-owners of the business. Similar to a sole trader, there is no legal separation between the business and the partners.

- Advantages: share the risks and liabilities with the other partners, diversity in terms of individual's attributes and what resources can be brought into the business.

- Disadvantages: share the business profits with the other partners, potential disputes between partners, can be held personally responsible for another partner's negligence or carelessness.

Again, registration with HMRC is required and it's recommended to have a separate bank account. Again, ensure you are aware of your personal liabilities. In this entity, you are jointly and severally liable. You will also need to monitor your annual turnover to ensure the threshold requirements are met with regard to VAT registration.

For taxation purposes, business profits are shared in accordance with the partnership agreement and each partner is taxed on their proportion similar to that of a sole trader. A self-assessment return will be required.

Limited company

Is a legal entity in its own right. Individuals own shares in the company by which they can exercise control.

- Advantages: indefinite existence as the company can continue beyond the lifetime of any one member; the company bears its own liabilities therefore protecting the owners; bringing people into the business through the medium of a limited company can be much easier.
- Disadvantages: additional requirements in terms of administration and deadlines, company information publicly available at Companies House.

This is set up as a separate entity to you as an individual and can limit your liability, but not in every circumstance. As a compliance requirement, you must report your annual accounts to Companies House.

As a separate entity, the company is taxed separately. The company is liable to Corporation Tax on its profits at a published percentage. Potentially, monies may be withdrawn by the company owners through salary and/or dividends, which will be subject to tax and National Insurance on the individual. There are potentially tax planning opportunities available to individuals in terms of how they structure the withdrawal of funds.

These are the most common structures but others are available. Your choice of a structure will largely determine how your business tax and personal income tax liability will be calculated and paid. Please ensure you take professional advice based on your own circumstances.

This section references the requirements for a business based in the UK. As a reminder we recommend that you always seek guidance from local professional advisers to understand your local laws and policies wherever you are located.

This is not an exhaustive list, but covers the most common areas. It is recommended that you seek the advice of a tax professional to discuss your personal circumstances.

Step three: planning your business

Writing a business plan is like writing your blueprint for success. The only difference is that you can add to it, change it and keep it as a live document so that you can capture your developing vision and planned strategic delivery on a regular basis.

Your business plan also plays an integral part in setting up and will be required by third parties along the way, such as the bank manager and investors. It also provides you with clarity when communicating to your stakeholders as you bring them on your side. Some people prefer to start with a highly visual tool such as a mind map or mood board, so their motivations are integrated with growth plans. Once this is done, there is a common business structure to follow to ensure all the elements of the business plan are included:

- business summary
- description of your business
- market analysis
- products and services
- marketing strategy
- management plan
- financial data.

Remember, there are professionals you can call upon for help on any of these elements, such as market researchers and accountants. These professionals will help you stick to an annual review of your business plan as well, so you can stay on track or make changes as required.

Step four: positioning

Market and product research is essential to make sure you are positioning the product or service you have to offer to the correct audience.

A SWOT analysis (strengths, weaknesses, opportunities and threats) will help you understand your business and becomes more powerful every year you complete it for comparison with previous years.

Solid market research provides a foundation on which to base your key decisions. This will include your customers, competitors and gaps in the market. It should be done on two levels – your own specifically designed research and using information that is already in existence. Your data should be largely quantifiable and make use of numbers, rather than qualitative.

Remember, the reason for market research is to ensure you have the right offering, to the right audience, at the right price and time. It is a common conversation with my clients to ensure their product development progresses in line with their market development.

You should aim to make it clear what your business does and what benefit it offers.

Step five: promotion

And now for the fun part, telling people about your business! You are the human embodiment of your business and it's true that people buy from people, so you're now the first step to promoting it to the market. The marketing strategy section of your business plan will help you move forward with promotion and decide how and where you will appear:

> Online: website, social media, paid-for advertising, PR, emails.
>
> Offline: networking, leafleting, magazines, local advertising, business cards, stationery, speaking opportunities and exhibitions.

The key to successful promotion is to record everything you do, monitor your investment and return and amend where necessary.

Step six: whom to inform

There are many parties to consider when starting a business, including:

- taxation and National Insurance
- bank account
- PAYE scheme (if required)
- VAT registration (if applicable).

Additionally, for a Limited company:

- Companies House registration, then annual return as a confirmation statement.

This is not an exhaustive list, as there may be other registrations that your specific business may need to consider, such as:

- health and hygiene
- health and safety
- property-related (rates, licences, fire, etc.)
- data protection
- insurance company.

We will look at the plan, positioning and promotion in the following chapters.

This section references the requirements for a business based in the UK. As a reminder we recommend that you always seek guidance from local professional advisers to understand your local laws and policies wherever you are located.

Remember this

Know who you can trust

Who can you actually trust in business? It appears there are two distinct characters. The ones you can trust and those that falsely want to build a relationship with you for dishonest purposes.

How good are you at identifying who you can trust? You can't do everything in your business. You will need to do business with others and also delegate, so you need to trust people and therefore be able to place your trust in the right people. You will never get it right every single time, but provided you review and learn from the experience it is less likely you will make the same mistake again.

How do you make your assumptions about who you can trust? Is it a gut feeling, or do you make good decisions in some other way? How quickly can you make a judgement about how the actual experience in time fits your initial assumption? One way I suggest is to have levels of trust and at each level you move the relationship forward or delegate more.

Choosing and navigating the next step

With so much to do, how do we choose the next step and have confidence it is the right one? You may find yourself at a crossroads, overwhelmed by options and unsure if that next step is the right decision for you. This framework is to help you choose your next move amongst those countless possibilities and reduce procrastination. Assess your current situation and evaluate your finances, market position, customer base, talent, operational processes and competitive landscape. Identify your SWOT.

Establish a clear vision that you truly believe and can communicate with ease. What are your goals and aspirations? Define the desired outcomes. This will serve as a guiding light when evaluating options.

Prioritise: with your long-term vision in mind, identify the key goals you want to achieve in the short/medium term. These goals should align with your vision, keep you on that trajectory and address key areas such as revenue growth, market expansion, customer satisfaction, innovation or operational excellence.

Research the options by considering potential strategies, initiatives and opportunities that align with the goals. What does your market research, competitor analysis and customer feedback tell you to gain insights into emerging trends and demands?

With a list of potential options, evaluate them based on the alignment with your goals, potential risks, anticipated return on investment (ROI) and how SMART these options are (specific, measurable, achievable, relevant, and time-based). Consider the financial implications, resource requirements and the impact on your team and customers.

Seek thoughts from trusted mentors, industry experts or advisers in your network. Their experience and external perspective can provide valuable insights and help you avoid potential pitfalls. Engaging the thoughts of others who have faced similar challenges can be instrumental in making your informed decisions.

Before committing to a particular path, consider conducting small-scale tests or pilots. This approach allows you to validate your assumptions, gather feedback, and assess the viability and potential impact of each option. Data-driven insights provide valuable evidence to support a choice.

Reflect on the potential risks in terms of likelihood and consequence. Every decision carries some risk. Develop contingency and mitigation strategies to address the risks effectively. Take calculated risks.

Do not lose sight of your core values; reflect on these throughout the decision-making process to ensure that the chosen path aligns. Make decisions that are consistent with your principles and build long-term trust and loyalty amongst employees and customers.

After careful evaluation, make a confident decision, take action, executing the plan. Closely monitor progress by continuously evaluating and measuring against your key performance indicators (KPIs). From this evaluation of the outcome, adjust your approach as needed based on real-time data, market feedback and emerging opportunities.

Three ways to find the strength to say no!

This can be a tough one for entrepreneurs, especially those new in business, or those easily attracted to new opportunities (the next big shiny thing). Let's explore these questions for you.

How easy do you find it to say no?

For those new in business, it might be very difficult to say no for fear of losing out on a new customer. It may be very easy to say no to opportunities or situations outside of your comfort zone. I wonder, though, does this help you develop as a business owner, or grow the business you envisaged?

Agreeing to work with someone who doesn't truly fit your ideal customer profile may damage your love for the work, despite earning the money. It may in the end cost you more time, money or productivity, or take your skills in a direction you don't want to concentrate on.

Can you say no to someone who doesn't give you the respect you deserve? A persistent late payer, a non-communicative customer, etc. Can you say no to a prospective new employee who shows promise, but isn't the right fit, right now?

Is saying no ignoring your instincts or simply protecting your business?

It's true, it isn't a natural instinct to say yes to something that scares you or no to something when you don't want to rock the boat, hence entrepreneurs build the ability to say no and step out of their comfort zone. They have worked on becoming strong enough to fight their natural instincts. I feel that if we can't master the art of saying no, we will never have the business we desire as we will be consistently taking two steps forward, too many back. Often, we end up serving other people's agendas rather than thinking of our own goals, purpose and reason why.

Here's how to find that strength

First, we have to understand what we want and therefore what we do not want. Thereafter, with systems in place and confidence in our choices, we are more able to say no or at least understand how we can learn from future communications, when the opportunity to say no next presents itself.

Tip: when you're clear in your reasoning to yourself, it makes it easier to communicate your reasons to the person or opportunity.

Next, keep your 'wants' or end goal front of mind. It's about being able to identify whether the opportunity that presents itself will help drive you closer to what you want, or take you off on a tangent, or even backwards. When you have a crystal-clear objective, interruptions and distractions are so easy to see.

Try to allow the time and employ strategic questioning to help you assess the opportunity.

Will it get you closer to your end goal or objectives?

Will it cost you time, money, productivity or ethics? Or will it save or enhance those things?

What value will it bring to your business and customers?

If you trial it, make the final decision fast: 'scale or fail fast'.

Tip: not all opportunities are distractions, some will be highly beneficial to you, your business and your customers. So, take the time to properly assess what's being offered to you.

Business is simple but not easy

Business is simple but not easy and we often make it more difficult than it sometimes needs to be.

How can you simplify your business and focus on those areas of your business that give you the outcomes you desire?

One way is to take smaller, well-considered steps towards your vision, goal and objective.

> 'You don't have to see the whole staircase, just take the first step.'
>
> – Martin Luther King Jr[1]

This quote is a popular one for good reason. Far too many people are presented with an idea of their future and feel so daunted by the end goal, the big step, that they become overwhelmed or disillusioned.

Your vision may seem so far away from your starting point that you begin to question your capability and even passion to get you there.

For me, you first have to clearly define what 'Success' looks like for you. Success is not what an 'influencer' or anyone else tells you it is. Then create a step plan. What needs to be done? What will the business need to look like in a year's time? What is my focus for the next 90 days? What are my actions for the next 30 days?

A 'step change' is often needed. Step change is defined in *Collins Dictionary* as 'a significant change, especially an improvement'.

If you want something different, then a change has to happen and often that change is greater than we anticipate, hence not everyone easily succeeds with their desire to develop and grow. A change doesn't come easily hence the reference to a step change.

As you work through your focused activities, you will begin to see some sort of flow, which will generate energy, momentum and enthusiasm for the process.

It's in the numbers

Very often our key performance indicators (KPIs) come back to a number. Of course as a business owner, we have to know our numbers. Not just the numbers in our annual accounts but those that drive the success of our business.

---

[1] King, M. L., see: https://www.goodreads.com/quotes/1063592-you-don-t-have-to-see-the-whole-staircase-just-take.

The eight key steps that the more successful businesses undertake each year without fail to best manage their financial performance are:

1 **Plan** – forecast your business performance.
2 **Measure** – actual performance vs forecast and KPIs.
3 **Review** – review and measure the annual performance of the business.
4 **Evaluate** – period to period, month – quarter – year on year.
5 **Compare** – benchmarking against your competitors and industry (was a good year unique or commonplace?).
6 **Value** – how has your recent performance impacted your valuation?
7 **Analyse** – reflect on your numbers and consider how much more profitable and valuable your business could be.
8 **Improve** – establish a plan that improves your performance and that can be implemented.

Look to capture your plan on one page

To help you simplify your business and narrow your focus towards your high pay-off activities, try this one-page plan.

This captures your vision, mission, goal or objective, your targets and the activities you need to execute on one side of the page.

What is your vision, mission, goal or objective?

This may be a longer-term vision or a shorter objective or goal.

What are your targets or key performance indicators?

Write down all the targets that have to be delivered in order to achieve that vision, mission, etc. What are the measures that will confirm you have achieved that bigger picture vision, mission, etc?

For example, if you wanted to double the size of your business, then is the measure a turnover target, the number of customers, the number of employees, the size of your premises, etc.?

What activities do you need to execute?

Considering the vertical, for each target consider and write down the activities that have to be executed to ensure you hit that target.

So, taking my example, if to double the size of your business, you need X new customers at an average sale value of Y, then what are the focused activities that you have to execute in order to achieve that target?

This tool helps you to have an activity focus rather than waiting for the outcome, which sometimes may be disappointing. With the one-page plan, if your targets and activities are well considered, then you should be able to simply focus on the activities. If you deliver them, then the targets should be met and then the vision, mission, etc. delivered.

The one-page plan certainly highlights what needs your focus, time and energy whilst also highlighting that anything else is often a distraction or interruption.

Is buying a franchise a good option?

Buying a franchise can be a good option for some entrepreneurs, but it's not the right choice for everyone. Here's an overview of the key advantages and disadvantages to consider.

Advantages of buying a franchise:

1 **Proven business model:** you're investing in an established system that has already been tested and refined.
2 **Brand recognition:** franchises come with instant name recognition and an existing customer base.
3 **Training and support:** franchisors typically provide comprehensive training programmes and ongoing support.
4 **Lower risk:** franchises generally have higher success rates compared to starting a business from scratch.
5 **Buying power:** you can benefit from the collective purchasing power of the franchise network.
6 **Easier financing:** banks may be more willing to lend money for a known franchise brand.

Disadvantages of buying a franchise:

1 **Limited flexibility:** you must follow the franchisor's rules and regulations, which can restrict your autonomy.
2 **Ongoing costs:** you'll need to pay ongoing royalties and fees to the franchisor.
3 **High start-up costs:** initial franchise fees and set-up costs can be substantial.
4 **Reputation dependency:** your business can be affected by issues with the broader franchise brand or other franchisees.
5 **Contractual obligations:** franchise agreements can be restrictive and difficult to terminate.
6 **Shared profits:** you must share a portion of your profits with the franchisor.

Whether buying a franchise is a good option depends on your personal goals, skills and financial situation. It can be an excellent choice for those who want to run their own business with the support of an established brand and system. However, it may not suit entrepreneurs who prioritise complete independence and creative control.

Before deciding, carefully research potential franchises, independently speak with any existing franchisees, review their disclosure documents, and consult with a lawyer and accountant to ensure you fully understand the commitment and potential returns.

Remember this

Try things

Procrastination can stifle the development and growth of any business.

You will find as an entrepreneur that there will be advice coming to you from all directions, whether that is a colleague, associate, online article, newspaper, customer or supplier.

Quite often the advice will be contradictory, and you end up in fear of trying anything because somewhere you are told every idea is a bad idea.

Try things for yourself. First, test them small in terms of numbers and the level of investment. Then, tweak the activity from the initial results and test it again in a small way. Review your measured results before deciding if it works or not. Then, and only then, understand if it actually works for your business or not.

> ### I wish I knew this before I started my first business
>
> You don't need to know everything before you start.
>
> Please accept you will never have all the answers. In the start-up phase it is a common feeling, and resulting behaviour, that we have to wear *all* the hats in our business. One minute we are selling, then delivering, then updating the accounts before undertaking some marketing when we have a moment. However, deep down we know we are not the best to do certain roles in our own business because of our skill, experience and knowledge.

Key points

- Are *you* ready to start your own business?
- How will you test the water?
- What is your strong reason why?
- Be clear on what work/life balance means for you.
- Are you ready to make the 'step change' often needed to start your business?

Additional resources

Books
Ferris, T. (2009) *4 Hour Work Week*. Harmony.

Podcasts
Modern Wisdom Ep878 – 15 Harsh truths from history's greatest founders with David Senra.

Websites:
www.enterprisenation.com.

CHAPTER 3
PLANNING YOUR BUSINESS

So far we've considered your mindset and whether you are ready to start your own business. The good news is that you have continued to this chapter where we will now start to look at the practical considerations during the key start-up phase of your business.

Here we will look at your objectives, how you will differentiate to create a market opportunity for you and take some initial considerations that will help you to form a strong foundation from which to launch.

> 'A goal without a plan is just a wish'
>
> – Antoine de Saint-Exupéry[1]

What does your destination look like?

If somebody handed you a road atlas and asked 'what's the best way to get there?' the first question you'd ask is 'where are we going?'.

It's the same in business. If you don't know where you're heading, there's little chance of you taking the best route to get there.

Decide your destination first.

Consider what you love, what you (or your future team) are good at and what will pay you well.

What is the business model that will deliver this for you?

---

[1] Saint-Exupéry, A., see: https://www.goodreads.com/quotes/87476-a-goal-without-a-plan-is-just-a-wish.

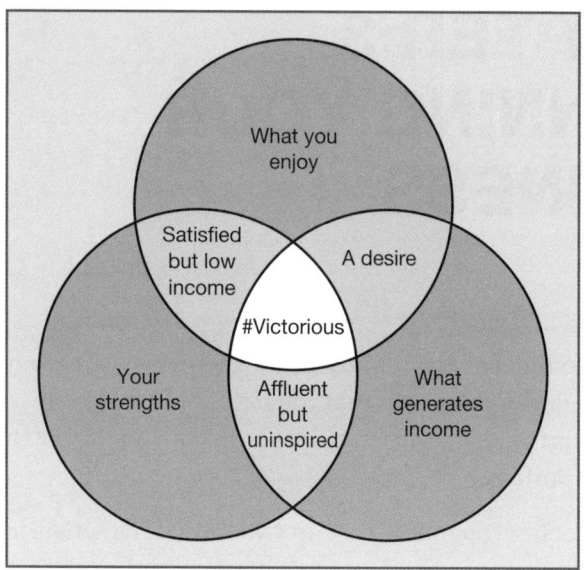

Next, decide when you'd like to arrive at the destination, then map out your route.

You may map out the journey step by step, which direction, what checkpoints, where I can stop for a break if needed, etc.

Of course, today we may just programme the Sat Nav that already knows the best route, quickest way, and what to avoid. Even this technology needed time, experience and a plan to provide a way.

But let's remember that even your Sat Nav alone *won't* get you there. You can't just set the destination and hope; you also have to drive.

Once you know where you're going, it becomes so much easier to work everything else out.

Are you clear on your destination and the best, easiest, quickest route to take?

Aim for a destination where you make the money you want or need, which delivers happiness and with minimal effort asap.

P.S. Effort if not hard work! Work smart, work effectively and efficiently.

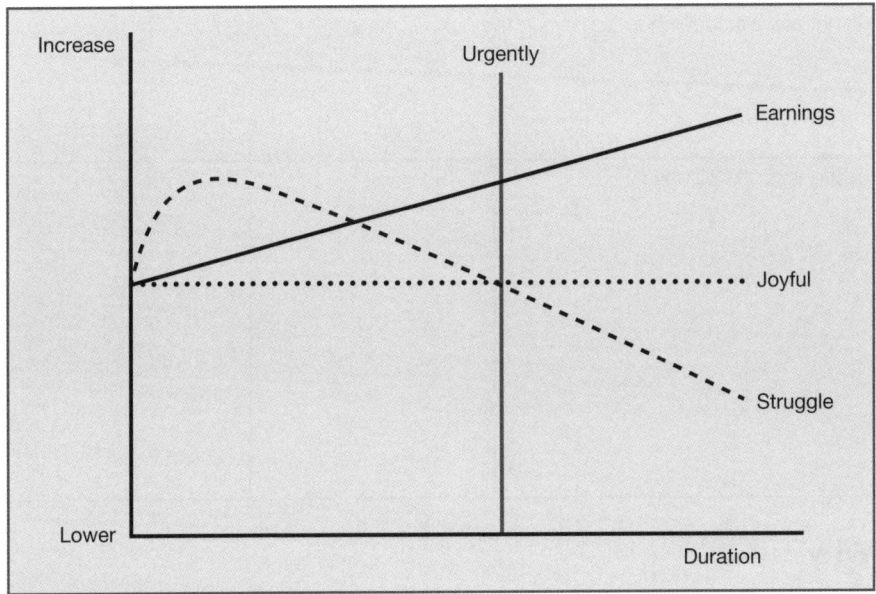

Is your desired outcome too far away?

From my experience of working with hundreds of business owners, the gap between the now and the desire is often far too big and contributes to the reason why we may procrastinate, stutter, bail out or not actually end up with the outcome we desire or deserve.

Together with the lack of a plan to get there, this is a common reason for not achieving the goals, objectives or New Year resolutions. The desire is too far away, and the step is too big to feel, sense, see and actually make. The gap is too wide, so there are too many obstacles to stop us reaching that desired point.

Can you break down the big picture, the vision, the goals, the objectives into smaller steps?

Consider the required journey and the flow of activities, and develop a plan of priorities that creates a series of smaller steps to make up the gap from where you are now to where you want to be.

As an example, you may have an x year objective or goal. Work out points to achieve along the timeline that keep you on that trajectory to that bigger desire, then break that down into 90-day, 30-day objectives.

What are you looking to achieve in the next 90 days?		
Actions for 0–30 days	31–60 days	61–90 days

Why?

With smaller, achievable and realistic steps it is easier to visualise the action to be executed, consider any obstacles to plan for, feel the journey step by step and, importantly, celebrate each small stage as a win.

You can more easily feel, see and sense interruptions to the immediate part of the journey and it's more obvious to you than a distraction to a longer-term goal that you can't easily relate to at this stage.

Much of our journey to achieving our desired point is around our behaviours and habits that influence our activity. Achieving smaller steps is easier rather than hitting a wall and then easily slipping back into the old habits or way of doing things, those things that you wanted to change or needed to change.

I've seen that business owners often find it easier to identify what needs to change and build an association with what needs to be done in the short term rather than the consideration of the long-term desire such as an exit plan.

If we deviate slightly on a small step then we do not go too far off course. If we deviate on a big step, by the time we get there, then we may have found we are way off target. You can also refine a smaller step more easily as it feels like a slight change of direction to the same destination not changing the destination.

James Clear in his book *Atomic Habits* uses the example of an aeroplane taking off from one side of USA and how a minor percentage change in the directional compass at take-off would mean a 200+ mile differentiation when they reach the other side![2]

Busy business owners have so many things to think about and do not like to be consumed or overwhelmed by having one single focus, big goal or vision. A smaller step is achievable whilst they can also still keep an eye on all the areas of high pay-off importance. You can have multiple small focuses rather than just one single large goal.

Regularly achieving smaller steps rather than waiting to achieve a big step fuels greater positive thoughts over negative thoughts and that compounds to impact our energy and motivation.

Momentum in business or life in general is important and for sure it feels good. This is what you get with the compounding effect of such smaller steps, within a system and tackling the right flow.

Achieving smaller steps along the way helps you change your identity to the purpose and engage with execution. It is then more difficult to slip back into older habits.

You become engaged to achieve a step, rather than just want it, because you know it's not the end it's just a step along the way influencing the ease of the next stage.

This approach also creates evidence that you can do it rather than waiting x months to establish if you can or you can't. This then influences your belief, energy and motivation.

For sure, you don't change behaviours and habits overnight! A meaningful change is required and a plan, system, activity focus creates a journey you want to take, feel you are progressing along rather than it feeling like just a light to aim for at the end of the tunnel that never gets closer.

---

[2] Clear, J. (2018) *Atomic Habits*. Penguin Random House.

> ### Remember this
>
> **Break down your journey into smaller steps**
>
> You can't just launch your business without any thought or planning.
>
> Break down the steps taking your business from concept to market.
>
> 1. Confirm your value.
> 2. Do your research.
> 3. Create your prototype or minimal viable product.
> 4. Test the market.
> 5. Consider your intellectual property.
> 6. Design your business model.
> 7. Know your numbers.
> 8. Build your brands (business and personal).
> 9. Create your marketing plan with strategy and tactics.
> 10. Launch it!

Who has the pain, problem, fear, want, need or desire that you are looking to solve?

One of the biggest reasons for business failure in the start-up phase is taking a solution to market that nobody wants.

Tip: ensure that your product development constantly aligns with your market development.

Find out what fits the market, start to develop the offering, then explore further details with the prospective customers that you would want to attract.

Too often, a product or service is established based on what the founder would want or would buy themselves, but remember you are not your customer!

Do you have a good idea of the people who will buy your product or service, the solution that you are proposing?

Look to build out the profile, the avatar, of your preferred buyer/s and consider the persona of the buyer. From this profile, put yourself in their shoes and consider their pain, problem, fear, want, need or desire that you can then solve with your offering.

Their pain may be financial, emotional or related to productivity and process.

What are the problems that your audience are currently experiencing that you could solve?

Most people have a fear that they want to avoid, so what is that for your audience?

Similarly, your audience will have a want, a need and things that they desire, but in what order? Can you find what they need but don't actually realise at this time? The businesses that thrive have focused on a need over something they want or desire.

However, we cannot dismiss the feelings of wanting something as they are more likely to influence their initial interest, as they are things that they are identifying with at that moment of making the initial decision to consider your product or service.

You may then need to test this with the market or complete your market research, which I will come onto shortly.

Who are you developing the solution for? (Avatars)
What is their pain, problem, fear, want, need, desire?
What is the solution in their words? How will it benefit them?
What are your competitors offering to this audience?

Why would they buy from you?

A common fear of start-up business owners is that they have nothing tangible and only the confidence in their product or service to convince their audience to buy from them in preference to the competition.

Don't forget your history!

You would not go to a job interview and have a blank CV with nothing to talk about. Therefore. consider what is relevant from your past that your prospective customer needs to know. Why are you the 'go to' expert and why can they trust your offering as the solution? What does the product actually do for them?

Yes, some of your customers will prioritise their purchase on the quality and buy at a price that they consider to be the value. I'll assume that what you are offering is quality, and pricing will be covered later in the book.

Most customers will buy from you because they get to know, like and trust you. Therefore, how can you expedite that level of engagement with you or your offering?

Building a reputation for reliability and consistency is essential, but trust positioning is something to have at the forefront of your communication with a prospective customer. From the moment they touch you, what is their experience, and will it encourage them to 'like' you? How can you build trust?

Trust positioning may include sharing testimonials, reviews or the logos of your existing customers or those related to your professional accreditations. Demonstrating that others know, like and trust you goes a long way to convincing a prospect to lean towards you.

For example, I'm your ideal customer and you've brought me to your website. On browsing the page, I see that you have also worked with a business similar to my own. As your prospect, my immediate thought leans towards trust, by feeling that if they can trust you then perhaps I should also.

Ultimately, the customer experience will influence their buying choice. Do you or your team respond quickly to enquiries offer excellent customer service, a frictionless checkout process, and know the customer expectations you should be looking to exceed?

Is there a market ?

Exploring your market to establish if there's demand for your product or service is essential and it is an area taken too lightly in the pre-start stage.

Good market research reduces your risk by obtaining information that supports the key decisions you will need to make about your business. It will save you many hours of worry and pain, whilst you effectively plan the direction of your business based on factual information.

All successful businesses have a close understanding of potential and existing customers and the marketplace they work in.

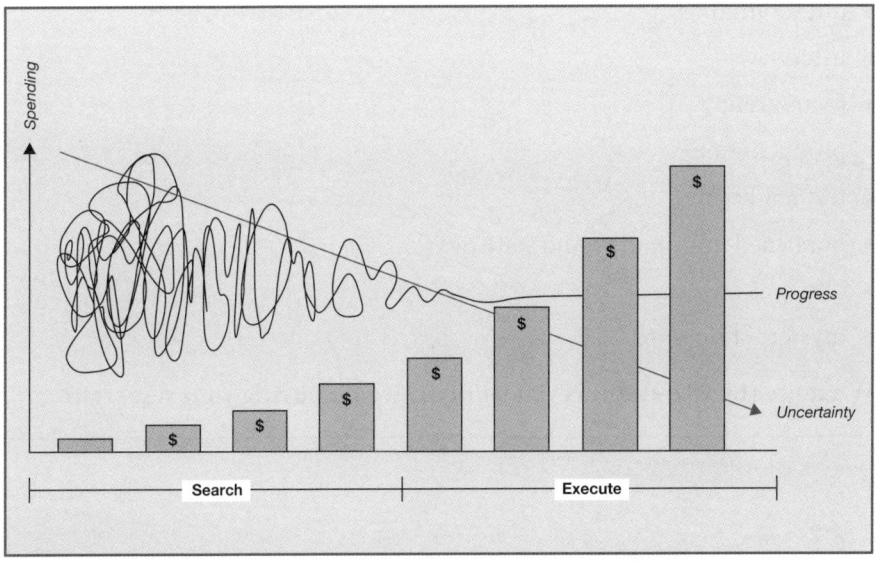

This knowledge allows you to target customers, identify new opportunities, effectively sell and importantly compete with others. Performing market research on potential customers *and* your competitors will help you understand how to make a difference.

The research should cover a number of key questions for your business but, as a minimum, should establish that there is a market for your type of product/service and that the market would buy from you based on your unique selling points.

When asked, many business start-ups will say they have undertaken their market research. However, when this is explored further it is usually with family and friends who repeat what a great idea it is and of course they will buy from you! Some have also established numbers from the local census that the population is X,000s; however, they have no idea if they will actually buy from them.

Market research is commonly broken down to primary and secondary research. It is common to see good desk research, from the comfort of your PC, but often the best research is reaching out and engaging with your prospective, ideal customers.

As an example, your own research could include:

- questionnaires
- interviews
- focus groups
- product tests
- test marketing
- published information and statistics
- observation
- mystery shopping.

What are the 10 questions you want answered during your research?

1	
2	
3	
4	
5	
6	
7	
8	
9	
10	

As an example, here are the questions you may ask as a web designer:

1. Do you currently have a website and if yes, then why/for what purpose?
2. Do you have someone to manage this for you? Can you do your own amendments?
3. How much did you invest initially and do you have an ongoing fee?
4. What is important to you about a website design?
5. If you rebuilt your website today, what would you do differently?
6. If your website could do something else, what would it be?
7. As a user of websites, what influences your engagement with that business?
8. What are your most important website features?
9. Do you integrate AI or utilise any plug-ins or external software API links?
10. What frustrates you about your website?

How do I complete my market research?

This may sound obvious but ask! I say this, as too many businesses, whether at start-up or when perhaps launching a new product or service, simply assume the likely responses and feel that they know what the customer wants or needs.

Yes, I would encourage you always to put yourself in your buyers' shoes, but you have to sample and test your potential audience for any learning or at least confirmation.

Many start-ups will ask friends, family and maybe close associates, who often will obviously support and encourage, as they feel it is their responsibility.

Many growing businesses feel that they know their customer but fail to ask how they would react to a new product or service development.

Look to identify your market and ideal customers; research a sample and ideally call them or meet them to ask a series of considered questions, with the objective of obtaining the insight that confirms that people will pay for your product or service and why.

As an example, try to establish the following:

- Can you profile and define the type of customer that will buy?
- How many potential customers are there in your catchment area?
- How much are they prepared to pay?
- Do they already buy your kind of product or service from your competitors – if yes, why?

- How best to let them know what you have for sale.
- What do they want from your product or service or what would encourage them to buy from you, such as the benefits and value to them?
- What do your potential competitors do?
- Which competitor has the largest market share and why?
- From feedback is your offer clear to the buyer?

You can complete primary or secondary research, but I encourage you to not restrict your findings to just desk research.

The method you use will very much depend on who you identify as your ideal customers in your preferred markets, how accessible they are and what you think will gather the best response.

How many people should you ask? Well, enough! Ask enough people until you have no new information or lessons from the responses.

Also analyse your competitors.

Undertake your own competitor analysis to see how your competitors approach the market with their product or service. Consider your direct competitors, those that are best in class, those that you aspire to be, but also those that are 'stealing your pound'. For example, where your audience currently consider to spend their money for what you are solving.

You may have a different approach for your solution, but your competitors have started their business and had some wins so, after reviewing your observations, you'll have a great place from which to start and this will save you from having to re-invent the wheel!

Secondary research involves analysing data that has already been collected, typically by other organisations or researchers. This includes studying reports, articles, statistics, and data from reliable sources. *It will also include your 'desk research' such as reviewing websites or analysing reviews.* It is helpful for understanding market trends, identifying broad industry insights, and benchmarking against competitors.

Primary research involves collecting original data firsthand from your ideal customer/s. It's tailored to answer specific questions or investigate particular matters. This type of research is particularly valuable for gaining insights directly from target audiences and gathering current, relevant data. *For example, surveys, focus groups, interviews and market testing. Observation or 'mystery shopping' experience can provide a level of detail you are unlikely to find with any secondary research.*

Positioning your solution

What makes you truly unique in the eyes of your customers? Do you know why a prospect will choose to work with you or buy your product?

Knowing the answer to these questions will prevent the shock of when customers don't choose you and helps you show up in front of those who would.

You will best position your business by understanding three things:

1. What your customers want (established via research).
2. What your competition do well or what they are not good at (via your competitor analysis).
3. What you do best.

Market and product research is essential to create your target avatar and make sure you are positioning the product or service you have to offer to the correct audience. This will ensure you are speaking to your ideal customer when detailing your offering.

Solid market research provides a foundation on which to base your key decisions. This will include your customers, competitors and gaps in the market. It should be done on two levels – your own specifically designed research and using information that is already in existence. Your data should be largely quantifiable and make use of numbers, rather than qualitative.

Remember, the reason for market research is to ensure you have the right offering, to the right audience, at the right price and time.

With this knowledge you can now position your offering in a way that people want to buy because you are presenting a solution to their pain, problem, fear, want, need or desire.

When verbalising your offering at a networking event or in a sales conversation or writing copy for your website or marketing assets, put yourself in your prospects' shoes and consider the words that capture their interest, hook their attention and pull them towards you with interest.

You should aim to make it clear what your business does and what benefit it offers. Talk from your prospects' position and not your own, so look to replace any self-references to I or we and refer to the impact for the potential buyer.

At this stage you may only have a list of features of what your business offers, so the best way to convert those features to benefits is to link them with the words 'which means that'.

Utilise this table to convert yours and establish your benefits.

(Feature) ... which means that ... (= Benefit)

Feature	Benefit

Like you, your prospects will only buy from you once they know, like and trust you. Therefore, how can you establish a relationship and build trust with your audience?

If you show empathy and understanding of your prospects' situation, then you will more easily build a relationship with them. If you share testimonials, case studies, logos of other customers or accreditations plus awards you've won, then you will create trust. But show empathy and understanding by sharing how they benefit from your features.

Six considerations for any business

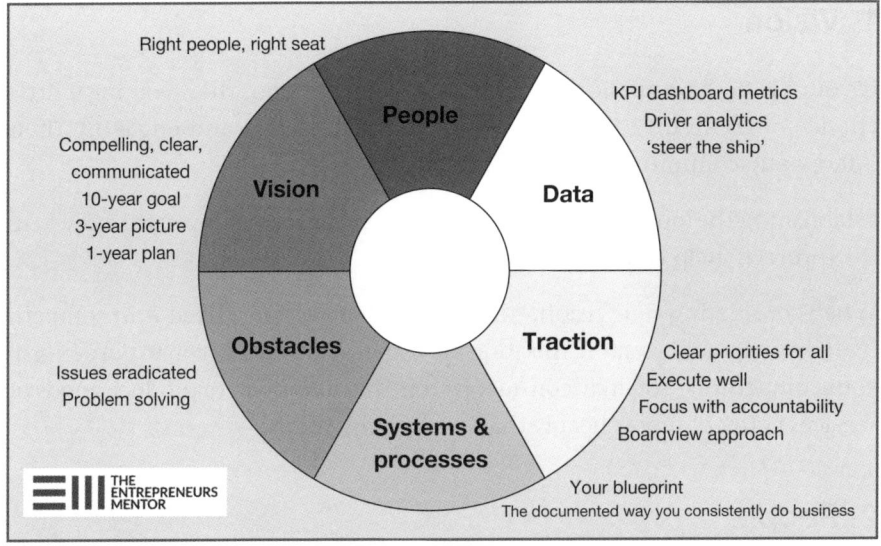

As you develop your business from an idea to start-up, look to keep in mind these six key areas of any business.

1 **Vision** – keep this front of mind and as a basis of your decisions.
2 **People** – what talent do you need around you and how do you hire them?
3 **Data** – utilise information and data in your business to make decisions that improve your business.
4 **Traction** – how will you create traction for your business and maximise your opportunities?
5 **Systems and processes** – build a business that does not rely on you. Create written processes for your people to follow as 'the way we do things around here' that can be continually developed.
6 **Obstacles** – be mindful of potential obstacles to your plans. Assess your risks early and plan activities that solve the issues before they arise.

Let's take a look at each of these six areas in a little more detail:

1 Vision

If your vision and mission are not crystal clear to you, then you have little chance of communicating them to your stakeholders and engaging their interest and commitment.

Establishing the 'purpose' of the business often engages your people (now or in the future) to help you deliver the vision.

When considering your vision, you are likely to have considered your competitive advantage and your organisation's attributes that enable you to outperform your competitors. You may consider factors that allow you to produce goods or services better or more cheaply than your competition.

2 People

Look to ensure that you have the right people in the right seat. This includes your internal and your external 'team' members. You will see many successful entrepreneurs reference the importance of surrounding yourself with talent and ideally those who can do things better than you!

Consider your team structure even before you have a team. What does your organisational chart need to look like? Start with a blank piece of paper and map out your ideal organisational chart without any emotion. Don't consider any names or personalities that already exist in the business or those you are considering. Instead, reflect on what is right for the business and then add the key responsibilities for each role. The responsibilities that when executed would provide you with a return on your investment in that role. From here, you can start to place names against positions and responsibilities. Finally, compare the ideal to what you have now, considering the action for any gaps or surplus.

If you need to hire, then for the role consider three areas: (1) the job description (2) the person profile and (3) your return on investment. Together, this considers the impact required and desired.

How do we know if we have the right people? Consider the role. Understand the skills and competence required for an individual to make an impact in that position. Then this helps you review if the current jobholder is the right person or the applicant fits the requirement.

Your leadership is critical to the culture of the business. There are different leadership styles. Find yours. Adapt it for your team and continually develop in an agile way.

3 Data

Data is all around you. For example, the data you have at your fingertips includes your customer interactions, operational delivery, people performance and marketing outcomes.

What are the metrics that identify you are progressing as planned or desired? Consider this as if you are the captain of the ship. As a business owner, much like the captain, you don't want to be doing everything, but you do want reassurance that your team are undertaking what is required. The horizon often cannot confirm the destination but all the dials and indicators in front of you confirm you are heading in the right direction. What do you need to steer your ship? What are your success drivers? What are the activities you need to have in control rather than waiting for an outcome that is often established too late for any impactful action? For each measure, consider that each dial has a red, amber and green zone. If they are all green, then you are very likely to end at your desired destination. All red, then something needs to change the course. What data do you need to feed into your dials?

What data do you have at your disposal? The obvious to which most businesses reply is Google Analytics. In itself that is a good start, but how much do you understand the devil in the detail about your web visitors, their behaviour and actions?

What other data do you have access to? For example, market research, your finances, visitor numbers, sales statistics (such as your average sales value, which products or services sell best, what are the reasons for purchases), and your waste (not just physical rubbish but the impact on your organisation's productivity).

4 Traction

Business traction refers to the progress of a company and the momentum it gains as the business grows.

It is helped by having clear priorities for all stakeholders – including the owners, shareholders, team, suppliers, customers or any other stakeholders impacted by your business.

To gain traction, you will have a plan for your new business activities, your operational excellence or a strategy that leverages your opportunities. The key here is to execute well and in a timely manner.

Often a business owner can be impatient for results, so when considering the traction potential for your business, here are a couple of considerations.

First, what is the impact on your earning potential vs the time to see the desired impact, considering the cost of any required investment?

Second, your market share versus your market growth rates, which is a consideration of how you generate and best use your cash.

As a practical reflection of all the key areas in your business, think about the boardroom. Imagine you had a team sat around the table or at least a spare chair for each key role. Consider what you need to know, measure and understand, as if they or you were reporting to your own board. What would you want to know from sales, marketing, operations, finance, etc.? Put yourself in each individual seat and consider what would be needed to keep a check on performance and progress.

5 Systems and processes

Combine your critical processes to create your business 'know-how', your documented way that you consistently do well in your business.

Your systems and processes are your activities and procedures that engage your people to get the job done, right first time, in line with expectations and to the promises made.

The book *The E-Myth* refers to seven essential systems – Marketing, Lead Generation, Lead Conversion, Customer Fulfilment, Management, Leadership and Finance.[3]

You can't do every system first, so consider those most critical for your business and utilise your team to create them.

Tip: an easy way to build your systems is to utilise a new hire. As you induct and train them, ask them to write up the system to check their understanding. On receipt you have a written system!

When creating a system, consider the outcome first and work backwards. This helps you best consider what is needed upfront to ensure everything runs smoothly and efficiently in its execution.

---

[3] Gerber, M. E. (1988) *The E-Myth: Why Most Businesses Don't Work and What to Do About It.* Ballinger Publishing.

6 Obstacles

This is to encourage a reflection on the obstacles you face and the solutions to overcome them.

You could argue this is a bit of a catch-all area, and to some degree it is, as you have already considered the other critical matters in the previous five areas. Considering your obstacles in advance helps you bring clarity on the prioritisation and those actions required. It also helps you to eradicate issues and solve the problems or challenges that you are likely to face.

This may involve the following:

- How you are using the assets of your business – your cash, people, equipment, etc.
- It could be internal or external factors or a combination of both.
- Is it product- or service-related?
- It may be linked to your suppliers or customers.
- Does it impact your sales generation or the delivery of the promise?
- Or does it enthuse your collaborators or motivate your competition?
- And what about the risks to your business?

Considering this final point, creating a risk register will help you to consider and evaluate the risks to your business and your livelihood. Analyse where you are vulnerable, the potential obstacles and what are the critical challenges to your business. Then rate them on how likely they are to occur and what level of consequence an occurrence would have on the business to highlight any action needed.

Your SWOT analysis

A SWOT analysis is a powerful tool for understanding your strengths and weaknesses, and for looking at the opportunities and threats you face. The areas you will consider provide an excellent basis for reviewing your business strategy and the future direction of your business or a new proposition.

It will help you to identify:

- areas of your business that are performing well or have been well planned
- where improvements are needed to remain competitive because your competitor/s are better

- new opportunities
- gaps in the market
- any threats to your business
- your value, USP and differentiator.

By undertaking a SWOT analysis you *really* get to know your own business.

What makes SWOT particularly useful is that the process can be undertaken by an individual or a group. With focused thinking you will identify your main strengths and form your strongest 'unique selling points'. It will also uncover opportunities that you can look to take advantage of now and not later. You will also better understand the true, revealed weaknesses of your business, so you can manage these and eliminate threats before they are harmful.

When reviewing each area, consider all elements of the business from finance and management to production and marketing.

Strengths:

- What advantages do you have or what do you do better than anyone else?
- What do people in your market see as your strengths?
- What factors mean that you 'get the sale'?

Weaknesses:

- What could you improve?
- Are there areas you should avoid?
- What are people in your market likely to see as weaknesses?
- What factors lose you sales?

Opportunities:

- Where are good opportunities for you?
- What are the interesting trends you can maximise?

Threats:

- What obstacles do you face?
- What is your competition doing that you should be worried about?
- Is changing technology threatening your position?
- Are political or environmental decisions likely to impact your business?
- Could any of your weaknesses seriously threaten your business?

Internal:

- Strengths: attributes of the organisation that are helpful to achieving the objective.
- Weaknesses: attributes of the organisation that are harmful to achieving the objective.

External:

- Opportunities: *external* conditions that are helpful to achieving the objective.
- Threats: *external* conditions that are harmful to achieving the objective.

Here's a template to help you analyse your SWOT against your competitors

Choose a competitor who is best in class, another you aspire to be and someone who is an alternative indirect competitor who is 'stealing your potential sales'.

SWOT worksheet for your business	
Strengths	Weaknesses
Opportunities	Threats

	Strengths	Weaknesses	Opportunities	Threats
Your business				
Competitor 1				
Competitor 2				
Competitor 3				

Once you have completed your SWOT analysis, ensure it is USED by considering:

How can we Use each Strength?

How can we Stop each Weakness?

How can we Exploit each Opportunity?

How can we Defend against each Threat?

> **Remember this**
>
> **Utilise your strengths and work on your personal development**
>
> An entrepreneur is confident in their ability and plays to their strengths whilst usually hiring other skills around them. They are also very honest about those strengths *and* the areas for their personal development.
>
> Regularly undertake an analysis of your strengths, weaknesses, opportunities and threats for the circumstances and role you are undertaking for a specific task.
>
> What do you need to work on? Consider completing a gap analysis of your skills in areas such as sales, marketing, finance, operations, leadership, etc. and highlight to yourself some areas for focus.
>
> However, remember you do not have to be a chameleon of all roles, and you can gain support by outsourcing or delegating many of the activities in your business.

Take the helicopter view and think strategically

To think strategically involves stepping back from the day-to-day and seeing the bigger picture. This is often referenced as the 'helicopter view'. It is an opportunity to consider any long-term implications whilst aligning your thoughts, plans and decisions with your goals.

This approach can help guide your thoughts and ultimately the business towards long-term success, making decisions that align with your overall vision whilst remaining adaptable to changing market conditions.

The sort of thinking to undertake when you step back for this purpose is:

- Assess how the business is performing against its measures and key performance indicators.
- What is the current market landscape? What are the trends telling you, how do you currently compare with your competitors and is your SWOT still relevant to today's market?
- Reflect on your long-term vision and goals. Review, reflect and evaluate. Is it still the right thinking for any changes you've recently experienced, or are expecting in the future, that may influence your business?
- Review your *success drivers*, those critical factors that move your business in the desired direction.
- Weigh up the internal and external factors that impact your business. Control the controllable by considering the internal capabilities and capacity whilst being aware of the external matters that will or could impact your business in either a positive or negative manner (e.g. politics, technology, innovation).
- Focus on areas with the highest potential impact with the minimal amount of resources.
- Consider the strategy and model for the next phase of your business. Create a roadmap to move in the desired direction towards your desired destination and to achieve your long-term vision. What are the key initiatives to implement, what are the next milestones and what resources will be required?
- Prepare for future challenges and risks to the business. Conduct 'what if' scenario planning, review your data and consider how to stay agile whilst developing contingency plans for potential outcomes.

In addition, reflect on the six key areas covered earlier in this chapter.

Such considerations will help you to create a business plan that is effective and not just a paper exercise.

> ### Remember this
> #### Keep the big picture in mind with your daily actions
>
> *Entrepreneurs* are *big picture thinkers.* They are creative and take the long view. They can quickly see patterns in complex problems and like to come up with new ideas and new projects.
>
> Remember the big picture, the reason why, whilst also encouraging the planning of your next smaller step. For an entrepreneur, who is a big picture thinker, the small steps can sometimes be difficult, especially if they have a low tolerance for the details and tedious work.
>
> Yes, both are important, but you can only start to work out the small steps if you know the big picture you want to achieve. If we simply get our head down and take continuous small steps, by the time we look up we may have gone in the wrong direction, or we will not recognise or like where we have ended up.
>
> Are you doing something today that may create an obstacle for you in your future?
>
> Consider that big picture and then break down the steps to know the high pay-off activities you need to undertake.
>
> Entrepreneurs do not dwell on the past because they know that they cannot change this, but learn from it, adapt if needed and plan the next moves.

Your business plan

Writing a business plan is like writing the blueprint for your success.

Some will say it is only required when you need to raise finance, but if you fail to plan then plan to fail.

Your business plan is not just a document that is only written when requested by a third party like your bank manager. It should be a live document, capturing your business idea, vision and plans that you should then revisit on a regular basis.

Keep it as a fluid document that you can change, so that you can capture your developing vision and planned strategic delivery on a regular basis.

A good business plan will bring together all those ideas buzzing around inside your head in a logical way whilst committing your ideas to paper. In preparation, it will fuel your idea, take you through a thought-provoking process and help you identify the areas that you need to consider more carefully.

By comparing an existing business plan against the business plan to take your business forward, it will help you identify the strategic actions to be executed for the changes needed.

It is always a good action to look back at your business plan after a couple of months to see if you have implemented your plans and ideas. If not, then review why not.

A good, well-considered plan is one of the cornerstones of a successful business.

The level of detail in your business plan will depend on the nature and size of your business plus the time and effort you are willing to put into its preparation. The most effective business plans make it clear what the business will focus on, identify the financial implications of the business and help overcome problems before they arise.

Be realistic rather than optimistic when making assumptions, particularly financial projections. When you make such assumptions, remember to make a note of these so you can reference back at a later date how you had forecasted such information.

In preparation, always start by making a note of your initial thoughts on paper. That may be simple notes or scribbles or using a structure such as a mind map.

Your business plan also plays an integral part in setting up your business and will be required by third parties along the way, such as the bank manager and investors. It also provides you with clarity when communicating to your stakeholders as you bring them on your side.

Some people prefer to start with a highly visual tool such as a vision board, so that their motivations are integrated within any growth plans. Once this is done, there is a common business structure to follow to ensure all the elements of the business plan are included:

- business summary including your key points, aims, objectives, motivation
- business description
- products and services including what you are offering and why customers will buy from you

- your key people summary
- market analysis
- the marketing and sales strategy
- management plan and key responsibilities
- financial data including the financing plan
- IT, premises, legal.

As mentioned, please review your business plan on a regular basis as a live working document. The review of your business plan is a critical stage. Are you achieving the financial forecasts that you set yourself? Does your product or service look like you initially visualised or have you forgotten a key element? This review enables you to be aware and take action.

There are professionals you can call upon for help on any of these elements, such as market researchers and accountants.

Creating your strategic business model

As mentioned, the level of detail in your business plan may depend on the nature and size of your business plus the time and effort you are willing to put into its preparation.

Much also depends on the stage of your business and if there is any purpose beyond your own planning, but your business plan does not have to be a book or essay. It may be as simple as a one-page document, using a tool such as the Business Model Canvas. This is a tool that I have recommended for the last 20+ years and is a widely adopted and trusted strategic management tool used by millions globally.

The Business Model Canvas was developed by Alexander Osterwalder and Yves Pigneur. Osterwalder initially proposed the nine 'building blocks' of the Business Model Canvas in 2005 as part of his PhD research, which was supervised by Pigneur at the University of Lausanne.

The official template can be downloaded from Strategyzer.

This one-page planning document gets you to consider nine critical business building blocks in your business. The single page consists of a series of linked boxes that fuel various considerations for your business, including your customers and how you find them, your offering and how you deliver it plus the revenue and cost structure, to name a few.

When completing the canvas, look to use different colour pens or Post-it notes which represent categories of required action. For example, green for all is good, amber for something that needs action, and red for something we can put a stop to.

Let's take a look at the nine boxes.

Value proposition

This is the central box that underpins your entire business model. It is a promise of value to be delivered, communicated and acknowledged. A belief from your customer about how your value will be delivered and experienced. It paints a picture of your brand and tells your customers why they should do business with you and makes the specific benefits of your products or services crystal clear from the outset.

What is it that you're offering, to whom and why? How are you going to solve their problems and improve their situations? It is your unique selling point that gives you the differentiation in your marketplace and creates your value.

The canvas can be split into two. The right side is how you take your value out to market and attract your key customer segments whilst building the desired relationships at the various stages of your customers' journey. The left side is about the resources you have to enable you to deliver your promise, albeit internal or external.

On the right-hand side:

Customer segments

Who are your ideal customers?

Here is where your avatars and buyer personas appear. Who are they and why would they buy from you? What are their pains, problems or fears? What do they care about? Do they make emotional or financial decisions with regard to your product or service?

If you are looking to attract other businesses in a B2B marketplace, then your avatar will be built around the profile of the type of organisations you are looking to attract. The persona will be based on the buyer, the person with the power to make the decision or who has the purse strings.

This box leads subsequently into …

Customer relationships

What do your customers expect from you? How does the relationship evolve?

Do they expect to speak to you in person or on social media? At which points of your customers' journey can you build the relationship? Does the relationship change during their journey with you?

Your initial relationships will be building trust as you generate awareness of your business and your prospect starts to consider your offering. After the sale, the relationship will be different as you build loyalty and advocacy for further purchases or referral.

Here is where you can also gain feedback, which helps you to continually develop that all important value proposition.

Channels

How will you take your proposition to market? Where do your ideal customers spend their time?

What channels or platforms will you use to take your value proposition out to your customer segments? Where do they hang out? How will you reach them and engage with them? Do they come from recommendations, are they likely to type their question into a search engine, or will they come across your service on social media?

The channels you choose will help your customers understand your business, distribution and sales. It helps raise awareness of your services or products, allows your customers to evaluate you before purchase and to find post-sales support.

And finally, on the right-hand side of your page at the bottom is ...

Revenue streams

Your business income as a result of sales of products or services.

Often referred to as turnover, your revenue streams will be driven and developed by all the activities in the right-hand boxes. Think about these three main things.

1 **Source** – who is paying you?
2 **Reason** – why are they paying?
3 **Method** – how are they paying? For example in advance with specific payment terms, one upfront payment, upon delivery?

Do you have more than one revenue stream? You may have clients on a contractual agreement at the same time as having short-term or one-time-only customers. Perhaps you run a training business and sell advice manuals on your area of expertise, but also offer a done-for-you service. Consider any potential secondary revenue channels for your business.

Let's now look at the left-hand side of your page.

This side is for the key elements you need to help you deliver your promise, your value proposition.

Key activities

What are the activities that you have to do to deliver your value proposition, reach your customers and generate revenue? What are the key activities that create your value and enable you to perform well?

External partners and internal resources

Who and what makes up the structure of your business?

This will include the wider team of people that are key to your business, so not just the ones on your payroll, but also people who are external from your business that still need to be communicated with: suppliers, subcontractors, supply chain, support networks, etc. that make up your partners.

When reviewing external partners, look at what they can bring to your business and what would motivate them to work with you.

This is also the opportunity to look at how your business would continue to run if you were to step away or are unavailable due to holiday or illness. Consider your people, your systems and processes, business assets, lines of credit and intellectual property. These are your internal resources.

Tip: be wary of one – if you are heavily reliant on one key resource or partner and something happens to that one, you could find this to be a stumbling block that is detrimental to your productivity.

Cost structure

Important costs to operate your business model.

What are the most expensive things that make your business run effectively? Reviewing your expenditure list can help you make sure that the things on that list are considered to be an investment not a cost. Some costs can be stripped out from your expenditure list so you can focus on the things that you need to make a return on.

For example, paying an accountant is considered more of an investment than a cost, because the benefits of using an external partner for this service offsets the cost of doing it yourself. Renting an office is another cost that can be considered an investment if you have a team or meet clients regularly but could be a cost that can be removed if you work remotely.

This one-page business model allows entrepreneurs like you to visualise your business and the key elements within it that shape your strategy. Once you have completed it, you can begin the next step of the business planning – to map out your key activities and start to drive change and growth.

Your value proposition

A good value proposition should encourage your prospects to lean towards you with interest.

Your ideal customer/s should read your value proposition and feel it resonate with them.

The term 'value proposition' essentially means that you can state your value with intent to make your company, product or services attractive to customers. And it's not always easy to do off the top of your head!

Have you ever been asked, 'what makes you different?' If you've ever heard responses like, we care, we listen, or we have excellent customer service, have you believed them? I mean, would you choose a company that doesn't listen, care or have good customer service?

What makes you different your unique selling point (USP)?

When you look back at those definitions, you can quickly tell that your USPs can't be clearly communicated in a few words or a catchphrase. Here are some thoughts to give you a head start on considering and writing your value proposition:

Making your business stand out with a value proposition starts with understanding your existing customers.

Ask yourself or them: 'Why did they buy from *you* why did they choose *your* product or service rather than your competitor's?

Know your features and benefits inside out. Ask what's in it for them.

When you know their pain, problem, fear or aspirations and what they're trying to fix or avoid, you can demonstrate a solution using your features and benefits.

If you're still not different enough ask why and establish the how.

For example, a benefit could be considered 'We listen'.

Q: How are you good listeners?

A: Because we save time in meetings by using Zoom, Google Meet or phone calls for our clients.

Q: Why do you need to save time?

A: Because time is precious and we don't want to waste a minute of theirs and spend our time working for them, not travelling.

Now all of a sudden, 'we listen' has become, 'we understand how precious time is, so we make our meetings as efficient as possible with online meeting platforms or phone calls. And we prevent unnecessary pollution every time we stay off the road too!'

In a statement such as this, you can also demonstrate an understanding of their pain – time management, what they're avoiding – lost time, and your personality comes through too – you care about the environment.

You also have to go into 'child mode' and keep asking why, why, why ... The deeper the dive you take, the greater the success you'll have at finding the real differentiation that creates your stand-out value. Customer service is a great example of continually asking why to establish what is unique about the service delivery or impact for the customer.

Remember, what makes your business different is often you; your why, the culture of your company and how you make your customers feel about working with you.

- Do you give away a lot of free content? Why?
- Are you working towards net zero? Why?
- Do you have a strong corporate social responsibility? Why?
- Do you make it easy for customers to do business with you? How?
- What is the culture in your company? Why?

The aim of a value proposition is to make someone lean in with interest when you speak. Drill down to establish your unique values and find a way to clearly communicate them.

Again, Strategyzer offers a useful canvas to build out your thoughts.

The 'Value Proposition Canvas' is formed around linked sections – the customer profile and the organisation's value.

First, consider the tasks and jobs your customer wants or needs to accomplish. Then consider the gains they will experience and the pain they may encounter.

- Gains – the benefits that the customer expects and needs. What would meet and exceed their expectations?
- Pains – what are the negative experiences, emotions and risks experienced by the customer whilst in the process of getting the job completed?

- Customer jobs – the tasks your customers are trying to perform or execute, problems they are trying to solve and the needs they wish to be met.

Then, analyse this information to establish how you relieve your customers' pains and deliver their desired gains.

- Gain creators – how does your solution offer value to the customer by creating gains?
- Pain relievers – what pain is alleviated for your customer by using your product or service?
- Products and services – the products and services that offer value as they create gain and relieve pain.

Managing your time with effective goal planning

Let me start with a little quiz:

Number of weeks in a year?	52
Number of days in a week?	7
Number of total hours in a day?	24
Number of available hours in a year?	8,760 (365 × 24!)
If we deduct 8 hours sleep per day and don't include all weekends? 16 × 5 × 52	4,160 hours remain.

Is this any different from you or me? Of course not, so how do you use the hours given to you to the best of your ability?

> 'If you are like most people today, you are overwhelmed with too much to do and too little time to do it. You will never be able to do everything. You will never be caught up.'
>
> – Brian Tracy, *Eat That Frog*

> 'Effective management is putting first things first. Organise and execute around priorities.'
>
> – Stephen Covey, *7 Habits of Highly Effective People*

In summary, the books reflect on the need to be selective, focus on the most important tasks first and the importance of prioritisation.

There are many time management techniques that you can use such as time blocking, the Pomodoro technique, the Eisenhower 'Priority' matrix, the two-minute rule of Getting Things Done, the Pareto analysis and of course many others. However, such tools, methods, techniques, strategies and models will only work with your discipline. If you have discipline, most things will work; if you have no discipline, none of them will.

Many people spend their day firefighting and being attracted to those things that 'appear' important and urgent (e.g. emails, telephone calls, interruptions, distractions), rather than the important but not urgent (e.g. working on the business, your proactivity). I encourage you to focus the use of your time on your priorities and drive your diary commitments by your goals and objectives. If you are asked to do something that does not fit with your goals or objectives, then ask yourself why you should do it.

Here are some of the reasons to be a goal planner:

1 Evidence that setting goals provides the focus that leads to performance.
2 Provide you with a measurement of progress.
3 Fuels our motivation and inspiration.
4 A focus that leads your priorities and effective activity rather than procrastination.
5 A purpose of your reflection (daily or by activity).
6 Easier to identify when your time has been wasted.
7 Provides greater clarity of when you are interrupted, distracted or having your time hijacked.

I encourage you to find your passion, understand your motivation with clarity and establish goals that make a real difference. This will fuel your activity, the right activity.

These high pay-off activities should then drive the content of your diary. Look to schedule these activities into your diary over the next 1–31 days. Not everything has to be achieved in the next day or few! Look to create blocks of time in your diary such as 30 minutes, 1 hour, 2 hours or 3 hours. Now write in your 'not negotiables' including time for yourself. Also include some time for firefighting, as we have to be realistic whilst always retaining control of our valuable time. Next take things off your 'to-do' list and allocate them into those blocks of time. You won't allocate everything off your 'to-do' list but that's OK!

Tip: if you have scheduled a list of important activities for the day, when your time allocation for one task expires, move on to the other important activity. You may need to reschedule completion of the other task, but don't forget that you scheduled the other 'important' things for a reason also.

Goals are not everything and an action plan is only part of the journey. It is the *right* activity that provides the focus to keep moving in the positive direction.

There are four things most business owners do not really consider when thinking about their goal planning. You will see a step change in your goal planning by implementing these:

1 **Benefits** – what will you gain from achieving your goal? How will you feel? What is the knock-on effect of achieving the goal?
2 **Losses** – you may be more driven by the losses or you will be looking to avoid the loss. What will you lose by not achieving your goals? How will you feel? What is the knock-on effect?
3 **Obstacles** – what are the obstacles that are likely to stop you from achieving your goal? We can often easily list these! Share your goal and ask a trusted friend what they think will also stop you. List everything.
4 **Solutions** – now consider a solution for all the obstacles you've listed. Once you have these solutions, build them into your goal activity plan. Again, if these are well considered, your checklist of activities will include the solutions that avoid the obstacle from ever appearing in the first place and therefore avoid knocking you backwards.

These four areas create and maintain the motivation and desire to achieve your goals.

Here are 12 stages of effective goal planning:

1 Decide exactly what you want to achieve and ensure it is realistic and achievable.
2 Write it down and keep it visible as a reminder every day.
3 Agree a start date today or in the future and commit to a deadline date that again is realistic. Work backwards from that point to set realistic dates of achieving the small steps.
4 Consider, and write down as a reminder, the true benefits of completing your goal. What is the gain of committing to this goal and achieving it as you plan?
5 Consider and write down the pain you would experience by not achieving the goal. What would you lose if you did not stay on track and complete the goal?
6 Consider the possible obstacles you will face along the way, those obstacles that you consider or you can visualise actually stopping you from achieving your goal.
7 Then consider the solutions to those obstacles. What do you need to do to ensure that those obstacles never occur?
8 Identify what help you need and who you need to advise or involve to help you achieve the goal. Is that a family member for support or an associate to deliver skill areas you do not possess?
9 Break the goal down into smaller steps and reference your high pay-off activities. Build in these activities in a step-by-step format and include the solutions you have considered in step 7. This forms your checklist. Work your way down the checklist, ticking off the proposed activity when it is completed and, as mentioned, the obstacles are less likely to occur as you work towards the achievement of your goal.
10 Get organised. Take the steps from your plan and schedule them to your diary and to-do list.

    Tip: be fair to yourself. Ensure you schedule them for a day that you can actually deliver them not a day when you will be in meetings all day!
11 Measure your activity and track your progress with honesty.
12 Enjoy and celebrate the success of achieving your goals.

Give this template a try

The goal is .... (SMART)

Today's date / /   Planned achievement date / /

Benefits and losses   Obstacles and solutions

Who else needs to know?

Action   *By whom*   *By when*

How will you track progress?

Make the best use of your time

You are key to the business growth or survival in the initial stages, so it is important that you know the value of your time. For example, if you value your time at say £100 per hour, then this focuses the mind when you are undertaking tasks that can be outsourced later at a cheaper rate. It also keeps you focused on those activities that give you the best return for your time investment instead of firefighting.

Look to use a diary to allocate your time and a 'to-do' list to prioritise your activity. This can be manual or PC-based software.

If for your business success it is important to undertake continuous marketing activity, like it is for most businesses, then mark out time in your diary for this activity, just like an appointment that you would stop other work for. You have classified the activity in your diary as important, so do not let it get cancelled on the day due to something else that has been brought to your attention.

A 'to-do' list is most effective when you categorise your list with the most important actions at the top, knowing therefore as you work down your list that you are doing the most important things first. This reduces the attraction of doing the easier things or just those you like to do. Each day write down those important actions that have to be done and then prioritise them for action.

To help you identify what is important, you should regularly (at least monthly) sit down and review your goals and objectives. When you know these, it is much easier to consider whether an activity is important, because you ask yourself the simple question 'does it contribute to my goals and objectives?'.

Constantly consider and understand where your time goes

You may reach the end of the day and think, 'what have I actually done today?' It's easy to be busy all day, but it's not so easy to be as productive. If you use a time-tracker you might see that your productive hours aren't meeting your expectations given how long you've been working! Therefore, the question is, where does your time really go?

If you have clarity on your HPAs then you will find your time less hijacked as the distractions and interruptions become more obvious. Try this simple tool that shows you what you may be getting distracted by during the day so that you can identify solutions as to how to prevent that happening in the future or at least identify the distractions that are causing the most amount of time lost and taking away your focus.

It's a list ... the interruptions and distractions log

Take one piece of paper and draw a line down the middle. At the top of the left-hand side, write Who? And on the top of the right-hand side, write Why? You might also like to add a smaller third column for day/time to help identify when you're most interrupted – could it be first thing in the morning, after lunch, or after school, for example?

Who?	Why?

You'll see who distracts you the most and you can manage that person with a plan. You will also see the most common reasons why and you can reflect on what needs to change to avoid a distraction in the future. Is it permission or authority? Is it something you don't need to be involved with? Is it something that in hindsight you've encouraged?

If you keep this log for a few weeks, you'll begin to establish a pattern and, once you have a pattern, you can look at ways to disrupt it.

Tip: try introducing 'stand-up' meetings for the team to share their needs or intentions for the day/afternoon. Standing up prevents people from getting too comfortable and feeling like it could be a longer meeting.

Another way for disrupting the interruption pattern could be shutting your office door at times you know you're most productive or most distractable. Turn off notifications, silence the phone, and set up auto responders on emails explaining that you will respond within a set time of the day. Protect your valuable time.

Additionally, trust in your delegation or outsourcing. Really you cannot do everything!

Poet Edward Young said, 'Procrastination is the thief of time.'

This is a saying that resonates with most people. Are you putting off doing something, rather than being distracted? Are you the one who is interrupting your own day?

We all procrastinate but we should all aim to keep the times when we do to a minimum.

Procrastination can be down to the lack of clarity in your direction or the plan. Therefore, you can procrastinate over the right course of action to take or the execution of an activity. However, with a clear vision, goal or objective, you can reduce your temptation to avoid doing one task in favour of another by referring to the plan.

We get around procrastination with two main techniques:

- **Keeping our goals in mind** – what do you want to achieve, is it achievable, when do you want to achieve it by?
- **Accountability** – what is the consequence of not achieving your goals, are you accountable to anyone else? Is anyone else depending on you?

Tip: spending one minute planning your day can save you five minutes. One hour of planning your week can save you around a day!

A brilliant tool for keeping your goals in mind is both simple and beautiful ... the vision board.

Display your longest-term goal and your short-term goals in one place. Perhaps make it your desktop background or stick it up somewhere that you will see it every day. Talk about them, share your desires, wants and needs with friends, family and networks, put them out into the universe – whatever works for you, keeping your goals in focus will help prevent procrastination.

At the end of the day, having the right mindset to work effectively without distraction or procrastinating over a task is what will give you back your time. Are you ready to do business?

The basic principles of effective time management in business are:

- Don't put more hours in, but make the ones you have more effective.
- Know the value of your time.

- Be clear on your goals.
- Plan short-term and long-term goals and activities to meet them.
- Log your activity when you feel less productive.
- Practise repetitive actions to create positive habits.
- Identify your 'prime time' of the day and use it wisely.
- Avoid meeting for a meeting's sake.
- Organise your workspace.
- Deploy a not-to-do list!

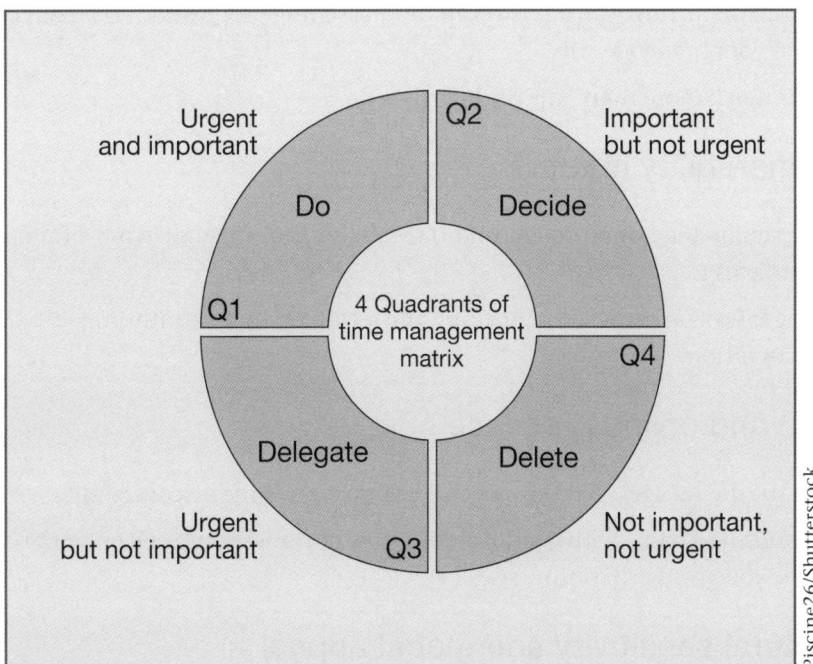

What's in a name?

This is a question often asked when new businesses are starting out. However, it is a question to ask for strategic purposes when naming the business (or even a service or product).

The name of your business isn't just a label; it's the first chapter in your company's story, the initial handshake with your market, and a powerful tool in your brand positioning. Your business name will significantly influence your brand's perception, success and connection with your audience. Remember a first impression is often made instantly, and many will assume they know what you do from your name!

A business name is often the first interaction potential clients have with your brand. It sets the tone for customer expectations and brand personality.

Your branding

- Your name acts as a beacon for your brand's identity, values and offerings.
- It's an opportunity to embed your unique selling proposition (USP) directly into your brand identity.
- It is much more than how the logo looks!

Memorability matters

- A memorable name aids in brand recall and can increase word-of-mouth marketing.
- The ease of pronunciation, spelling and recall can significantly impact brand recognition.

SEO and online presence

- In the digital age, your business name impacts online discoverability.
- Choosing a name with good search engine optimisation (SEO) potential can give you an edge in online searches.

Cultural sensitivity and global appeal

- Consider cultural connotations and language implications, especially if you plan to operate globally.
- A name with positive universal appeal can ease international expansion.

Legal considerations

- The importance of ensuring your business name doesn't infringe on existing trademarks.
- The process of securing your business name legally and digitally (e.g. domains, social accounts, etc.).

Research real-world examples

- Analyse successful brand names and what makes them effective.
- Learn lessons from names that didn't work and the pitfalls to avoid.

Choosing the right name for your business is a critical decision that requires thoughtful consideration of many factors, from market appeal to legal protection. It's not just a label but a reflection of your brand's story, values and vision.

What do I need to consider when thinking of the business name?

Your chosen business name will appear everywhere, such as your website, stationery, advertisements, uniforms, signage and email footers. The most important initial consideration when thinking about your business name is to remember that the name will help form someone's critical first impression of you.

Choosing a name is perhaps an area that many new business owners enjoy. It allows you to be creative and start to think about how your business will be recognised and represented. However, you need to be more objective and decide upon a name that considers and reflects your business, its image, your values and how your business will be positioned in the market.

Other considerations

Do you want your own name or initials included? Will it need to reflect what your business does? Are you avoiding long words or jargon or acronyms? If exporting overseas, what does the name mean in those markets? Will the name be as good in the future or will it date quickly?

If you are trading as a Limited company, then the word 'limited' has to be disclosed with the full corporate name together with any specific trading name.

A further consideration is whether the business name is already being used. Another business may own the rights to that name and ask you to stop using it. If you are a company, then you may not be able to register the business at Companies House if the name, or similar, already appears.

There are also 'sensitive words' that need official permissions, such as those that suggest your importance, status, connections or specialist activity, as they may create a false impression about your business.

Once you have considered the best name, then we suggest you test the name on others, as sometimes the business name can mean everything to you as you see the full picture; however, a neutral third party may think that the name is poor, irrelevant to your core business or it may mean to them something totally different.

If you are considering applying a trademark to your business name, then a made-up name works well, as it is therefore less likely that someone will have an interest in that name compared to an industry-recognised term.

Some businesses like taxi firms or construction-related businesses sometimes rely on directory listings for their new business leads, so a name beginning with a number or A is usually preferred to then appear at the top of these directories.

Business insurances

What type of insurances do I need to consider?

There are many insurance considerations, some of which are compulsory and others are optional. For example, if you employ someone, you must have employers' liability or, if you have any vehicles, then you are legally required to have appropriate motor insurance. Then the optional insurances that need to be strongly considered to manage your risks are areas such as liabilities. What if someone claimed for tripping in your premises (public liability), the advice you gave was considered to be incorrect (professional indemnity) or your business experienced a loss of some sort (equipment, money, goods in transit, loss of stock).

If you have identified key people in your business who would be difficult to replace (like yourself), then you should consider key person insurance. Your insurance adviser will also talk about business interruption insurance. So, for example, after a fire, yes the stock was insured but what about the days that you were not able to trade due to the premises damage?

If you are working from home, you should check your domestic insurance as it may not cover you for business purposes and could invalidate your policy.

A good insurance adviser or broker should be proactive in the identification of your insurance needs. It you are in a specialist industry, then you may benefit from finding an insurer that specialises in that sector.

Here's a checklist of the key insurances that you should consider for your business based in the UK:

- ☐ Employers' liability
- ☐ Motor insurance
- ☐ Public liability
- ☐ Product liability
- ☐ Buildings and contents (fire, theft, damage)
- ☐ Professional indemnity
- ☐ Contract insurance
- ☐ Credit insurance
- ☐ Key person cover
- ☐ Legal expenses
- ☐ Business interruption
- ☐ Portable equipment
- ☐ Business money
- ☐ Goods in transit
- ☐ Loss of stock
- ☐ Specialised requirement (e.g. retailer's shop front)

This is not an exhaustive list but covers the most common areas. It is recommended that you seek the advice of an insurance professional.

Why legal considerations are crucial in business

Navigating the legalities in business may seem like navigating a minefield. Yet, understanding the 'why' behind legal considerations is not just about compliance. With the right, proactive advice you may save yourself thousands in the long run. We often think about risk mitigation, but it is also about creating a framework of trust with your stakeholders, your operational continuity and maintaining your competitive advantage in a landscape that is continually changing legally!

Don't trust the word of your 'friends' and seek legal guidance to secure your interests. Protect yourself, as people may have other agendas, not what they say, or they change priorities over a short period!

Your legal considerations are not merely a defensive strategy, it's a proactive approach that enhances every aspect of your business operations, from how you engage with your customers to how you protect your innovations.

Here's a list of just some of the legal considerations you may need to make in your business.

- If you employ staff, whether they are full time, part time or casual workers, you have implications relating to the employment law. This is a huge area and one you should seek professional advice upon. Quite often the right set-up and documentation can save time and money in the future. Some of the main areas covered by employment law are around fair recruitment, management and dismissal procedures, providing written conditions of employment, minimum wage compliance (which is reviewed regularly), disciplinary and grievance procedures, and policies that cover areas such as discrimination rules, maternity and paternity leave, and rules on absence and sick leave pay.
- Protect your relationships with suppliers or customers for things you buy or sell – showing considerations of ownership, responsibilities and expectations. Care should be taken as a verbal contract can be considered in some situations.
- Trading terms and conditions – ensure you can rely on your documentation. Have you reviewed the small print? Do your terms ensure you control your own product or service?
- Partnership agreement, or if a company a shareholder agreement, protecting the interests of the owners in the case of dispute, death or separation.
- Premises requirements – do you need planning consent for structural requirements or use of the property? Have you taken advice on the rent or lease contract? What are your rights, especially in shared premises? What are your responsibilities for repairs?

- Intellectual property – do you need to protect your ideas with patents, copyright or trademarks?
- Protecting the consumer – are you responsible for product defects causing injury or damage? Have you considered the trade descriptions act including false representation such as a product description?
- Franchising – have an expert review your franchise agreement.
- Recovering bad debts – don't be afraid to use legal methods to recover monies due to you. A good customer is only one that pays.
- Software licences – are they held and does your use comply with those licences?
- Regulations specific to your industry sector have been considered.
- Data protection – if you are processing and storing personal information, then you should register with the information commissioner. Be careful as there are a number of scams offering to do this for you, but it is simple to do the registration direct at www.ico.gov.uk.

Protecting your business idea

This section is for those in either of two camps. First, for those who worry about sharing their idea in case it is stolen by someone or second, for those that think it will never happen to them, as it may.

Protecting your innovative ideas is crucial, and the more unique your idea appears, the more people will want to know more and even copy it.

The protection of your idea and the know-how, your intellectual property, not only protects your business for long-term success but also avoids the need to sometimes start all over again.

The first, often best, way to protect your business concept from potential threats is to consider your legal protection. This may include the registration of your intellectual property to confirm your legal ownership of the idea. This will include trademarks that protect your brand name, logo and slogans and patents that safeguard your unique inventions and technologies. You can also secure your original creative works with copyright and utilise the protection of your 'trade secrets', which maintains confidentiality of valuable business information.

- **Patents** – protect new inventions; how they work, what they do, what they are made of and how they are made.
- **Designs** – protect the overall look of a product including the colour, shape, texture and material.
- **Trademarks** – protect brands, such as your business name or logo, and can consist of a word, phrase, picture or a combination of all these.
- **Copyright** – protects written, dramatic, musical and artistic works including photos, recordings, software and databases.

Two minimal actions you should take are background checks and Non-Disclosure Agreements (NDAs).

Checks should be conducted on potential employees, partners and investors to minimise the risk of someone you bring close to you in good faith from stealing your idea.

Look to use NDAs when sharing sensitive information with potential partners, investors or employees. These are legally binding contracts that prevent the unauthorised disclosure of your ideas by those parties to others.

Also be practical and safeguard your idea by limiting the sharing of your idea and work on a 'need-to-know' basis within your organisation. We get excited about our idea and want to tell people about it, even boast about it, but be cautious about making disclosures to the public before you have secured the proper protection.

Although it may not always create any form of agreement or contract, it is certainly encouraged to document everything. Maintain records of your conversations around the development of your idea including conversations, meetings and emails. It is also good practice to follow up a conversation, casual or formal, with an email or written note. You may be able to use such documentation if you need to prove ownership in the situation should a dispute arise. Formal protection is certainly something to consider, but it can be a lengthy process to resolve with likely additional legal, or even court, costs.

Be vigilant and be observant for infringements.

When you have something unique that requires protection, then regularly check for unauthorised use of your intellectual property. Keep a check on the various channels, such as social media, competitor websites and online marketplaces, and even monitor the dark web.

If you suspect infringement, consult with an intellectual property lawyer to explore your enforcement options, such as cease-and-desist letters or legal action.

The implementation of such protective measures can significantly reduce the risk of your business idea being stolen or copied.

What is a supply chain?

A supply chain is a commercial link between a company and its network of supplier organisations to produce and distribute a specific product or service to the end buyer. This may involve people, activities, information and resources involved in the provision to bring the offering to market.

The supply chain is likely to be involved in your planning, procurement, purchasing, production, transportation and logistics, storage, distribution, customer service and returns.

As an example, the chain could look like this for a retail business: sourced raw material producer supplies – logistics – manufacturer – storage – distributor – retailer – retail customer.

A good supply chain is a collaborative process planned across all the required functions. It concentrates on the desired process first, then considers efficiency, effectiveness and costs, with the purpose of looking to improve the process and reduce the cost of sale.

Many businesses are now considering their ability to demonstrate ethical practices. For example, what materials are used to produce the product or who is producing the raw materials or manufacturing the product and whether they are fairly paid whilst working in respectable, safe conditions.

As a business responsible for the relationship with the end buyer, a key role is your supply chain management. This is the management of the flow of goods and services and includes all processes that transform raw materials into the final products.

What considerations should I have when choosing suppliers?

This is an important consideration as your supplier could have a big impact on the reputation of your business.

Choosing a supplier is much more than deciding who is the cheapest. Your choice should also take into consideration the potential relationship, good and open communication, delivery, flexibility, quality, reliability, value for money, their history, their financial security and service, especially the after-sales service. For example, if you want to deliver to your customers within a few days, then your supplier may offer you quick, reliable delivery rather than the lowest price, so know what factors are important for your business before you start your search for the supplier.

You will also have to consider the number of suppliers that you have. A small number is easier to manage and you may be able to combine deliveries. However, can you afford to rely on just a few? Ideally, you are looking for suppliers that want to work with you for the benefit of both parties.

Tip: businesses with a single element in their supply chain and no alternatives suffered during Brexit and the pandemic due to delivery restrictions.

If you do not know where to find your suppliers, then before simply making an internet search, ask your contacts for any recommendations, review any trade press or look up any trade directories and establish who your competitors may be using.

Once you have decided upon your supplier, then request a meeting and advise them of your expectations to agree any service levels in advance. It will also be an opportunity to utilise their expertise and receive some guidance on orders. Start to build a relationship with the supplier that will benefit you in the future.

If you need to import your goods, then seek specific specialist advice to consider the countries you are importing from, the payment terms and how to control the quality. Most suppliers will want you to enter into a contract or provide you with their terms and conditions. Please ensure you read and understand the small print, especially relating to any notice periods for stopping their supply.

IT matters

Tomorrow this section will potentially be out of date, as technology, software and hardware are changing so fast.

IT matters because it will bring efficiencies in your business that will save you time and money. Due to the rise in technological solutions, there has never been a better time to start a business, so I encourage you to think about what you could utilise now and also keep an eye on developments in the future that may help you develop your business.

What software do you need to do what you do and deliver the promise to your customer? What can you automate to save valuable resources? For example, how will you record your accounts information and make it easier to manage the financials in your business? What is available to suit your business and help you manage your prospects' journey and customer relationships?

As the technology is advancing so quickly, you can only really consider what hardware and software set-up you need now, whilst also having a plan for the future that you can see. Make a list of the features you need now and what would be desirable to help you develop the business in the future. This takes the emotion out of the buying sequence and you buy what you need. Too often I've seen businesses buy the trendy equipment to only find it doesn't really do what they want in the way that they want it to. If you find a solution that ticks all the boxes on your feature list, then surely that is the one to invest in?

When setting up your IT infrastructure then I encourage you to review two further matters. Your security and the potential of your systems integration. Cybercrime is rife and will not be going away, so ensure your systems are safe and secure, especially if you are holding customer data. Even a few days' disruption can be painful, but there are many examples when businesses have lost their entire database and stored documentation resulting in them having to start all over again. When looking at your IT systems, this is a point to consider your risk management and the need for IT support.

If you are holding data, especially customer data or sensitive data, then you may need to register under the data protection regulations.

A recommendation is to keep your data safe with regular backups. You can do this in various ways, such as saving your data onto a remote disk or to the cloud. Whichever solution you choose, look to make it automatic so that it just happens.

Tip: test the backup every so often. You don't want the first test to be at the time you need it and it fails.

Premises and location

Your initial premises are an important consideration, and many factors will influence the decision such as permissions, planning consent, insurances, communication needs, location of labour, building regulations, fire protection, disabled access, smoking laws, environmental concerns, security, flood planning and crime prevention, to name a few.

Premises such as a warehouse or a production area may be critical for the business, but you may be a service business that you wish to start from home.

For many small businesses the use of home is a serious consideration as it is simple and saves costs.

We suggest that you consider all the requirements that will make your business operate to the best of its ability in terms of efficiencies, overheads, facilities available and location. Write out lists of what the premises 'must have' and what you would 'ideally' like, but happy to sacrifice, and this will make your search and choice much easier and, importantly, correct for the current purpose.

To find the appropriate premises you can look in the local press, search in your preferred location, contact commercial property agents or sometimes the local authority has a database of available premises. During your search try to find out what potential neighbours are paying in rent and rates, as this will help your own negotiations.

The choice of premises could be a key ingredient to your success, but don't run before you can walk and take on premises that are surplus to the immediate start-up requirement, unless your business plan demonstrates use of the surplus space in the near future or you are securing a premium location with available resources.

If you are going to start from home, consider an area that you can separate from your personal and family life. Can you lock the door and not be tempted into the office at any time? Is your business documentation secure from others' eyes? Where will you meet customers? We also recommend that, if you work from home, you still dress for work and create the right mindset for the day ahead. You should also check your mortgage deed or tenancy agreement to ensure there are no restrictions in doing this.

If you decide to take office space that is not critical to the operation of the business, then take care with the rent or lease agreements that you are asked to sign. You may want flexibility in the early years to increase or downsize your space without being tied into long-term arrangements.

If you need or desire to have premises for your business, then you have the option to lease, rent or buy the premises. We recommend that you seek your own professional advice to consider the financing options, affordability and any legal or tax implications.

What equipment investment do you need?

Getting your business equipped covers many areas including the furniture and IT requirements, machinery, storage, fittings and even vehicles. Obviously, much will depend on your type of business and location. Your competitor research may help you with this consideration.

The starting point is to consider your operational process and list all the equipment you will need. You should then consider equipment that helps your functionality and efficiency.

Once you have a list of equipment requirements, then consider whether you want to purchase this equipment as new or second-hand. Many new businesses purchase 'nearly new' equipment, but you should consider the lifetime of this used equipment and the ability to finance its purchase if needed.

Purchasing your equipment outright may be the only option or sometimes the right choice. If you want to finance the purchase with a lease or a hire purchase arrangement, then it can sometimes be more difficult if your asset depreciates quickly over a short period.

For example, a children's play centre will need the play frame, but as soon as it is installed it will lose most of its value overnight as it is personal to that installation.

When selecting your method of finance, you should also consider the ownership as sometimes you will not own the equipment until the final finance payment has been made.

It is recommended to discuss the different options with your accountant and the pros or cons on how depreciation of assets, capital allowances and finance costs will impact on your accounts or tax position.

Tip: you should ensure that you and any colleagues are fully competent in the use of the equipment or seek appropriate training. On purchase also make sure you collect and safely store your equipment guarantees.

Health and safety

Every business owner has a responsibility for health and safety to primarily operate a business that creates a healthy and safe environment for the staff and visitors, even if it is just yourself.

Some businesses will also have to consider the disposal of gases, liquids, chemicals and substances or even noise.

There are minimum standards for all businesses and, if you employ more than the stated number of staff, then you should have a written health and safety policy and communicate your policy to all staff.

You should undertake risk assessments at your premises to identify hazards and risks, then determine how these will be controlled to avoid injury. Common assessment considerations for all types of businesses are slips, trips and falls, display screen equipment, portable electrical equipment, fire and first aid provision.

If your business involves the preparation or sales of food and beverages, then you should speak to your local authorities about the required food hygiene standards.

Other considerations include your insurers' requirements or equipment providers' recommendations for regular inspections.

If you do have an accident in the workplace, then these should be recorded in an accident book, and in certain circumstances they are reportable to the enforcing authority (RIDDOR).

The health and safety executive has a very informative website for reviewing your specific responsibilities. If in doubt, please take professional advice as planning to prevent circumstances is better than having to deal with any consequences after an injury or accident.

It is therefore recommended to have a day-to-day management procedure with records evidencing your proactive actions. For example, do you check your first aid box regularly? Do you comply with the food hygiene standards?

Tax explained

Tax can be a complicated subject and is very personal to each individual, so it is recommended that you take professional advice from someone like an accountant before you start to set up the business. It is also recommended to take advice on the latest allowable expenses and non-allowable expenses relating to your tax liability computation.

The tax considerations depend on the type of entity that you choose for your business, such as:

Self-employed/Partnerships

A self-assessment tax return is required by HM Revenue & Customs for each tax year. The return must be submitted by the end of the following January. Income, profits and other investment information is included. Income tax is calculated and is paid to HM Revenue & Customs before stated deadlines. National insurance contributions may also be payable.

Limited companies

As a Limited Company you must complete an annual company tax return. The company is taxed on its profits with the resulting Corporation Tax liability payable nine months and one day after the end of the company's accounting period. Where shareholders receive dividends from the company, they will be taxed on these as part of their self-assessment personal tax return.

VAT

This is a tax on turnover, consumption and on imports of goods. It is applicable to the vast majority of business types and entities. When you are registered for VAT, this must be charged on all taxable sales at the applicable rate.

There are different VAT categories to charge, standard rate, zero rate, exempt rate and those supplies outside the scope of VAT.

Depending on the scheme, VAT returns will need to be completed on a regular basis, which in most cases is quarterly. The return includes all VAT that has been charged to customers less VAT on purchases during the period. The net amount will then need to be paid to or is due from HM Revenue & Customs.

Your VAT may be calculated in different ways. For example, cash accounting, a flat rate and annual accounting methods may be applicable to your business. Again, it is recommended you take specific advice from your accountant about these schemes.

PAYE

Pay-As-You-Earn (PAYE) is a payroll deduction system in which tax is deducted from a person's income when paid by the employer. The amount withheld is determined by a tax code which applies the taxpayer's individual tax liabilities. The employer is responsible for calculating and collecting the employees'

PAYE & National Insurance at the appropriate percentage and must pay this across to HM Revenue & Customs by a deadline in the following month.

The employer is also liable to National Insurance on amounts over the earnings threshold. An annual form P35 is required by HM Revenue & Customs, which reconciles PAYE/National Insurance deductions to amounts that have been paid.

Employee benefits

Where an employee or director is provided with benefits from the business, e.g. a company car, this must be disclosed on an annual form P9D/P11D. The benefit will be taxed on the individual as employment income and the employer is liable to Class 1A National Insurance. The P11D's and covering P11D(b) must be submitted to HM Revenue & Customs and the relevant amount of Class 1A paid across by a specific deadline following the tax year end.

This section references the requirements for a business based in the UK. As a reminder we recommend that you always seek guidance from local professional advisers to understand your local laws and policies wherever you are located.

This is not an exhaustive list but covers the most common areas. It is recommended that you seek the advice of a tax professional to discuss your personal circumstances.

Digital transformation – what, why and how

What?

Businesses are increasingly focusing on digital transformation and leveraging technology to transform their operations, processes and customer experiences.

This has included adopting cloud computing, big data analytics, artificial intelligence (AI), machine learning (ML) and automation and the one that every business owner will have come across by now, 'Making Tax Digital'.

Productivity via digital channels and automation is now becoming a consideration alongside hiring the next person. Look to reflect on tasks that can be more effectively automated before delegation or outsourcing.

Digital transformation is revolutionising the way many businesses operate, bringing significant impact across various industries. They are transforming their business model with the aim of continuous improvements, driving a competitive advantage and ultimately achieving a greater return on investment.

Why?

By adopting digital technology, businesses can automate manual tasks, streamline processes and optimise operations thereby providing the benefit of increased efficiency and improved productivity.

However, they're not only saving time but also reducing human error through decreasing the need for repetition, whilst still delivering consistently to the process model thereby allowing employees to focus on higher-value activities.

In short – let the machines do the repetitive tasks, so you can put your brain to use on the exciting ones!

How?

Let's use cloud computing as an example. Cloud computing enables businesses to access, store and share data securely, so they can collaborate with their supply chain and employees in real time and scale their resources as needed.

Analytics is another excellent example. Digital transformation also empowers organisations to make data-driven decisions by leveraging advanced tools to analyse large volumes of data. This can help businesses gain valuable insights into customer behaviour, market trends and operational performance, enabling them to make informed strategic choices and stay ahead of the competition.

Furthermore, digital transformation has a profound impact on the customer experience. With the rapid increase in digital channels, businesses can engage with their customers in a personalised and meaningful way.

Through data collection and analysis, companies can better understand customer preferences, anticipate their needs, and deliver tailored products or services, much quicker than ever before.

For instance, a business may use the data in their e-commerce platform, and add industry data, to leverage recommendation algorithms to offer personalised product suggestions based on their type of business, individual browsing and any purchase history. The customer then only sees marketing messages that are relevant to their needs, delivered at the appropriate time.

Additionally, digital technologies enable businesses to provide seamless, integrated, customer-centric, multichannel experiences, allowing customers to interact with the business through multiple touchpoints such as websites, mobile apps, social media and physical premises. This integration of channels enhances convenience, accessibility and overall satisfaction, driving customer loyalty and retention.

> **I wish I knew this before I started my first business**
>
> ### Time is your most valuable asset
>
> This was my biggest lesson in my early years. I wanted to help everyone. I wanted to be everyone's friend. However, in reality it was to my detriment, as I could not focus on myself and the high pay-off activities that I really needed to concentrate upon. I encourage you to learn one thing. The ability to say 'No'. No to the wrong client. No to the things that will waste your time. Focus on what truly matters and look to automate, delegate or outsource the rest. Be clear on how you should be spending your time. With the clarity of knowing what you should be doing today, interruptions and distractions become obvious. Invest part of that time to reflect and continually analyse if there is a better way to utilise your most valuable asset.

Key points

- Are you clear where you are heading and is it realistic?
- Plan your exit from day one and build the business with this in mind.
- Are you clear on who is your customer and why they would buy from you?
- How do you differentiate from your competition to create your value proposition?
- What are your strengths, weaknesses, opportunities and threats?
- How will you complete your effective market research?
- Ensure your business plan is written in a focused, succinct manner that provides clarity and focus.
- What is the value of your time and how will you protect this most valuable asset?
- There is so much to consider, but do it well as it will save you pain in the long term.
- How will you embrace digital transformation?

Additional resources

Books
Gerber M. E. (1988) *The E-Myth: Why Most Businesses Don't Work and What to Do About It*. Ballinger Publishing.
Wickman G. (2012) *Traction: Get a Grip on Your Business*. BenBella Books.
Tracy, B. (2017) *Eat That Frog*. Berrett-Koehler.

Podcasts
HBR Ideacast from *Havard Business Review*.

CHAPTER 4
HOW TO UNDERSTAND YOUR NUMBERS

It's a fact that most business owners don't like the numbers in their business with the exception of the amount they are invoicing or selling! Let's get you comfortable with the uncomfortable and perhaps even get you to the point that you love your numbers!

In this chapter, the aim is to help you to better understand your financials, grasp the 'real' numbers in your business and appreciate the factors that will impact your profitability and critical cash flow. By the end of this chapter, you will have more comfort in your financials whilst having an understanding of the numbers that support your decisions and impact your success.

What do the numbers in my accounts mean?

If you don't like numbers then you are not alone. It is common for entrepreneurs to not like or understand their numbers. This chapter aims to give you the understanding of your numbers and what you should look to consider from a financial aspect.

If you don't have the head for, or interest in, numbers then look to get someone alongside you who does, either internally or as an external adviser.

Let's start with your financial reports and what they mean.

Every business is split into the following elements to enable you to 'balance' your accounts and check on the profitability of your company:

Balance sheet

- **Assets** – what you own. Defined as an item of property owned by a person or company, regarded as having value and available to meet debts, commitments or legacies:
  - fixed assets – building, machinery, vehicles

- current assets – your bank balance and cash plus those that can more easily be converted to cash such as debtors (money owed to you) and stock.
- **Liabilities** – what you owe as an obligation arising from a past business event. Defined as a thing for which someone is responsible, especially an amount of money owed:
  - current liabilities (short-term) – tax owed, overdraft, loans, creditors (money you owe to people like suppliers)
  - long-term liabilities – long-term loans like mortgages.
- **Capital and reserves**:
  - profit from the year
  - retained profits from previous years
  - share capital *(if Limited company)*

Profit and loss account

- **Revenue** – a summary of your sales value from your revenue streams. Also referred to as your turnover or income. This is work you've completed and invoiced, product sales, payment receipts without invoice, sales of assets, other income and interest.
- **Cost of sales/cost of goods sold/variable costs** – those are the costs to the business that are related to your income, so the more your sell, these direct costs increase:
    - purchases – materials, stock
    - direct expenses – labour, marketing, advertising.
- **Expenses/overheads/fixed costs** – other purchases and ongoing costs you have for the day-to-day running of the business such as wages and salaries, premises costs, expenses and depreciation.

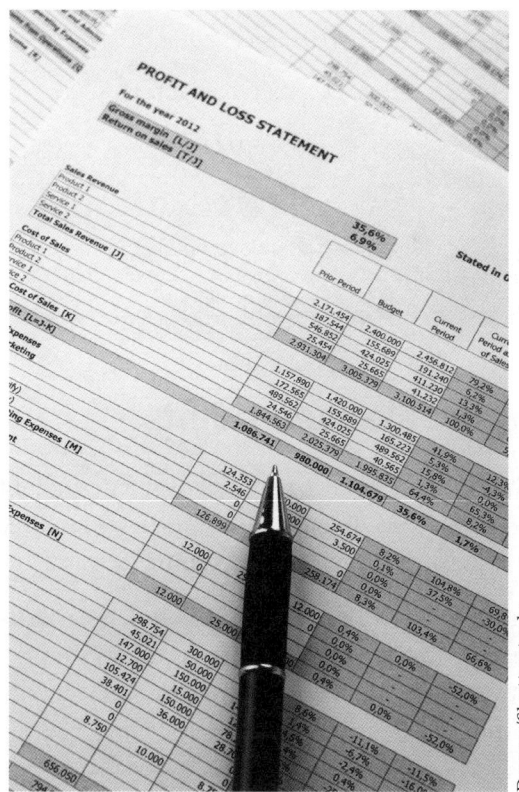

Drazen/Shutterstock

For your internal management reporting, you can show your accounts in the format that you desire. This is recommended to give you clarity on your numbers and how your business performs. However, for tax returns and accounts submission in the UK, there are recognised formats governed by the financial reporting standards (FRS). Don't worry, your accountant will know!

> **Remember this**
>
> Number of customers
>
> x
>
> Number of times they buy
>
> x
>
> Your average order value
>
> = revenue/turnover
>
> Less
>
> Cost of sales/variable costs
>
> = gross profit
>
> Less
>
> Fixed costs/overheads
>
> = net profit

Know your break-even point

This is the minimum level of sales required over a period of time to meet all your fixed and variable costs. In basic terms, the level required to stay in business in the early years or retain your profits going forward.

The calculation of your break-even point is much easier for some service businesses, especially in the start-up phase, as this is simply the sum of your fixed costs, the overheads you have to pay every single month, and what you need to cover with your sales revenue to break even.

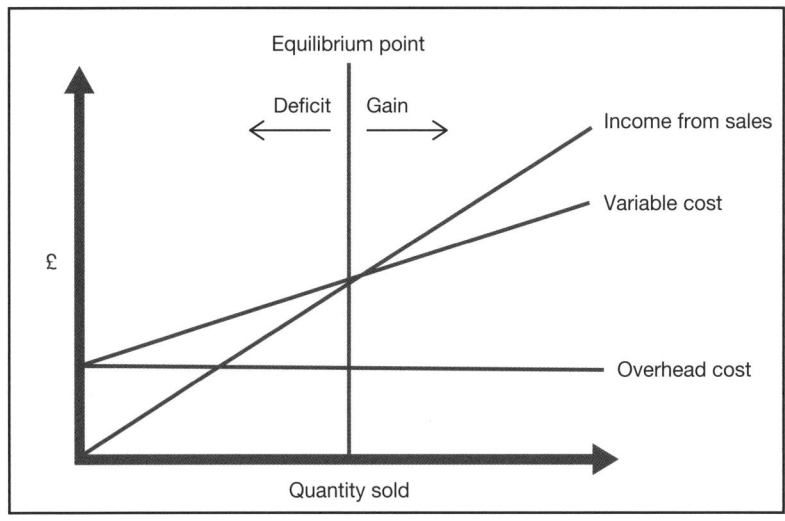

Many businesses will have related cost of sales or an associated cost of delivery.

If you outsource your service delivery or offer a product, then you will have to consider the cost of sales to calculate your break-even point.

For example, as a service business, how much of your fee charged to the customer will you then pay your subcontractor or a member of your team to deliver?

If you are offering a product, how much will it cost you to buy the raw materials and build it to supply the product in its completed form?

If you are a reseller of a product, then how much does it cost you to buy the product at a wholesale price before you sell it on?

In these scenarios, you will need to calculate the percentage profit margin and allow for this cost of sales to calculate your break-even.

For example, if your cost of sales is 50 per cent, then you will need £2 for every £1 to contribute to paying your fixed costs to break even.

Don't forget to include what you want, or at least need, to pay yourself in the calculation. I'm sure you will want to pay yourself as well as covering all your costs at break-even!

Here are five steps that enable you to apply your break-even analysis in practice:

1. Identify all fixed costs (rent, rates, insurance, subscriptions, salaries).
2. Determine variable costs per unit (materials, direct labour cost).
3. Set your selling price.
4. Apply the formula to calculate your break-even point.
5. Use the result to inform your business decisions and your goal setting.

Here are some raw examples to support your calculation:

Service Business Revenue for a One-Person Business Solely Delivering the Offering

Revenue	£5,000
Cost of sales	Nil
Gross profit	£5,000
Fixed costs	£2,000
Net profit/desired	£3,000

Service Business or Product Sold with 50 per cent gross Profit Margin

Revenue	£10,000
Cost of sales (50%)	£5,000
Gross profit	£5,000
Fixed costs	£2,000
Net profit/desired	£3,000

What's your break-even?

Knowing your break-even point helps you to set your sales targets and calculate your pricing. It will help you allocate resources in line with your margin or direct costs and ultimately assist in evaluating your business viability and profitability.

Let's calculate your break-even:

Net profit/desired	
+ Fixed costs	
= Gross profit required	
Gross profit margin (x%)*	
Revenue required to break even *including paying yourself what you need*	

* *Your gross profit margin is the percentage of your revenue that is profit after your direct expenses and cost of sales.*

> ### Remember this
> #### Benchmark your numbers against your competitors
> How is the business performing in comparison to the industry sector? Are you doing well, or could you do better? Are your results due to the impact of the sector or the economy rather than just your performance?

Cash is king

If you've not heard this phrase before, then it's one you will come to hear more often when running a business. It is certainly one to keep front of mind:

Turnover is vanity, profit is sanity, but cash is king.

Ultimately, if you don't have cash in your bank account to pay your costs and liabilities, then you will struggle to continue to trade, even if you are still selling, delivering or waiting to be paid for work completed or products sold.

Your goal should be to build your reserves with free cash that provides you with the working capital that you can reinvest or provide you with a level of comfort that you may desire as you move forward to scale your business.

Free cash is a term used to designate the 'spare' money you have in the business, the cash you have collected from your sales and allowed for your tax liabilities. It is the cash a business has left over after paying for its operating expenses and capital expenditure and what the business then has for future choices such as dividends or bonuses, reducing debt, or investing in future growth opportunities.

Understanding and managing your cash flow is crucial for any business owner. With effective cashflow management, the business remains solvent, and you can maximise your growth opportunities and avoid unnecessary debt.

Remember, while profits are of course important, maintaining a positive cash flow is essential. Cash truly is king.

Most things come back to a number

Far too often businesses are focusing on the wrong numbers. Too many management dashboards contain the wrong numbers.

The monitoring of the following areas is all good to know for the identification of patterns and trends:

- turnover
- cash
- margin
- profit
- value
- market share
- number of customers.

However, these are all results or outcomes of other activity in the business. The focus on measuring outcomes does not give us information during a period that will help us influence the performance of the business during that period.

Instead of simply measuring such outcomes, look to focus on the numbers, and the related activities, that drive your desired results.

Additionally, identify your key performance indicators (KPIs) and understand what drives your success. What activities influence your outcomes? These are activities you can leverage if you need to improve performance during a period. They are activities that you measure that reduce your surprises at the end of a period.

Here are some examples of such 'Success Drivers':

- new lead contacts to the database
- referrals received
- prospect meetings held
- conversion rate
- average income per new customers
- pipeline value
- number of leads, sales, products sold, etc.
- capacity
- productivity time per project
- average order value
- profit margin per sale, per day, per week.

As an example, the most common factors that make up our revenue are the number of people we sell to, the number of times they buy and the average sale value. Consider the breakdown of the numbers that influences your future revenue.

Ultimately, most things come back to a number.

At first glance, you may think some of these are not numbers, but most come back to a numeric of some sort. For example, customer service, how do you measure it? 5 Star? What about your team, X out of Y in a survey were happy scoring out of 10

- customer happiness (complaints, testimonials)
- team happiness (measure, turnover, years of service)
- proactive calls/visits made
- proactive contacts with introducers
- delivery of service level agreements
- chargeable hours
- hours on training, R&D, idea generation
- number of customers won/lost

Whilst we are talking of the numbers you can measure in your business, here are some additional measures that you may wish to consider that impact your cost and cash drivers:

- debtor days (the average amount of time it takes to collect the money owed to you)
- average cost per customer, per sq. ft, per unit
- your customer acquisition cost – the cost per customer recruited
- team productivity
- average invoice value
- stock turnover days.

Your seven critical numbers

In any business there are seven critical numbers for your proactive management to see continual improvement.

1 **Profit and loss.** How much profit did you make last year or in a period? This should be easy to find; simply deduct your expenses from your income.
2 **Operating costs.** How much do you have to spend to keep the business running whether you made a sale or not?
3 **Gross margin/Gross profit.** This number comes from net profit plus operating costs.
4 **Cost of sales.** This number is created from anything and anyone related to a sale. It will also change in line with your sales, whereas operating costs will largely remain the same.
5 **Revenue.** Your revenue is your sales income (less VAT and any local sales tax).
6 **Average order value.** Take the revenue last year and divide by the total number of sales made.
7 **Number of customers.** If you have a high turnover of short-term clients, you can average this number over last year or you can work on the number of retained customers.

Additionally, look to take a holistic approach when working on the development of your business, with an eye on your numbers. The greater the profits, then of course you will find that you have more choices for other matters in the business (e.g. recruitment, operations, promotional).

Everyone likes the sound of business growth, but please make sure the profit growth is going in the same direction as the sales turnover growth. There is a business model for high customer volume and low margins, but for the majority of start-up businesses it is not worth increasing your business turnover and working harder if it is not bringing you the profits.

At the start-up stage, it is important that you have systems and controls in place to maximise the development of your business or there is a danger that profits may be eroded as quickly as the sales grow. How will you manage the increased business? Will you need more staff? Will you need different premises?

> **Remember this**
>
> **Make the numbers work**
>
> It is common to dislike numbers, but have a burning desire to measure and understand the various 'real' numbers and make sure that they are 'working' for the future success of the business.
>
> The 'real numbers' are not just the financial numbers or the analysis of trends that you would undertake whilst reviewing a set of financial accounts but also understanding the underlying success drivers for the business and those outcomes.

What number is most important to focus upon in my business?

As mentioned earlier in this chapter, cash is king and critical for the operation of your business. After all, you only run out of it once! However, there is one key number in your profit and loss account. After all, you need profit or investment to provide you with the referenced positive cash flow and to have the working capital needed to operate your business.

There is in fact no single universal metric that applies to all businesses, because the 'most important number' depends heavily on your industry, stage of growth and strategic goals. However, there is one number to focus upon. I'll come back to this in a moment, once I've acknowledged some additional thinking.

The number for your focus may depend on:

- What aligns with your stage and strategy: early-stage businesses may be focused on traction metrics whereas a growth business may look at sustainability and profitability. A mature business may be looking at EBITDA (earnings before interest, taxes, depreciation and amortisation) or 'free cash'.
- Industry-specific crucial measure: for example, production, profit, cash burn rate, customer satisfaction, customer acquisition cost and customer lifetime value.
- Measures that reflect your core value proposition: for example, reoccurring revenue, production efficiency and optimisation via time utilisation rates.

Some companies identify a single 'north star' metric, one that best encapsulates the value they deliver to customers and how that correlates with revenue.

The one number for most businesses, the most important number is *gross profit*. Why? Anything below your gross profit number is (or should be) fixed by their nature. First, your 'fixed costs' that are your ongoing costs associated with the business whether you make no sales or multiple ones. These may change slightly but generally they are fixed for the period ahead (e.g. rent, rates, insurance, admin, staff, software licence fees, etc.). The other number below your gross profit, which I also suggest should be fixed in your mindset, is your bottom line 'net profit'.

Gross profit − fixed costs = net profit

Or net profit + fixed costs = gross profit required

This is the bottom-line net profit you want to make for your return on investment for all your hard work. This number is to provide you with the income for the lifestyle you desire and an amount to reinvest in the business. This should be fixed and not negotiable.

Therefore, the gross profit number you need to hit is the number for your focus. If you hit that number, then you will pay your overheads and receive the profit return you desire for yourself.

Another reason why this is your 'most important' number is because you can now pull levers above this to make your business work. For example, increasing the number of customers, improving the average order value, reducing the cost of sales and improving your margin return. What is often missed by many business owners is that if you improve your gross profit margin with such levers, you won't need as much revenue as you thought!

Many businesses will chase revenue (sometimes with good reason) but often without any consideration for what makes the business easier to run. You may chase the golden £1 million revenue, which too many people reference as a 'successful' business, but without managing margins and costs you may find that the resulting profit still won't deliver what you really want!

If you have multiple products or services, when considering your profit margin look to maintain an eye on your profit per product, per service or per department. For example, as a restaurant, what is the profit per individual dish you offer? You will want to keep an eye on your customer makeup and product mix to ensure you are maintaining a consistent margin across potentially various different price points.

This analysis may help you to identify a product or service that returns a higher gross profit margin and therefore could potentially be part of your strategy to include within your primary offering to market. It will also identify when you need to review your pricing or costing around a specific product or service that may be pulling down your overall margin.

Remember this

When considering the black and white financial numbers in the business, don't forget to analyse your financial ratios.

Are margins being retained? Is the team productive as a people cost vs turnover? Are the debtor days or stock turnover days improving? What are the debt ratios? What is the return on investment?

What numbers do you need to measure and make happen for your success?

Finding the money to start and raising finance

Your new business could be financed in a number of different ways and quite often a combination is used. There are numerous types of business finance available from a whole variety of lenders.

Preparation is part of the key to success in raising finance and securing the right price for the transaction. A well-prepared and structured business plan with professional input is invaluable. From their experience they will guide you on what the lenders want to know.

Independent assistance in raising finance will ensure banks/lenders offer their best price for a transaction as they will know that they are in competition with other providers.

Asset finance can play an important part in the funding of any business. In this case, you borrow against the asset purchased, such as a vehicle, and you now pay monthly assisting cash flow as you don't have to find the full balance in advance. *You should take professional advice when borrowing money; check the real interest rate and read the small print.*

Invoice discounting and factoring play an important part in funding the working capital needs of many businesses by immediately advancing monies against an invoice value. You do not have to wait 60 or more days to get paid and therefore your business cash flow is under control, which is vital in the early growth stage.

Another option is to consider external investors. They will want a share in your business in return for their investment and a repayment plan for the monies lent, but they will also bring expertise that you may desire to the business.

Variable rates, fixed rates, caps and collars; there are numerous interest rate products to consider. With expert advice, the terms and funding types need not be confusing. Getting the finance structure of your business right needs thought and care.

Depending on your business and its location, there may be grants or subsidised loans available to you. As the type of grants and the available funds change so often it is recommended to have a conversation with your local support organisations to establish if any applicable grants are currently available for your business, in your area.

Key considerations in relation to your choice of finance should be:

- speed of decision
- price – interest rate and fees
- security required
- convenience
- flexibility
- quality of service.

You will improve your success in raising finance if:

- you know who to speak to
- ask for the right type of finance for the transaction
- understand your business gearing (the amount of debt, in proportion to capital, that the business uses to fund its operations)
- understand interest cover
- have a good credit history
- obtain professional advice.

A common source of finance for most start-ups is their family and friends. If this is a consideration for yourself, then ensure you keep the agreement formal and ideally in writing. If it remains informal, then the terms may get changed or early repayment may be requested as their circumstances change but you are not in the position to honour that early.

Here are the main methods that start-up businesses use to raise their business finance:

- family or friends
- bank – overdraft, loans, commercial mortgages
- credit cards
- invoice discounting and factoring
- debt finance
- grant support
- equity finance (e.g. investors)
- peer-to-peer lending

- asset finance
- hire/lease purchase
- finance lease
- operating lease
- contract hire
- sale and leaseback
- supplier/supply chain finance
- pre-sales.

There are many types of finance available and ways to generate finance for your business. It may not be easy to raise finance, but there are always new lenders entering the market with different propositions to consider.

Please take the advice of experts before taking on debt for your business. Ensure that you understand how the charges and interest are made up and you are comparing like for like, but not just getting attracted by the headline.

Keeping accurate financial records

Maintaining proper accounting records is vital in terms of monitoring how well your business is doing. Ensuring you are paying the correct amount of tax is a legal requirement!

A good financial accounts system will include receipts, payments, invoices, bank statements and till receipts (where applicable), all of which should be kept in a tidy manner with a cashbook and daybooks maintained.

Historically, these were manual books or ledgers, but there are now numerous accounting packages to make this easy for you.

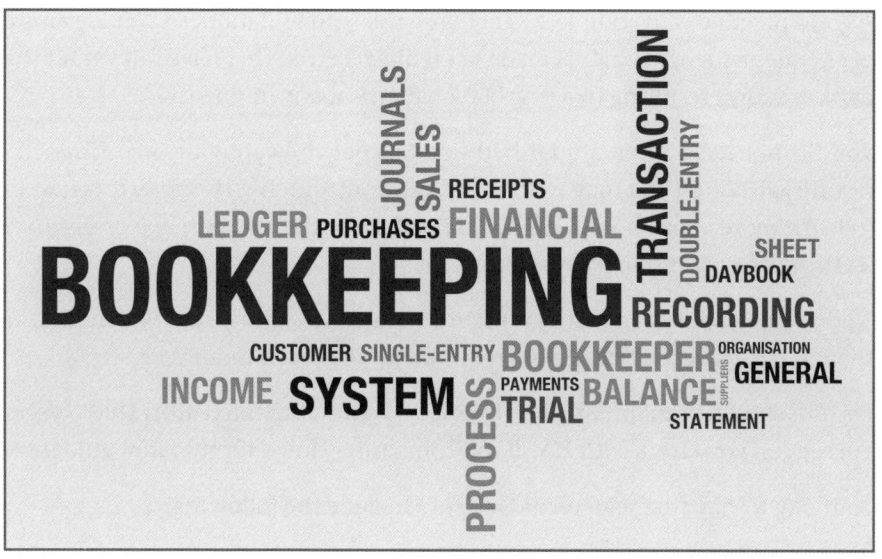

Software packages are available to help maintain the company's financial records.

The system you choose does not have to be a software package, and many business owners use Excel spreadsheets or even manual bookkeeping records if they are not VAT registered. With the requirement of online VAT submissions to HMRC, a software package is often used as you grow and become VAT registered. Your choice of package will depend on how much information you want to obtain from your records. A good financial system will be able to tell you how profitable your business is and easily track monies owed to you or the liabilities you are due to pay.

Your day-to-day finance operations should be systemised to make life as easy as possible when you need to complete your records. For example, where will you safely keep all your credit card or petty cash receipts? When and how will the sales invoices be raised?

For VAT purposes, accounting records should be prepared in order that VAT returns may be completed.

A good practice is to complete a regular bank reconciliation, so you are aware of cheques issued, payments made or credits received that have not yet hit the bank account, resulting in a true bank balance at any moment.

You do not have to be a qualified bookkeeper to keep your own financial records, although you may wish to consider outsourcing this role. If you wish to learn more about bookkeeping yourself, then the local college or distance learning providers offer very good courses.

A good financial system with accurate accounts will always save you money, as there is then less corrective work required by your accountant.

Records should be maintained for a period of years after the year end has passed. We suggest you check with HMRC or Companies House for the latest guidance.

Your day-to-day financial records should include the following:

- day book (ins and outs)
- sales invoice template
- sales invoice file
- purchase invoice file
- bank statement file
- petty cash book
- credit card management
- asset register
- VAT returns
- other records personal to your business.

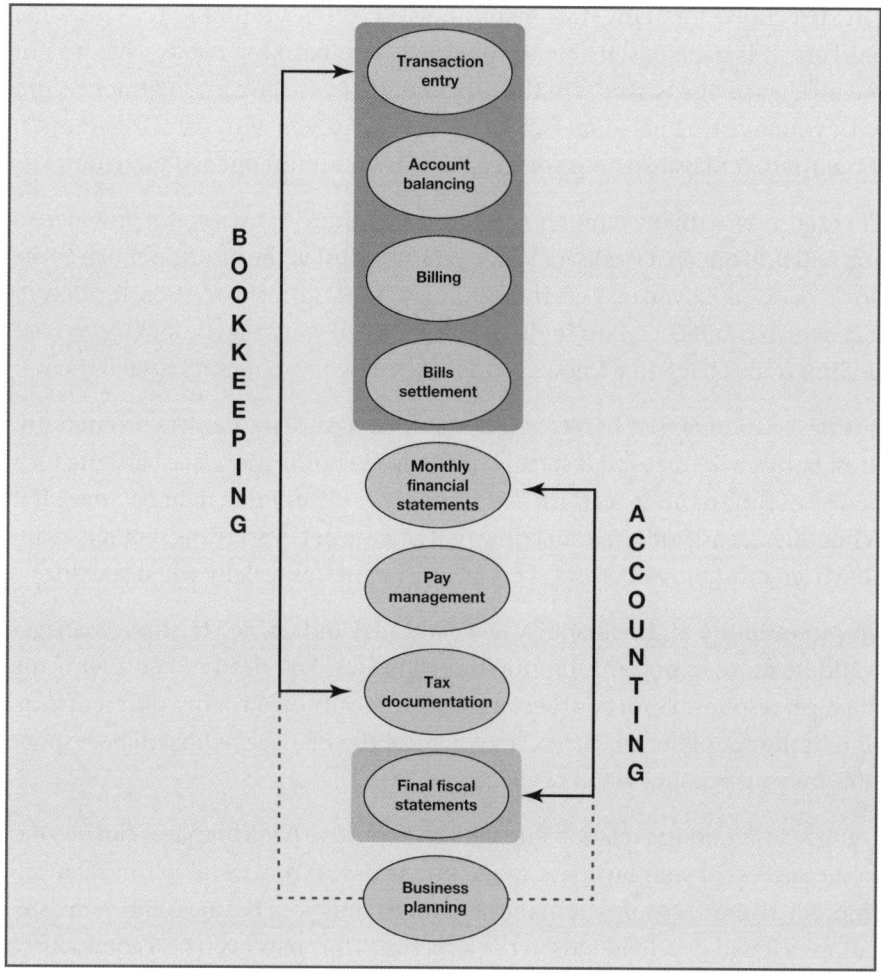

Choosing a bank account

This is not a decision to take lightly. The need to make a change of bank accounts later is time-consuming and can be disruptive for a business once it is established. Getting it right first time is not critical, but it is an important consideration.

Do your research, as with any supplier. Ask business acquaintances, friends, accountant contacts and business and finance advisors for their recommendations.

Visit different banks to test the quality and level of service offered at the time of your visit. Prepare a list of questions that cover the main business banking issues you will have with your business.

The first choice for many start-up businesses is often the proprietor's personal bankers. It is usually sensible to split these two banking needs – i.e. 'to not put all eggs in one basket'. On the other hand, if you have a good track record with your existing personal bank, this may assist you with securing finance, if required. It may also help you get a business account opened more quickly.

There are now so many more choices for your business bank account provider, so you will find one that works for you, but be mindful of the future as much as the now. For example, you may get free banking at start-up but no relationship or contact, which could be important in the future when you could be looking to raise finance from a bank that knows you as much as what your numbers tell them.

Business customers pay bank charges. Ask for a copy of the bank's current tariff. Most banks will offer small start-up businesses commission-free banking for a period of time or under certain conditions (e.g. minimum credit balance). If it is not offered, ask for it. We all know that price is not everything, but it is available from most providers and every penny counts, especially when starting.

The accessibility and availability of a dedicated and trained business manager could be more important for growth businesses. You need to consider if the manager responsible for your account will be locally based or in a different location in the county or country. Can you meet the manager who will be responsible for your account when needed?

A good close working relationship with a supportive bank manager can be vital to the success of your business. Make sure you work and develop this relationship. Take time to ensure the manager understands your business and your aspirations – it will pay dividends in the long run. They may even be a good source of referrals for your business!

The business banking sector is highly competitive and there is no need to settle for a level of service and price that you are not totally satisfied with or first offered.

Key considerations:

- What do I really want from my business bank?
- Number of local branches available and their opening hours (if you need to pay in money on a regular basis).
- Convenience – including on-line banking.
- Range of services on offer.
- Price of those services.

- Accessibility and availability of the manager and support team.
- Quality and speed of service.
- Speed of decision making and consistency.
- Confidence in the people who are handling your business affairs.

Choosing an accountant

The considerations are very similar to those for your potential bankers. One check is to ensure that all those calling themselves accountants are in fact qualified and able to do the job for you and have professional indemnity insurance cover for their advice to you. Look to see if the owners of the accountancy practice are members of one of the official accountancy bodies.

All qualified accountants should be able to complete your statutory accounts and tax computations for you whilst giving you professional advice and making the required compliance submissions to the relative authorities.

It is common for accountants to now position themselves as business advisers, but ensure they are proactive as it is often the case that you may not know the questions to ask before you get the advice they can offer. If they only respond in a reactive manner, then you are likely to lose out as you don't know what to ask.

Ask those that you trust for any recommendations and meet your potential accountancy suppliers to establish if you can work with them, if you like them, if they can deliver your expectations, and offer you a range of services to support your business.

Budgeting and forecasting for your business

If you do not have a plan to achieve, how will you know when you have done so? Keeping control of your finances is key to your business success, and a financial projection of your business idea is a recommended management tool. Once established, you can review the actual performance of your business against your forecast and identify why you have performed better or not so well.

A good budget forecast will note any assumptions you have made for reflection and also help you make decisions with confidence whilst allowing you to manage your business finances more effectively.

Building an effective forecast will help you truly understand the numbers in your business. For example, the different elements that contribute to your revenue such as the number of sales and value per sale.

Annual accounts are prepared after the year end, sometimes a few months later, and are therefore not always useful for planning purposes. It is much more effective to have a forecast and complete regular management accounts to provide you with the actual performance against that forecast.

Budgets and forecast plans are not just for the bank! They should be 'live' documents that you are working with on a regular basis. They are documented expectations of your income and expenditure in a given period.

Profit forecasts are used to plan the performance of your business. From start-up to growth or just survival, the forecast tells the business owner what has to be delivered to achieve the overall proposed performance. This may be a sales target or perhaps a cost budget.

To establish a forecast, you need to predict your likely sales, direct costs, overheads and other costs such as financing. But all these should be calculated, sometimes with assumptions, and not guess work. If you guess then how can you truly measure performance and how will you justify your plan to a prospective lender?

When considering your sales for a period that you are forecasting, don't forget to allow for any seasonality. Do you or your industry see spikes and lows in patterns of sales across a year or chosen period you are forecasting?

Many of the costs and overheads will be easier to predict as they may be subject to contracts, quotes, salaries, property costs or even a percentage of the sales.

It is best to be realistic and have a profitable forecast that you exceed rather than an ambitious forecast that just breaks even as you cannot achieve that level of sales. Be SMART, specific, measurable, achievable and realistic within a time period. Remember turnover is vanity, profit is sanity, but cash is king.

Cashflows are a useful tool to monitor the availability of cash within the business. Cash is the lifeblood of any business, and it is therefore vital to know that your business will have enough cash to pay its creditors and expenses when they fall due. Cash is king! It is like the oil in a car engine; no matter how powerful your engine is, if the oil runs dry the engine seizes up. Cash in a business is exactly the same; no matter how profitable it is, you cannot run dry! A cashflow forecast is usually projected over a period of 6 or 12 months, although you can look at shorter periods if necessary.

In simple terms, cash flow is the movement of your cash over a period of time.

For example, let's look at a new order. You receive the order on day one. You order the goods from your supplier on day two with the payment terms of 30 days. On day five, you receive the goods and supply to your customer. On day 10, you raise an invoice to your customer again on 30-day payment terms. Let's jump forward to day 32, when the supplier is due their money but you will not be paid until at least day 40, thereby creating a cashflow situation that has to be managed and met. Hence why funds to start your business or 'free cash' later enables you to best manage this working capital requirement.

The cashflow budget is different from your profit forecast as it considers when the actual cash spend or cash receipt is expected. For example, a telephone bill is received and paid quarterly but is for a service that is used monthly. Therefore, in your profit forecast it is shown monthly, but in your cash forecast it is shown when payment is due, say quarterly.

Start with a profit forecast and then create the cashflow forecast based on the customer and supplier payment terms. Care should be taken as some things appear in a profit forecast that do not show in the cash flow and vice versa, such as capital injection, depreciation, finance repayments, asset purchases and VAT.

A good cashflow forecast will show you the working capital requirements of your business that will enable you to continue trading whilst you generate the continuous income.

In summary, a good forecast will show you if your business idea has substance and, once you have the forecasts, use them as live documents to measure your performance and control your finances.

There are some common phrases used in planning such as:

- **Opening balance** – this figure is the ending balance of the previous month.
- **Total income** – this is the total income figure for the month, both sales and other income.
- **Total outgoings** – this is the combined total of the outgoings. Usually split between direct costs and overhead expenses.
- **Net cash flow** – this is the difference between the total income and the total outgoings.
- **Ending balance** – this is the balance at the end of the month. This figure is obtained by adding (or subtracting if it is a negative) the net cash flow to the opening balance of the month.

CORPORATE BUDGET TEMPLATE

[Entity name]

Summary

	July		August		September		October		November	
	Planned amount	Incurred	Planned amount	Incurred	Planned amount	Incurred	Planned amount	Incurred	Planned amount	Incurred
Total Revenue	$0	$0	$0	$0	$0	$0	$0	$0	$0	$0
Total Expenditures	$0	$0	$0	$0	$0	$0	$0	$0	$0	$0
	$0	$0	$0	$0	$0	$0	$0	$0	$0	$0

Revenue	July		August		September		October		November	
	Planned amount	Incurred	Planned amount	Incurred	Planned amount	Incurred	Planned amount	Incurred	Planned amount	Incurred
Operational revenue										
Type 1										
Type 2										
Type 3										
Type 4										
Type 5										
Type 6										
Type 7										
TOTAL	$0	$0	$0	$0	$0	$0	$0	$0	$0	$0

Expenditures	July		August		September		October		November	
	Planned amount	Incurred	Planned amount	Incurred	Planned amount	Incurred	Planned amount	Incurred	Planned amount	Incurred
Running costs										
Financial and Legal										
Promotions										
Asset reduction										
Dues & Subscriptions										
Insurance										
Interest Expense										
Maintenance/ Improvements										
Taxes & Licenses										
Telephone										
Travel										
Web										
	$0	$0	$0	$0	$0	$0	$0	$0	$0	$0

Choosing the right key performance indicators (KPIs) for your business objectives

We can have the vision, a desire to get there, even the plan and know-how, but it is as important to track your progress towards your goals and objectives. Such tracking enables you to see your progress, adapt when needed, know when you've got there and celebrate the smaller steps of the journey.

Key performance indicators (KPIs) are a valuable tool for measuring and monitoring. However, choosing the right KPIs, relevant to your business, can be challenging.

KPIs also help you make informed decisions. They can help you identify areas where your business is succeeding or those that need improvement. They measure the effectiveness of your initiatives.

Here are some thoughts to help you choose the right KPIs for your objectives.

Start by defining your objectives. What are the specific outcomes you want to achieve? These objectives should be aligned with your long-term vision and address critical areas such as revenue growth, customer satisfaction, operational efficiency, market expansion, profit improvement, etc.

Once you're clear on the direction, identify the key drivers that impact your objectives. Those critical components that must perform well for you to achieve your objectives For example, if your objective is to increase customer satisfaction, drivers could include customer retention, customer loyalty or customer feedback.

Consider your 'success factors'. What are the outcomes you want or need to deliver your desired objective/s?

Select KPIs that align and provide insight into the performance of critical drivers and help you track progress. When choosing KPIs, consider your stakeholders, such as investors, employees and customers. Ensure they are relevant and meaningful and provide the desired insights.

Are your KPIs practical and actionable? KPIs should provide insight into performance that can be acted upon. For example, a KPI such as revenue growth is an outcome and not specifically actionable, whereas a KPI such as conversion rate would be actionable since it provides insight into how to improve revenue growth.

Consider both leading and lagging indicators. These KPIs should be activity-based as much as outcome-focused. For example, you may want to gain 10 new customers as an outcome. However, you can only measure this at the period end. Whereas if you consider the linked activity-based KPI, then 20 quotes at a 50 per cent conversation rate would lead to the 10 and this can be monitored throughout so that you have no surprises at the end of the period.

Your KPIs should be easily tracked and managed from the data you have readily available. If data is not available, you may need to revise your KPIs or invest in other data collection methods.

Once you have chosen your KPIs, monitor them regularly with consistency and adjust them as needed.

Credit control – getting paid on time

Unfortunately, you won't get paid on time every time. It's a sad reality of our business culture in the UK that some businesses, and perhaps close to the majority, don't pay their invoices on time. However much you have your terms and conditions, with your payment terms clearly stated, there will still be businesses that will pay when it suits them for their cashflow purposes or when it is within their terms.

Here are some tips to help you get paid on time and not become a lender to your customers!

The first steps are to ensure that you have clear payment terms (e.g. paid within 30 days of the date of the invoice) and ensure these are clearly communicated with all your customers. If you are able, ask to be paid direct to your bank account, as this reduces any further time.

Payment terms

You need to ensure your customers understand how much they need to pay and by when they must pay you. Most businesses give a period of credit, but this will depend on your business.

The customer is more likely to pay you on time if your terms are clearly set out in writing from the start *and* you stick to them!

Depending on your business, you may have specific terms as defined in a contract with your customer or general terms and conditions that you may display on your website or quotes. These should quote your desired payment terms together with any other terms or conditions.

There are many types of payment terms used including:

- payment in advance
- cash with order
- cash on delivery and
- net number of days, which is when the payment is due the quoted number of days after the invoice date.

You should choose the best terms for your business. However, this is a balance between being paid as quickly as possible and meeting the customers' expectations, which may be governed by an industry standard.

The agreed payment terms should always be clearly stated on your invoices.

YOUR COMPANY NAME

BILLING STATEMENT

Customer Business Name,
Contact Person
Street Address
Locality
ZIP Code,
Region

Issue Date
Bill Number,
Purchase Order Number,
Tax ID,

Street Address
Locality
ZIP Code,
Region

Item Details	Units	Price per Unit	Tax Percentage	Total Amount
			0.00%	0.00
			0.00%	0.00
			0.00%	0.00
			0.00%	0.00
			0.00%	0.00
			0.00%	0.00
			0.00%	0.00
			0.00%	0.00
			0.00%	0.00
			0.00%	0.00
			0.00%	0.00
			0.00%	0.00
			Intermediate Total	€ 0.00
			Tax Amount	**€ 0.00**
			Final Amount Due	**€ 0.00**

Pay By
Special Instructions

You should also make sure *all* of your team are talking to customers on the basis of these terms; otherwise, you may find sales and finance teams talking at cross purposes.

However, this alone will not ensure you get paid, let alone paid on time.

Credit control is most appropriately considered as controlling your risk. Is your customer a good customer? Are you controlling when you are going to be paid or knowing the risk of potentially not being paid, whilst also understanding the risks to your business if you are not paid?

Depending on your business and the level of transaction value, you should consider a form of credit check on your customers. If they have a poor existing credit record, then it is unlikely to improve with you taking them on and it may be that they came to you as their existing suppliers have them on stop. This check could be by way of a bank or trade reference or a credit agency report.

You should then establish a set of steps to continually communicate with the customer until they have paid and understand the 'real' reasons for non-payment and when the payment will be made. This will include sending account statements, reminders and letters, and warning about the amount due, plus making telephone calls at the appropriate times. Do not be afraid of issuing letters warning of possible legal action.

Here lies a potential issue for some business owners. How to collect the money due whilst keeping a good customer relationship for future sales. Well, first a good customer is only one that pays, so you should be firm when chasing. If you are not comfortable with chasing the money then outsource this role, as debt chasing is a drain on your resources, so already a cost and you want to take action as effectively as possible.

To help small and new businesses, the UK Government has taken steps to try to help with the risk with the introduction of the Late Payments Act, which allows you to charge interest on overdue invoices, and they have also made changes in the court procedures to make that process of claims quicker to implement.

You should have a credit control policy that everyone follows. Sometimes you have to be realistic about their ability to pay and be fair, unless of course they are persistent liars! However, at all times you should retain contact, keep control and monitor the commitments given to you.

Look to agree and confirm your payment terms and procedures up front. Check on your customers' payment practice and whether they can meet your terms. If not, then you can decide how much you want to work with them and negotiate these.

Whoever your customer, they are not an ideal customer if they don't pay you. Don't be the bank for your customers and allow your critical cash flow to suffer for the benefit of others, as cash is king!

Keep on top of your credit control and make sure it does not get out of control.

Credit control is too often considered just for big business, but it is an important aspect of any business. Credit control is anything you do to reduce the wait between supplying a customer and getting paid. For example, after you've issued the invoice it's good practice to check it's been received (a classic excuse!) and they are happy, plus that it has been authorised for payment on the due date. Then perhaps remind them a day or two before the due date that it is becoming due.

You have done the work; you deserve to be paid. If you don't collect the debt, then it may become unpaid and classified as a bad debt that you may need to write off, losing the profit, losing the investment you made.

This table below demonstrates how much extra revenue you need to generate to cover a bad debt. For example, your profit margin is 10 per cent and the bad debt is £5,000. You will need an additional £50,000 of revenue to cover that loss. There's a motivator to chase it!

Your profit margin %	Bad debts					
	£100	£1,000	£5,000	£10,000	£50,000	£100,000
1%	£10,000	£100,000	£500,000	£1 million	£5 million	£10 million
3%	£3,333	£33,333	£166,666	£333,333	£1.7 million	£3.3 million
5%	£2,000	£20,000	£100,000	£200,000	£1 million	£2 million
10%	£1,000	£10,000	£50,000	£100,000	£500,000	£1 million
15%	£666	£6,666	£33,333	£66,666	£333,333	£666,666
20%	£500	£5,000	£25,000	£50,000	£250,000	£500,000
30%	£333	£3,333	£16,666	£33,333	£166,666	£333,333
40%	£250	£2,500	£12,500	£25,000	£125,000	£250,000
50%	£200	£2,000	£10,000	£20,000	£100,000	£200,000

To support you in chasing payments, you may consider payment technology to help people pay you quickly! Perhaps a direct debit via Go Cardless or a Pay Now button for card payments on your invoices (available via software such as Xero).

A financial ratio to regularly measure is your debtor days. The debtor days ratio shows the average number of days your customers are taking to pay you. It is calculated by dividing debtors by average daily sales. Keep it low and in control, ideally matching your payment terms (i.e. 30 days).

Once you have raised the invoice, ideally as soon as possible, here are some steps you can take to get paid:

- Check the invoice has been received and that it is authorised ready for payment.
- Seven days before the payment is due, politely remind the customer that payment will be expected on the due date.
- The day before, issue a statement with the due date as a reminder.
- If not paid on the day, pick up the phone to give a reminder and ask for the payment date (an email is too easy to delete and ignore).
- Build a rapport with the person responsible for deciding when to raise your payment.
- Get to know the excuses you are served and have a question to respond (e.g. I just need to get the payment authorised = Great, thank you, when do you think that will be?).
- Keep notes of conversations or promises that you can refer back to.
- Be persistent in your chasing. People pay people who chase and are known to chase!
- Still not paid, consider issuing formal chase letters every seven days with the seriousness and threat increasing to a warning of legal action.
- Thank the customer once paid. The appreciation creates a subconscious feeling for paying you next time!

The above may feel like many administrative steps that you don't have time for, but you can automate many of these reminders using software or delegate or outsource the task.

> **Remember this**
>
> A good customer is also one that pays!

Keeping score

You can have the forecast and all the controls in place to manage your finances, but time goes by quickly, so you want to keep your finger on the detail in a timely manner. The best way to keep score is to use scorecards. A business scorecard offers numerous benefits that can significantly enhance your organisation's performance and strategic management. It is a strategic tool used to monitor, measure and manage a company's performance across key areas.

Your scorecard should include a mix of activities (inputs) and targeted results (outputs). Some you may measure daily, weekly, monthly or other set periods.

Additionally, a good scorecard will help you identify what needs to happen to make any required changed. For example, the output may be a revenue target, but the detail may be captured by measuring the activity that makes up your sales revenue. Therefore, if you don't hit your revenue target, you can establish why (e.g. you didn't sell enough or perhaps you discounted too much and therefore did not hit that average order value).

Here are the main reasons why a business would implement a scorecard:

1. Clear alignment with strategic goals.
2. Track key performance indicators (KPIs).
3. Drive accountability.
4. Encourage data-driven decision making.
5. Identify trends and predict outcomes.
6. Improve communication and focus.
7. Measure customer and employee satisfaction.
8. Drive continuous improvement.
9. Enable scalability.

Six financial management tips for business owners

Effective financial management is vital for the success and the sustainability of your business. Here are some practical strategies that could help you to navigate the financial aspects of business.

1 **Create a clear budget and financial plan**
   First, I encourage you to start by assessing your current financial situation and set realistic goals to develop a financial plan or model that gives you confidence. What are you basing your decisions on? Creating a financial forecast that outlines your revenue streams, expenses and cash flow projections will provide you with a live document to track and manage your finances effectively.

2 **Understand and sensitise your numbers**
   Consider your budget and ask yourself 'what if' questions, then have versions of your budget that would show how you would adjust to cope should that situation occur. Doing so supports your confidence when dealing with such situations but also enables you to implement a change in tactics efficiently if needed.

3 **Monitor and conduct regular reviews of your finances**
   Monitoring and tracking key financial metrics really help you make informed decisions, so keep a close eye on metrics such as your revenue, profit margins, accounts receivable, accounts payable and even your inventory turnover if applicable.

   Regularly review your profit and loss statements, your balance sheets and your cash flow statements to gain a comprehensive understanding of your business's financial health.

4 **Review your expenses**
   Controlling costs and optimising expenses is of course crucial for maintaining profitability, so regularly assess your expenses and identify areas where you can cut costs, or find a more cost-effective alternative.

   Bear in mind, as soon as you consider an expense to be a cost rather than an investment it's time to consider removing that spend. Other ways to control costs include negotiating with suppliers to explore bulk purchasing options and embracing lean principles to eliminate waste and optimise your expenditure.

5 **Implement a cash reserve**
Building and maintaining a cash reserve is really good financial management practice. It involves having a cushion of funds to ensure you can navigate unexpected expenses or economic downturns or surprises in that those reserves allow you to have choices and help you feel much more comfortable with decision making. We learned during the pandemic that having sufficient reserves to fall back on is essential.

You may look for a three- to six-month cash cover of your costs in reserves, but much will depend on your risk profile.

6 **Take professional advice for financial management**
Seek professional financial guidance earlier than most do. Consider working with an accountant or a financial adviser who specialises in small business finances as they can provide insights to help you navigate complex tax regulations or offer strategic advice to optimise your financial management practices.

Financial management isn't just a one-time task; it requires regular review and adjustment to continuously evaluate your financial strategy and make necessary adjustments based on the changing market conditions, the industry, trends and your business performance. Staying proactive so you can make data-driven decisions ensures that your financial management practices remain aligned with your business goals.

By having a financial management strategy, you can ensure financial stability, have a strong foundation for your business's growth and know what you need to achieve to reach the point of success you desire. It is all in the numbers really!

I wish I knew this before I started my first business

Cash is king

The profits that you may be able to generate tomorrow mean absolutely nothing if your cash dries up and you can't pay your liabilities that are due today. It may not be the exciting part of your business, but know your numbers, keep your books accurately up to date and have an eye on your cash flow.

Understand the factors that influence the cash in your business. Don't be your customers' bank by not collecting what is due to you when it is due. Additionally, know your cash cycle and how it flows. For example, you use your cash to purchase raw materials, you then produce and deliver your offering before raising your invoice. You then chase and collect what is owed to you before splitting the 'pots' for tax and the profit that you can reinvest into further purchases, as the cycle continues and becomes more complex as you scale and grow.

Key points

- Do you know your numbers? If not, get good people around you.
- Turnover is vanity, profit is sanity, but cash is king.
- What are the key numbers in your business that drive your success?
- Do you need to raise any finance to start and, if so, how will you do this?
- Keep up-to-date accurate financial records.
- Mindfully choose your professional advisers as they are critical to you.
- Understand your tax liabilities as a business and as an individual.
- What does your financial forecast look like?
- What are your key performance indicators (KPIs)?
- How will you ensure you get paid on time?

Additional resources

Books
Michalowicz, M. (2017) *Profit First*. Portfolio.
Kiyosaki, R. (2011) *Rich Dad's Cashflow Quadrant*. Plata Publishing.

CHAPTER 5
HOW TO MARKET YOUR BUSINESS

This may be the chapter you have been waiting for! However, this chapter will not give you the 'silver bullet' to winning a constant flow of new customers. Sorry, but this does not exist; otherwise, everyone would be successful already!

This chapter will help you maximise your resources by considering the messaging and ways that you will attract the interest of prospective new customers and how you can pull them towards you.

What are you offering? What do you really do?

Before we talk about the how let's ensure you have ultimate clarity on what it is that you really do for your customers. What are you really taking to market as an offering and solution?

You have a product or service, but ultimately you also have a solution. A solution to someone's pain, problem, fear, want, need or desire. For example, as a website designer no one really cares that you can build websites even if they want one. They are more likely to be buying a platform that helps get eyes on their business, generates leads or provides a level of automation for the business.

It is important you have this clarity so that you can then position it in the marketplace; otherwise, it is very likely that you will waste time and money when executing the 'how'.

You may have started your business or you are currently gathering feedback to establish your minimum viable product (MVP), where you are considering what you do to generate revenue, for which audiences and for what value.

Are you sharing what you really do?

Think about that for a moment. What do you really do?

When you know your 'real' solution then you will find it easier to gain the interest of your prospects.

A further consideration to help you answer this question is to consider the gap in your market and recognise the unmet needs or underserved markets. What solution is your audience seeking that is not currently offered or not offered that well?

How should you be introduced?

Just imagine for a moment that in the room next door, to wherever you are right now, there are 500 of your ideal dream customers. They are all waiting to hear from you and in a short while you are going to be introduced.

What do you want the host to say as a way of introduction? How should they introduce you to 500 of your dream customers? What would engage them to hang on every word you want to share?

One consideration may be to include your personal brand messaging. What do you stand for, and what is your purpose, your 'go to' expertise? What about the impact or the contribution that you make? No one cares if you're a website designer, accountant, influencer, etc. but they care about how they can gain or avoid a pain by meeting you.

The answer to these questions will help you to form the start of your messaging.

I work with …	
Who struggle to …	
And would like to …	
What separates my service from others is …	
Because of this my customers are able to …	

Use this framework to build out your introduction:

I am …	
From …	
And I/we work with …	
Who have a problem with …	
What we do is …	
So that …	
Which means that …	

This may also be your elevator pitch.

As an example, this was my introduction when I owned a bookkeeping practice:

I am Mike Foster from A1 Bookkeeping and I work with pubs and restaurants who have a problem finding the time to keep reliable financial records.

As expected of a bookkeeper we complete their day-to-day record keeping, but we give back time to the owner enabling them to do what they do best whilst having reliable, accurate financial information to support their critical decision making.

Are your marketing foundations established?

The early years of running your own business are about creating a foundation, a solid jumping off point to propel you onto the next stage.

Often, the initial stages are sparked by your desire, but you are always creating foundations for the next step of your entrepreneurial journey.

Look to establish the right foundations from the start. Start with the end in mind. What do you have to do now that makes it easier and sustainable in the future?

Ask yourself if your foundation is strong. Do you have the right foundations and are they strong enough to support your growth? I've seen many businesses simply focus on sales and, as a result, their business has nearly fallen over, as the rest of the business was not structured to cope. Much like building a house, if the foundations are weak then there is every chance it will wobble and even fall over. That's like going out and winning loads of new business, but not having the operational model to deliver on your promise.

The best foundation for your business is one that is holistic. A holistic approach considering all elements of your business is often required to form the best foundation.

They're the fundamental elements that form the basis for a business and its eventual success. Yes, of course you can succeed without creating a foundation, but that's often luck and you have a better chance with a strong base. As an example, without a consideration of the foundations, you may end up with a business that is reliant on you and that's then difficult to change. A business that is reliant on you to operate will eventually drain your enthusiasm and passion. It can mean constant interruptions for help, multiple emails, phone calls and meetings that you needn't spend time on, missing out on holidays and returning to piles of hard work, and even dwindling revenue.

Every business is different, and a foundation plan may well be different for you, so here are some thoughts to help you create a solid foundation for your marketing and lead generation:

- Know what you want to achieve with a clarity of your vision.
- Have a strategic marketing document and a tactical operational plan. The effective execution of your marketing will depend on your ingredients, your mindset, the strategy, the tactics used and your resources in terms of your time, team and money.
- Have the talent or best advisers around you who support your plan and execution whilst filling the knowledge or skill gap you may have. If you don't know how to execute a marketing tactic such as paid ads and you have no desire or time to learn, then hire someone who does or outsource.
- Reflect on valuable research that confirms where and how you are to position your business into the market.
- Analyse your customer segments and profile your ideal customers so that your messaging is relevant, on point, relatable and empathetic.
- Be invested in tried and tested lead generation channels and tactics.
- Understand your customer journey, how the relationships evolve, and create a matching marketing and sales process.
- Understand your marketing maths; what budget is needed for what desired return.
- Know your numbers and those critical 'success drivers' for your marketing.
- Measure your performance on activity and outcomes. Have a process in place to review your performance and allow your team's innovation and creativity to continually improve your marketing and sales.
- Know how you truly add value to your audience and why people lean towards you with interest.
- Have clarity on what you really do and how you wish to position that 'go to' expertise. For example, are you offering a 'me' or an 'us'?

> **Remember this**
>
> **People buy from people**
>
> Within a business that offers a personal experience, primarily the purchase is made from an individual making the offer and not so much from the brand or business. Yes, certain brands can influence an individual's decision making, but we all know people who have never returned to a location because of the service received not because of the product.
>
> Entrepreneurs are very often people orientated, even if it is not seen at face value. They understand why and how p*eople buy from people* and achieve results though relationships.
>
> People tend to buy from people they trust, respect and believe. Entrepreneurs therefore are good at aligning their own values with others and demonstrating true empathy.

Strategic marketing – who, what, how

A marketing strategy is a process that will allow you to concentrate your resources on the best opportunities to increase sales and achieve a competitive advantage. It is common to see business owners over complicating their sales and marketing with huge planning documents that do not actually give them the focus they often need to take action. Instead, it fuels procrastination awaiting the perfect plan that will just 'work' (they don't!) rather than encouraging experimentation.

Of course, some businesses, especially larger, complex businesses, may need a more detailed plan, as is often found in the corporate world. That is often why a small business owner wants a plan of multiple pages when they start their own business, because that is what they know from how they were encouraged to work in the past.

An effective sales and marketing plan can often be captured or summarised on just one or two pages.

Here are some thoughts to help you do your strategic thinking and create your one- or two-page sales and marketing plan. A document you can share with others including your team, your stakeholders, your lender, your suppliers, etc. that provides crystal clear understanding of who you are looking to attract, and how, with what messaging or tactics.

Consider your objective. Why do you want a sales and marketing plan? What is it you're trying to achieve? Of course you will be trying to recruit new customers, but you may also be thinking that you need to recruit strategic partners or referral contacts. You may want your existing customers to buy again or refer you to others.

How will you measure the success of your marketing and sales? Think about your key performance indicators. What are you going to measure, in terms of your activity and your desired results? What is your value proposition? What's unique about you? What's your differentiator that gives you value in the marketplace?

Gain clarity on your market audience. Who are you targeting and what is their profile? What is the market opportunity? Capture your insight, your research and your understanding of the market whilst having clarification about who you are trying to pull towards you.

Who are you looking to attract? There is a saying that 'you get what you market', so if you market your business to everyone, then don't be disappointed when you get anyone. Do you have key customer segments? Can you describe your ideal customer? What does your customer buyer profile look like? What's the avatar of that buyer? With this information you can actually focus your mind, focus your attention with powerful messaging.

When thinking about your customers, or your prospects, consider their pain, problem or fear, want, need or desire and how you are addressing that. This creates an emotional connection with the buyer and demonstrates that you understand them. What are they looking to gain or avoid?

How are you going to position yourself into the market? What's your offering? How are you going to position your offering to attract those ideal customers?

Identify where your ideal customers hang out and consider the channels and tactics that enable you to 'fish in the right pond' and effectively, efficiently pull those people towards you with interest. For example, if your customers are online, are you using online tools and, if they're offline, are you using offline tools or does it need a bit of a mix?

Consider how you are building a relationship of trust and respect with your prospective customers. This is trust and respect for you, your business and your offering. Make sure that your sales and marketing process maps your customer journey. If your customer journey goes through the common stages of awareness, consideration, purchase, onboarding, loyalty and advocation, then where does your sales and marketing process map alongside?

Considering how to promote your business

One of the most common questions in business and often a source of frustration is 'How do I decide where to promote my product or service?'.

You could promote your business anywhere, but I suggest your marketing activity will be much more effective and resourceful if you have considered this within your marketing strategy. The majority of businesses have limited resources for their marketing in terms of time and money, so a strategy will help you maximise this.

Within a good marketing strategy, you should make considerations such as:

- Do you know your market?
- What is your vision of the ideal customer?
- What is your strategy and vision?
- What is your position in that market?
- And how do you plan to target your market, and what are your tactics?

Your customer base will contribute towards the success of your business and how your business is represented or perceived, so think about who you really want as your customers.

Look to profile your potential customer. For example, what is their industry sector, what size are they, where are they located, what is the personality of the owners, how much would they spend per annum, on what terms would they trade and how established are they? You can also segment your potential customers by knowing their demographics, their classification, their life cycle stage, or by their psychographic attitudes and values. You should also look to profile the buyer within your ideal customer business. Are they most likely to be male or female, what age, what do they drive, what do they read, etc. This will help you with your effective communication to them.

In terms of contextual marketing, you need to understand 'what' the customer is doing when they decide to purchase and 'where' they were. As covered in Chapter 3 'Planning your business', this is identified with effective market research. Look to establish the following from your ideal customer:

- Where are they buying now?
- Why from them?
- What do they get for their money?
- How often do they buy?
- What are their buying habits?
- Who influences the purchase decision?
- Do they buy on a want or a need?
- How was that product or service brought to their attention?

Some businesses can sell to anyone, focusing on the mass market, but this is certainly not a strategy for most businesses. If you narrow your focus it will mean:

- you can concentrate your marketing efforts in the places where your customers dwell, whether that is in the online or offline universe
- you can better understand their needs; where your product or service can help them and why or when they need them
- you will be able to start identifying product or service gaps
- you can easily adapt as you know your market environment.

To help you build your connected overall business strategy, consider the leading factors such as: how many customers will we have? Where will we work from? How will we deliver? What is our preferred type of work or main products? What is our niche? What will our employees or resources look like? What is our pricing policy?

Once you know more about your business positioning and your potential customers, you will be better placed to understand your position in the marketplace. For example, if you plan to open a food shop, you may have little chance competing directly with the major food outlets, so you will position yourself for a different customer, with a different offer to them; otherwise, it is likely to be about the price and the competitor's buying power will win. Simply competing on price is a dangerous race to the bottom.

Consider the 4 Ps of the 'marketing mix':

- product
- price
- place – the purchase location or distribution channel
- promotion – your chosen marketing communications such as advertising, public relations, personal selling and sales promotion.

These factors should also play a key part in your marketing strategy.

A good marketing strategy is one that effectively raises awareness of your offering and provides you with a flow of leads that are likely to turn into customers. A marketing strategy is a process that can allow you to concentrate your limited resources on the greatest opportunities to increase sales and achieve a sustainable competitive advantage. It contains the company's value proposition, key brand messaging, data on target customer demographics and other high-level elements.

From a strategic perspective, who do you want as clients, how will they get to know, like and trust you and what does your business represent?

Look to answer these key considerations to help you build your marketing strategy:

What do you want your business to be known for?	
Why are you marketing? (Brand profile, relationships, partners, sales?)	
Is your market business to business (B2B) or business to consumer (B2C)?	
Who do you really want as ideal customers?	
What is their emotion such as pain, problem, fear, want, need, desire?	
Where do they hang out?	
What influences their decision to buy?	
What do your ideal customers want from your offering?	
What key messages will pull them towards you with interest?	
Make a plan including focused tactical actions.	

Once you have a strategy, you can then select the right marketing tactics and tools to build traction and pull prospects towards you to create sales opportunities.

If you know what you really want and how to make it easier to obtain, then marketing to win new clients is like a tap. Turn it on when you need it or the best businesses just leave it flowing.

Seven steps to establish your marketing plan

Let's look at the effectiveness of your marketing investment. How do you market your business to the right people and create a constant flow of leads from your ideal customers?

Of course, marketing is a massive topic, so here are seven steps that will help you establish an effective marketing plan.

Step one: be clear on your objective (the why)

It may seem obvious that you want to win more business and increase your revenue but the motivation for truly effective marketing, not the common feast and famine, is born by identifying why you want these new customers. Is it more income for you personally that gives you more choices as an individual or as a family? If so, what does that provide you with and how would you feel if it was obtained? Or how would you feel if it wasn't? Is it to give you more options as a business, by increasing the critical asset of cash flow or capital reserves? Would the reinvestment of this cash see a cumulative effect of further growth?

Step two: understand your audience and markets

Look to identify your target market. Who is your ideal customer? We all have limited resources for our marketing in terms of time and money, so there are many benefits of focusing on your ideal customer. You will be more specific with your marketing tactics and also speak with more relevant messages. Reflect on the profile of the decision makers, the suppliers they use already, what publications they read and where they hang out. Research their situation, their goals and objectives, what they want or need, and find out what stops them from achieving their goals. This will help you establish what is causing them pain and understand what the impact of their problems or challenges is. All of this builds a useful profile for your focus.

When considering the market, reflect on the overall picture: how the sector looks, is there a regional difference, what are the expectations in the market and is there any gap for you to exploit? This is where your SWOT analysis comes into its own, enabling you to establish how you can utilise your identified strengths and exploit those opportunities in front of you.

Within the market, break down and understand your customer segments. Is that by a demographic, the ideal client profile, a niche or vertical market?

For a deeper understanding and to more successfully target your market, look to develop your 'customer personas'. It is good practice to name your personas. By humanising your target market, it's possible to gain a deeper understanding of the people you're hoping to engage with and relate to them.

To create a customer profile persona, you can start to narrow your focus using data and market research. Ask your considered audience using surveys, focus groups or interviews. See who your competitors consider to be their customer. Review social media feeds for trends or use analytics or tools to understand what people are searching for and the language they use. Then look to establish what they care about. Put yourself in your customers' shoes. What is their journey? What are their issues?

Step three: look to define your brand and its offering

Consider or use your team (if applicable) to agree on your 'core' brand values that drive your day-to-day operations. The things you live by, the things that help you base decisions, and the things that help you hire the right people.

Then understand your voice and develop your consistent brand tone of voice.

Over recent years, marketing and sales has moved to the digital world and this has been accelerated during the pandemic. No longer can we rely on our actual voice to control our communication, so what is your tone of voice that you can replicate online, through print and in person? This should be influenced by the audience you are talking to and their language. How will the brand tone of your voice be consistent? What sort of language reflects your personality? Do short, punchy sentences reflect your brand, or would longer words and phrases show a maturity and expertise that you want to convey? Your tone of voice needs to be consistent across all your brand assets. If not, your prospects and customers will be confused, and when they are confused they often look elsewhere.

To supplement your voice and give you consistency across your business, look to create a brand style guide. This would include any visual identity including imagery, colours, fonts, etc. that ensure that you communicate your brand with consistency.

Once you have clarified your audience, the market, your ideal customer and your brand positioning, it is easier to establish a relevant offering with the hooks that pull your prospects towards you with interest.

Step four: your marketing tactics

Don't move onto this step too early. Without a clear picture of your audience and a strategic approach, you could waste your resources in terms of time and money.

With a clear picture of your audience and what you are taking to market, in terms of a product or service, you will consider the most effective channels and tactics to use. You will more easily identify where your prospects hang out and can then use the most relevant tactics to build traction and generate leads.

To establish the tactics that work, you first need to consider the various different ways to build traction for your business, then test and measure a few before establishing the most effective ways to market your business with the best return on investment.

When considering the options you could use, be careful not to dismiss a marketing tactic because of your own personal feelings or experience. For example, you may not like social media advertising, telesales or never click on a Google ad because you know it's been paid for. However, they may be the best tactics for your business!

Step five: create a systemised process to pull prospects towards you step by step

Here there are two considerations. First, the actual lead generation, your marketing, that brings more prospects than ever before into your sales funnel. Then it's the lead conversion, your sales, that is the steps of your funnel to convert more leads into actual revenue earning sales.

Review your customer journey and consider the various stages of your sales process – awareness, consideration, decision, onboarding, fulfilment, loyalty, advocacy. The *awareness* stage is supported by your marketing activity for lead generation. It takes your potential customers from 'lurkers' to 'interested' to 'enquiry'. They then move to the *consideration* stage and from here onwards, I consider this to be your sales activity to maximise the lead conversion or encourage future sales. The initial stages from *consideration* to a positive *decision* and *onboarding* could be broken down into a number of steps. This is beneficial, as you can then measure the effectiveness of each step and if you find that your prospects are not moving through the steps or bailing out at a certain step, then you know which part of your process to review, tweak and improve.

Also don't forget the latter stages of the customer journey and how your marketing should continue to work. Too often businesses stop their sales process during the fulfilment stage. However, how does the relationship with your customer need to evolve to maximise the *loyalty* and *advocacy* that create more future revenue through further purchases or referrals to other new business?

Step six: measure, manage and evolve

This can be, and is often, avoided as some businesses feel that they've done all the research and hard work to create the marketing campaigns so have no need to monitor them. Others avoid monitoring because they don't want to see the results as, in their heart, they know it's not quite right.

This is as critical as any step before. It measures your activity and your outcomes to provide you with the insight to best understand your return on investment.

As mentioned in earlier chapters, you may measure your outcomes such as the revenue earned from a campaign but look to also measure the activity along the way, as it will save you £000s. If you are measuring activity, then you can tweak, amend or even stop an activity if it is not progressing as you thought it would.

Step seven: the activity plan

It's execution time! For this step, break down your activity on a per-week basis. Using a format such as a Gantt chart, establish which activities have to be executed, at what time and by whom. Use such tools to break down the huge task of your marketing into bite size chunks that can be more easily implemented.

Ten ways to generate leads for your business

You by no means have to implement *all* of these to be successful in lead generation. To scale any business, you need a consistent flow of leads. This may be from multiple methods, or it may be with a strong focus or investment of resources in one or two.

Let's look at these 10 ways in more detail.

1   **Know your customer**

    It goes without saying that a strong customer profile helps you aim the right message at the right person at the right time. You need to keep an eye on your customers' needs, wants, fears and desires to make sure you can provide what they need in changing times. The pandemic, or ever-changing economic climates, has shown how we have to keep close to the market and adapt to any changing needs or expectations.

    Profiling your ideal customer provides you with great information about the words you can then use to attract their interest and, importantly, clearly communicate how you can really help them.

    You should be able to create a profile that when read by your ideal customer they think, 'Yes, that's me you're talking about! You understand me, I want to work with you,' and they lean towards you with interest.

    Most buyers are sceptical. When they do their research, they need to connect with you, like you, trust you before starting to lean in and make an enquiry.

2   **Use LinkedIn**

    With clarity of who you are looking for, you can begin to search and connect with people who you want to engage with. As you would 'in person', exercise the highest etiquette standards and refrain from using sales techniques in your connection messages or even in your first two or three follow-up messages. A good tactic is to initially thank your new connection for connecting, and then give them something of value, something that will be of interest, perhaps a blog that shares your story and business ethos and a link to an interesting read for them or their business.

3. **Ask for referrals**

    Satisfied customers are often happy to share their favourite supplier or provider with others, but they just may not think to do it without prompting as they are busy people!

    You can also utilise your connections that have complimentary businesses to your own for referrals as it is very likely that they have a similar customer base. Ensure that when you are asking for referrals you are clear about the type of customer you want! When talking of referrals, establish what encourages your contact to make a referral to you. It may be as simple as a token of thanks. The 'what's in it for me' factor for others may be a financial reward or a reciprocal referral.

    Collecting testimonials and recommendations on Google, LinkedIn, TrustPilot and similar are also great ways of providing 'social proof' of your service, so don't be shy about asking.

4. **Nurture existing customer relationships**

    Too often a customer is forgotten once they've purchased. Consider your relationship as the customer continues their journey with you. You can implement certain automation tools to ensure you continue a relationship with past customers that will remind them of you, and prompt them to either buy again or refer you onto someone else. It's easier to take care of an existing customer than it is to find a new one, so remember to put some effort into that relationship rather than constantly chasing new ones.

5. **Have a rock-solid website**

    Your website is the digital shopfront where leads often go to be converted. The majority of your website visitors are doing their initial research, so it should convey your brand voice, be easy to navigate and help your potential customers make the decision to purchase. It can be written in a more formal tone than social media but will ideally avoid too much industry-related jargon.

    Don't be tempted to say too much, but say enough! Too much content can confuse the prospective customer or enable them to incorrectly pre-qualify themselves. Also ensure your copy talks about them and their pain or potential gain rather your 'I' or 'we' messaging that simply talks about yourself. No one really cares until you've hooked their attention and reason to want to know that detail.

For it to serve its purpose, your website should be safe for people to visit, so it's advisable to engage a professional designer to keep up to date with plug-in updates and security certificates, etc.

Utilising Google Analytics, or similar tools, shows you where improvements can be made, and your designer can help you navigate this. It also shows you which other digital platforms have referred users in and which search terms were used to find you online. This information will help shape your online presence in other places such as social media, magazine publications and affiliate websites.

6 **Give value in everything you do**

Lead funnels (or magnets), spark initial interest and can be used to capture email data so you can stay in touch with someone who has engaged with your content. Whatever you use as the offer, it should provide value, avoid sales language, and ideally go to a specific landing page so that you can track the online traffic.

Value can also be provided in all areas where you engage with potential customers and referral partners. Give tips, advice, share information that changes the way they view something for the better, give a gift; whatever it is share it on social media, in networking meetings and on your website as well.

7 **Show an interest in others**

Employ active listening, both online and in person. Could your product or service be of importance to them or someone they know?

Showing you're listening on social media is also important so your audience can see you care about what they care about and, more importantly, can help.

8 **Implement automation**

Some social media platforms include auto-response messages that help you provide answers to common questions quickly. Most customer relationship management systems (CRMs) allow auto-response emails to be triggered along the customer journey to save you remembering or having to find the time to do it yourself. Tools like online calendars allow you to set reminders for actions to be taken.

Be mindful to not over automate your communication as it can be obvious to the recipient!

9 **Be abnormal**

If you are the same as everyone else, then you struggle to stand out and capture the desired interest in your market, especially if you are starting up and competing against others with an established market presence. So, how will you market or grab attention in a different way? That moment when your prospect receives an email or sees a social media post ensures that you stand out.

For example, handwritten and coloured envelopes of an unusual size. Adding emojis to email subject lines. Social media posts, with images, colours and headlines that will 'stop the scroll'.

10 **Pay for them!**

You can pay for advertising to find leads. This can be online, or in print, and it can be very effective.

It's advisable to ask a professional to help with PPC (pay-per-click) advertising, to ensure they are set up correctly, running efficiently and tweaked where necessary. If you are running paid-for ad campaigns, have a think about the rest of your marketing and make sure the messaging aligns.

You can also pay organisations to give you a list of potential prospects based on specified criteria. The clearer you are about defining your audience, the better the list will be. These lists can provide names, addresses, emails, telephone numbers and much more. Do your research to ensure you obtain reliable, quality lists, but that is only the first part in lead generation. You now have to do something with that list!

Are you the best kept secret?

Your marketing should be a mix of tactics that keeps your strategy in mind at all times. In other words, who are your ideal customer/s, where do they hang out to help you identify the best channel or tactic to reach them, and what is the message that speaks to your audience?

You will also have a mixed audience to consider. Some that know you and others that don't (well not yet!). Whilst choosing your tactics, it is a good idea to consider if your targets are 'warm' or 'cold' contacts and if you are best marketing on a one-to-one basis or one to many.

A great analogy is the concept of your 'stadium'.

Inside the stadium are your biggest fans. They are already buying from you, they love you and are now loyal and likely to buy again. Some are even advocates for whom price is not the driver.

Just outside the stadium are two groups of people that are close to you. Those that are desperately trying to get in but missed the opportunity to buy at the time of your last offer, or they have just left early, as they don't need the encore.

Be mindful of the latter. They may be potentially losing engagement as they have not bought from you for a while or feel exhausted with the relationship. They need your attention to keep them in longer.

Then there are the people who didn't travel to the stadium. One part of that audience are those that know about you, the 'warm' side, but were not yet ready to buy, in a position to buy, or have not yet been given a reason to lean in towards you any further and consider a purchase.

The others, the 'cold' ones, is an audience that have never heard of you. To them you are the 'best kept secret' and they need awareness to even start to engage with you. How do you move your cold audience to a warm contact?

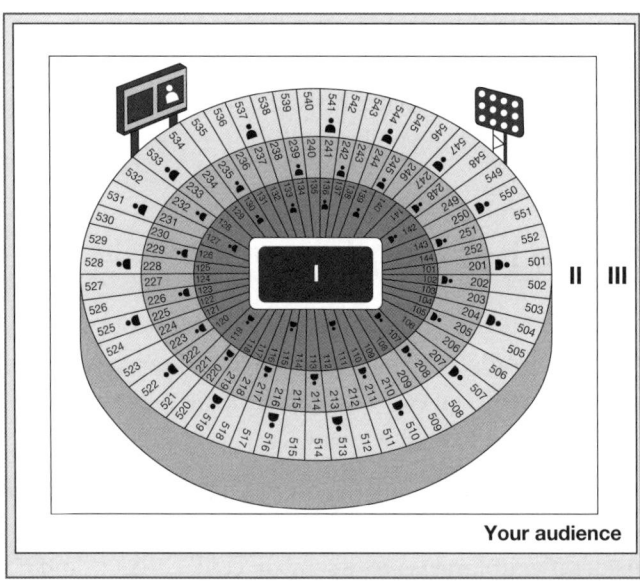

Your audience

Marketing through storytelling

It is important to build a relationship with your network of referrers and potential customers based on trust and likeability. The sharing of stories, anecdotes and some background information about us is important to build that foundation.

However, there is more to storytelling for marketing purposes than 'getting to know you'. Having a strategy underlining the stories you're sharing and that all-important goal behind it helps your story become effective at growing your network and, consequently, your business.

The following questions should help you lay down the outline of your marketing stories:

- Who are *you* and what do you *really* do?
- Who do you *help* and what problems of theirs do you solve?
- Why did you *start* your business and where?
- What gets *you* out of bed in the morning and why?
- What have *been* your greatest highs, lows and learnings?
- What is it *like* behind the scenes?
- How can *people work* with you or buy from you?
- *who* or *what* are you thankful for?

What is your end goal?

Why are you sharing this information? Is it so you can grow a networking community that you have an affiliation with? Is it because you need to find people who can support you in business? You want sales! Perhaps if you share more about your reason why, your backstory, goals and even perceived failures, people will recognise your authenticity and they will gravitate towards you.

All the above are great reasons to share your stories, and having that reason clear in your mind before you start writing will help you keep the story relevant, clear and interesting.

Are you marketing to one or to multiple prospects?

The marketing tactics you use may depend on whether you are promoting your business to an individual on a one-to-one basis or whether you are marketing to multiple prospects at the same time.

This may be referred to as the difference between lead generation and brand awareness, but this is more about who and how you are marketing to them.

Brand awareness marketing can be expensive, so always maintain the focus on the generation of leads even if you are marketing to multiple prospects at once.

Here are some examples:

- Marketing on a one-to-one basis may use tactics such as emails, telephone calls, direct messages via text or WhatsApp, voicemail, personalised video, direct mail or door-to-door knocking.
- For multiple prospect marketing, the tactics may include social media, paid advertising, video, podcasts, radio, webinars, print editorial or advertising and exhibitions.

How to reach your audience

To take your business to market and effectively reach your audience, you will often need a tactical marketing plan. This is not flippant, but the operative word here is *tactical*.

There are a series of steps you can take to ensure that your marketing is just that.

Do that market research to know your audience, to identify who you want as a customer and the best ways to attract them.

Also invest some time into researching your competitors to find out what works for them, what makes them attractive, or what customers don't like about them.

Once you know who you're talking to and what you're talking about (solutions to their pain, empathy and humour, etc.), you can work out what tools you'll need to convey your message in the marketplace.

The, marketing mix' refers to the mix of activities and platforms you'll use to raise awareness, gain interest and generate an enquiry.

Here are some ideas for your marketing activities. Which of these tactics would be best for your audience and when could you put them to use?

- Web pages and blogs
- Social media pages
- Online and social media advertising
- Print advertising
- Business cards and stationery
- Broadcast ads on radio or TV
- Direct mail
- Shopfront
- Email
- Merchandising and packaging
- Face-to-face meetings
- Events and exhibitions
- Telephone campaigns
- Word of mouth
- Sponsorship
- Networking for referral partners

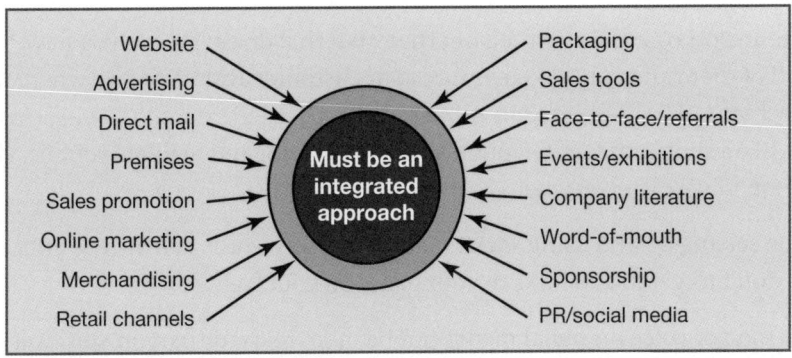

Let's look further at the most popular marketing tactics used by start-up business owners:

Website

Decide what type of website works best to display your product or service to your audience. A brochure website includes a few pages with a design element, an e-commerce website includes the functionality for customers to make a purchase, and a portal allows you to give access to certain areas with a log-in code.

What is your call to action? The website is the final stop, the online shopfront where people come to do their research and buy – but what does that 'buy' mean to you? Do you want your customer to contact you directly, download something, sign up, spend money or place an order? It's important that your customers clearly know what you need them to do and how to do it easily.

Are you using the right keywords and have the search engines like Google indexed your web pages? You may have the best website in the world, but it's no use to you if search engines don't know it's there. Keyword optimisation and search engine optimisation are important so that people can find you. Indexing is important so that Google can find you.

Your website has three types of visitors. Those that like to read. Those that like visual representation. The robots indexing your site!

Social media

There are lots of social channels out there, but that doesn't mean you have to be on all of them all at once! Remember your customer avatars and go where they expect you to be. Also bear in mind that social media doesn't have a closing time like a shop, office or telephone line, so monitor and regulate your usage so it doesn't take over your life!

When setting up and using social media, your keywords will also be effective. And don't forget to add links to your pages on your website.

Your tone of voice on social media can be more relaxed than on your website, but a good rule of thumb is if you wouldn't say it in a business meeting, don't say it online.

Online advertising

Pay-per-click (PPC) advertising and social media adverts are an effective way to reach potential customers. If they know you but haven't yet bought, then social media advertising may be best and, if they know the pain you are highlighting but don't know you, then paid advertising within search engine results may be the route to take. But again, refer to your tactical plan and choose the right mix for your customer.

Consider getting an expert to help you with both of these advertising strategies. They are not straightforward, and paid advertising is one of those things that could absorb your time and take you away from your key responsibilities. There is a science to the use of these tactics such as understanding the algorithms as much as the use of the platforms. You will need this understanding before finding your rhythm and return on investment.

Networking

We use networking for many reasons throughout our business lives, not just to 'sell to the room'. In a successful networking meeting, you can meet advisers, suppliers, referral partners (people you share a customer base with), friends, mentors and, last but not least, customers. Be brave, be you and get out there!

> ### Remember this
> #### Have multiple marketing methods but focus on the few not the many
>
> You have to be continually generating leads as without leads you have no one to sell to, no one to service and no one to retain.
>
> Stand-out entrepreneurs will have a number of marketing strategies, across multiple channels, using various tactics. Together, this creates a variety of activities at the same time to generate leads and drive revenue to the business.
>
> They won't be doing everything as they know what works.
>
> These strategies and activities will be both online and offline activities, but all undertaken in a consistent manner, with a consistent message, all working systematically as a habit in the business.

The 'work' in networking

Networking is not just about face-to-face events, such as your latest greasy breakfast or glass of wine at the social drinks. It is how you create and develop your network online and offline. For example, via Events, LinkedIn and one-to-one meetings.

There are many networking opportunities. You could attend a networking meeting most days for breakfast, lunch and dinner! However, it's not just about the next event. Effective networking for your business can perhaps be achieved without ever attending an event.

Break down the word 'networking' and you have some of the answers already.

- **Network**ing – identify a network of contacts and business influencers that can truly impact your business (e.g. they will buy from you, they will refer others to you, they have a synergy to work with you, they sell to the same market).

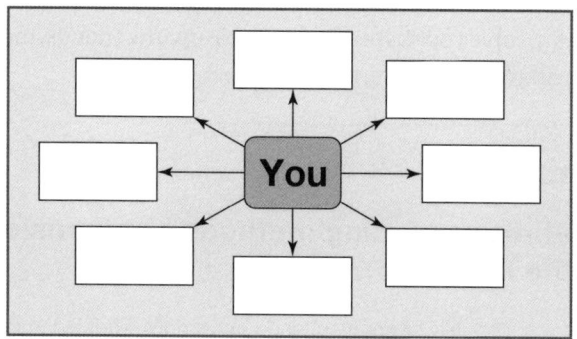

- **Net**working – cast a net and capture your contacts with the objective to convert them from a nice-to-know contact to an advocate of your business. Score your network contacts from 1 to 5, where a 5 is that they would refer you without being asked for a recommendation or they are ready to buy. For anyone who scores less than 5, what do you need to invest to uplift their score?

- Net**work**ing – the key here is proactivity. What can you do to proactively work on building the relationships and make regular contact with your purpose in mind?
- Networ**king** – if you get networking right, it can be the cost-effective king of your marketing strategy.

The key one is 'work'. Are you working your networking with persistence?

Here are some thoughts to help you maximise your networking:

1 Have more one-to-one appointments – an opportunity to find out more about others and explain your offering in more detail.
2 Educate people in your network about your business, its offering and the benefits.
3 Break your business down so people learn more about what and how you do it.
4 Share evidence, case studies and testimonials, as proof you can deliver.
5 Attend events (online and offline) consistently to build your relationships. You have to also work it when you arrive, not just turn up.
6 Do you give referrals as well as expect referrals? It's human nature to replicate a referral you have given.
7 Follow your nose – where is the money for you or the support you need?
8 Be clear on the type of business you are looking for. Be specific. Paint a picture that your network can easily visualise.
9 Are you saying the right things so people understand what you do and how they can refer you?
10 What do you need to do to develop those individual key relationships in your network?

NETWORKING

Calculating your marketing budget

There is a common phrase in business, 'you have to spend money to make money', so let's look at how to calculate your marketing spend.

Another common question often asked is what percentage of your turnover you should spend on your marketing. For many businesses this is *not* how to set a marketing budget.

Setting a marketing budget begins with a marketing plan. Everything in business is strategy-driven, because without a sound strategy and comprehensive set of tactics you won't be able to identify what needs your investment, what is a win and what doesn't work. As covered earlier in this chapter, the basis of a good marketing strategy is in identifying who your customers are, what you are offering them, where they are and how you attract them to your offering.

In selecting your tactics, establish if your customers prefer to take in information by watching, listening or reading. Maybe your new customers are visiting a shop or exhibition in person, or they are browsing the web or social media at home in the evening. This knowledge of your customers will direct what area of marketing you can invest in.

At this point, you can begin to build the plan and then put a budget against that plan by knowing or researching the cost of executing the identified marketing activities you need to undertake.

To extend those thoughts, you should also consider the integrated marketing activities you need to execute. Too often marketing is undertaken in isolation and another part of the customers' experience lets you down. For example, your audience may be strictly mobile users and high users of a social media platform. In which case you need to ensure your website is mobile adaptive, you can produce great looking content including videos, you have a scheduling tool and maybe some budget for advertising.

Marketing is not a golden ticket to doubling your customer base or offering a guaranteed return, but it is a sound investment for future growth. To effectively grow your business you want your marketing to provide a reliable flow of new leads. These considerations will help guide your marketing spend:

1 Your customer personas and what they want to hear from you.
2 How your potential customers like hearing from you.
3 What actions can you take to ensure you meet your potential customers?
4 How much time will the action take to implement?
5 Is using an outsourced resource a good investment to free up your own time?
6 How can you automate your actions?
7 How can you measure marketing success against spend?

For most businesses, your marketing spend can now be forecasted based on what tactics you need to use to pull your audience towards you and the resources needed to generate the revenues you desire (how much that costs in terms of time and actual investment). Some tactics will have a defined cost attached to them (social media, SEO, PPC) whilst others may need testing to establish the likely level of investment needed (paid ads, telesales, direct mail, email marketing, funnels). If you are testing a new marketing channel or tactic, I suggest testing small in the first instance.

In some cases, you may not yet have a marketing plan so it's difficult to price out the proposed activities as you don't know what they are at this point. You may be looking to set a marketing budget to establish what you can spend before thinking about how best to spend it. In this case, you should consider your 'free cash' for your marketing investment, your risk appetite, and how much you are prepared to spend to win the revenue you have budgeted for. Be careful of just setting a budget to spend for spending's sake, and spend wisely.

You can't market to everywhere all at once, so get specific, understand your audience, do what is right for them and, if it is costing you money rather than an investment providing a return, stop it, cut it.

How much should you spend to acquire each customer?

The Entrepreneur's Circle shares a formula to help you calculate how much money you need to spend on your marketing to obtain the number of leads needed to deliver the number of sales in consideration of your conversion rate:

1. How much is your average customer worth to you? Over their lifetime or the next two to three years, say.
2. How much would you pay to get one of those customers, taking into account their lifetime value above?
3. How many leads do you need to get a customer? If you sell to half of the people you speak to, you would need two leads to get one customer. What's your ratio?
4. How much can you spend to get a lead? Answer 2 ÷ answer 3.
5. How many new customers do you want next month?
6. How many leads do you need next month to get that many customers? Answer 3 x Answer 5.
7. How much marketing spend do you need for the next month to get that many customers? Answer 6 x Answer 4.

As an example:

What are your numbers?

Lifetime value	£5,000	
Prepared to pay	£500	
Leads needed to convert one customer	2	
= How much can you spend per lead?	£250	
New customers wanted	6	
Leads needed to get that number	12	
Marketing spend	£3,000	

Consider this – is the number one mistake a business owner can make trying to get their leads/customers/clients/patients as cheaply as they possibly can? If so they may be depriving themselves of the number one advantage in business, which is to create a scenario where you can profitably out-spend your competition to get customers.

> **Remember this**
>
> **Know your acquisition cost and likely return on marketing investment**
>
> How much does it cost you to win a new customer?
>
> For example, what was your investment in the advert and the creation of your landing page to sell the offer and track enquiries? Then how many enquiries did you receive that converted to a customer?
>
> Marketing cost / Customers won = Acquisition cost
>
> You should also then know the lifetime value to you of winning that customer (income per year x number of years retained as a customer). If the lifetime value outweighs the acquisition cost and cash allows, then it may be simply the level of investment to consider.

Fifty proactive marketing activities to win more customers

This list of marketing thoughts and ideas has been created based on observation of what helps many start-up businesses to find new customers on a bootstrapped budget.

You won't need, and it is not suggested, to implement all of the ideas, but the list is designed to fuel your thoughts and spark your ideas to take proactive action and attract the customers you want.

When considering the list, ask yourself whether you have to do it all yourself. What is the value to you of having an expert do this for you or at least give you some support?

1 Profile your ideal customer

This is perhaps one of the most proactive activities you can undertake, as it gives a purpose and value to all your other marketing actions.

Analyse your existing customers, especially those you love working with, and identify the commonalities. Consider your prospects and again profile the type of customer you would like to work with every day. Not just the sector they work in, the size of business or where they are based, but also consider the personality of the decision makers, what they were doing when they bought from you and why they specifically bought from you.

What are the common pains or problems that you can solve? What is the consequence for them of not taking action on this pain or problem?

Profiling your ideal customer provides you with great information about the words you can then use to attract their interest and, importantly, clearly communicate how you can really help them. When you are talking to someone who fits this profile with your marketing messages, you want them to say, 'That's me you're talking about! I want to work with you.'

Once you have identified a profile for your ideal customer, search for more businesses that match this profile. This will give you great focus for your marketing activities and maximise your resources in terms of time and money.

2 Maximise your use of LinkedIn

Before you start any activity on LinkedIn, please ensure that you have created an attractive and informative profile page that is attractive to your target prospects.

You can then use the search facility to find people or companies that you want to engage with and attract to your business. Can you follow them, like or comment on their status updates, communicate with them via the LinkedIn InMail tool, or perhaps get introduced by one of your existing first-level connections?

Use LinkedIn Groups to engage in conversation whilst sharing your expertise and experience. Use content that provides the reason why people will want to get to know, like and trust you, which they need to do before buying. If you cannot find a suitable group, then create your own group for your niche market and invite people to join the group to engage with your discussions.

When accepting a LinkedIn Invitation, do not simply accept the invitation to connect. Create a thank you message to send to all new followers and include information about your business with back links to your relevant online presence. Likewise, have a thank you message for new connections that accept your request to connect.

3 Show an interest in others

This applies to the use of social media as well as face to face. Show an interest in people and they will show an interest in you.

How many times have you commented on someone's update and within the next few days they have replicated the engagement?!

Be proactive and view other profiles on LinkedIn so they see you are viewing them, endorse people, make recommendations, like or comment on updates, congratulate them on anniversaries, etc. Of course there is a balance, as you do not want to appear as if you are stalking them, but likewise you just can't assume one action is enough.

But also pick up the phone, make a point of saying hello when you see people at events or ask after them with a colleague. Too often people rely on the ease of email and mobile communications, so being proactive and making the call from your mobile instead of sending the planned text message may just make a different impact.

4 Automate your response to enquiries

The more you can systemise with your marketing and make the activities a habit within your everyday business, the better results you will experience. One way is to automate the follow-up process after someone makes contact with you. This simple step will bring great results. Not only does it save you time but also ensures you do not miss an opportunity to communicate and therefore value the contact made with you. You also contact soon after the enquiry whenever it is or whatever you are doing and don't miss that golden moment of their interest in you.

From experience, you will know the words that help you convert interest, so why not replicate those again and again for future positive outcomes? For example, if someone completes a website enquiry form or provides you with their contact details in some other way, then you should have an automatic response to them. This should thank them for their interest and provide them with some initial information including links to relevant content on your website. However, do not stop at one automated reply, use software to generate a number of future touches to build your relationship.

This may need testing, especially if your audience requires a more personalised approach. If that is the case, see how you can mix the automation with other offline touches, and some tools will enable you to automate a step that reminds you to call them or write a letter.

5 Give something away to generate new followers

Create a giveaway that you can offer to generate new followers. You can make the offer both online and when you meet prospects face to face, perhaps as part of the sales process. However, ensure the offer is something of considerable value to your ideal customer. Is it a book, a white paper, a tool, a free sample?

Put yourself in your prospects' shoes or even ask them. What would they truly value so that in return they do not hesitate to provide you with their contact details? Encourage and request their contact details in return for the giveaway.

Offer this giveaway via a specific landing page on your website or a page with a separate domain, such as a 'squeeze' page. This way you can measure the outcome of your marketing activity to drive traffic to that page.

Use social media and your other marketing activities to generate awareness and interest in the offer that creates traffic to that page.

6 Use an unusual shape or colour in your direct mail

Make your mailing stand out from the crowd. What is going to make the recipient want to open your mailing?

This may be a non-standard size envelope or a promotional giveaway that is inserted and creates a bulge in the packaging and therefore curiosity. The envelope could be a different colour, other than white, to make it stand out from all the other mail received.

When the mailing is opened, what is different to grab the reader's attention? Is it another white page with black text or something different to generate an interest and thereby create a reason to engage?

7 Align with larger brands

Collaboration and the alignment with larger brands reflect positively on your business and create a sense of credibility and trust with others.

Strive to obtain your prospects' recognition of the brand alignment. This could be mentioning a project you are working on together or perhaps a collaboration such as a voluntary project.

Develop the relationship and create the content you will use to inform people of the alignment. Then tell people by utilising case studies or push out the news using press releases.

8 Actively listen in groups

Listen both online and in person. Listen on social media platforms or when attending your next networking event.

Actively listen to the people posing the question AND to those responding. Listen to what is being said and by whom. Could your product or service help them either to directly solve the point raised or indirectly provide support?

9 Distribute referral certificates

Create a certificate or a voucher making an offer that your referrers can pass onto their contacts as part of a recommendation to you.

For example, this could be a discount off the first purchase, a free review or initial meeting or some additional value.

Consider a two-part referral certificate. One part is completed by the referrer and sent back to you to claim a gift and the other part is given to their contact to take up the offer with you. Therefore, in addition to creating the offer for the prospect, you need to create an offer for the referrer.

Don't just rely on the certificate doing the work, as you have to create the 'reason why'. The 'reason why' a referrer would pass on the certificate as a recommendation and also the 'reason why' the offer will actually be of considered value to then be taken up by the prospect.

Consider the lifetime value of a referral to your business and the saving of any normal marketing spend to attract that customer. Does that give you a budget to create such an offer or consider a personal thank you gift?

10 Get to know your customers' contacts

People find it easier to make a referral or recommendation to people they know, so who does your customer know? Well, one source is their own customers and suppliers.

Gather information, observe, consider who you would like as a customer and ask your customer for a referral to that business or individual. They can't say they don't know them!

11 Hand the phone over

Consider how you generate the best telephone introductions from your referrers. Perhaps a lead goes cold between the referrer's conversation and the time you receive the referral and make the call yourself.

Therefore, try having a coffee with your potential or existing referrer and openly discuss potential cross referrals. Engage their interest in the benefit of referrals, the fact that you have customers with the same interests, and how you can each benefit from more customers.

You should then look to get them talking about their customer list and how your product or service could meet the pains and problems of their customers.

Next, consider the opportunity to be more proactive in the meeting and see if they are willing to call the customer and hand over the phone to you as an introduction of your business. You could offer the same in return, by calling your customers or contacts.

For this to work best, you have to have a good reason to call each other's customers with the true intention of passing over the phone as an introduction.

12 Start your own networking group

Have you been to networking events and questioned why you attended? Perhaps you met the wrong people or those attending were not right for your business.

Starting your own networking group provides you with the opportunity to control who attends and even invite your potential key business influencers to join for free. They will value the invitation and even invite paying attendees.

You could focus your group on your ideal referrers, your ideal customers or those in consideration of your niche.

Being the organiser also enables you to control other aspects of the event, such as who can speak at the event or where you meet, all of which could be beneficial for you.

In consideration of your own finances, you could also in return network for free! Well, free of a charge but of course an investment of time.

One word of warning is how you position yourself as the organiser. It gives you recognition and helps build relationships, but you could be known for organising the event rather than for the business you run.

13 Video your expertise and share it

Video is a powerful marketing tool as the combination of images and audio uses a mix of the senses we use to gather information. We use our senses, such as what we can see and hear, to transmit a signal to the brain, which brings all the information together to produce the whole picture. So surely a more accurate, perhaps genuine, picture is built when watching video compared to simply having the words that are open to further interpretation if read alone.

Video platforms such as YouTube are global, but you can market your video either locally or even simply direct your ideal prospects or customers to your content. There are other video hosting platforms, some without adverts, but the linkage of YouTube with Google searches cannot be ignored.

Use video to share your expertise and your personality, so people get to know, like and trust you.

14 Paid advertising

This may not be suitable for all types of business.

First, establish the invaluable information about your current web visitors and ideal prospects. What are the keywords they use and the type of copy they like to see? This can then be used across all your marketing copy including your paid advertising.

You can also run a paid campaign with such a low bid amount that you hardly ever receive a click to pay for, but you still receive the keyword data and other information to analyse.

With any pay-per-click campaign, you will want to generate good quality click through without paying too much for them, so look to use unique specific phrases that relate to your business and ideal prospect instead of the usual common key singular words. For example, instead of simply stating 'solicitor', create a campaign to generate leads for 'solicitor for a new commercial lease'. The amount you pay per click is likely to be much lower and yes you may receive a lower click through rate but the clicks you do receive are very likely to be of a much better quality, more relevant to your target market, and therefore you generally see better progression towards a warm lead.

Research how you can best use pay-per-click advertising to gain new leads for your business. Whether you offer a product or a service, whether you are B2B or B2C, there is a pay-per-click campaign suitable for your business. This may be paid advertising with search engines or advertising on social media platforms.

When testing your investment in paid advertising, look to run more than one style advert at the same time. This is known as split testing, where you run two or multiple adverts to test, measure, learn, improve and test again.

15 Gain your share of free PR

Everyone has a story to tell. So what is your story?

Start by understanding what your ideal customer reads and why. Is it online or traditional print? Is it the whole publication or a certain part? When you know this, you know the publications to target for coverage and where you would ideally like to see your content placed.

Build your story. Perhaps involve one of your customers and cover the benefits of working with you, but importantly the aim is to demonstrate your expertise with the readership of your target publication.

A successful plan for free PR is to have a story that is not time specific. Create your press release and send it to the editors of target publications read by your ideal customer. Send it with a covering note that advises the editor that they can use this article at any time in the future. This is because many editors will have some space to fill one day or for one edition and may just use your news.

You should also consider how to utilise radio, podcasts and online platforms, as much as the printed press. Build relationships and position yourself, as the 'go to' knowledge and expert in a specific area. Get yourself considered as the point of reference for a relevant news story or theme and get added to their contributor database. It may not be today you are asked, but it may be tomorrow.

Another proactive method is to hook onto the latest news stories. A news story breaks locally or nationally. Can you offer yourself to radio and TV as an expert for comment? To hear about the latest news, you can sign up with feeds from news agencies and similar providers. You can also use tools such as Google Alerts to advise you when keyword-related content is posted on the web.

Also look to position yourself in a timely manner. For example, you are a solicitor specialising in helping drink drivers, so look to offer articles and opinion about drink driving campaigns at the time each year when such stories are covered or as the latest news is released about incidents or convictions.

16   Maximise Facebook newsfeeds

Of course there is your own newsfeed, which should contain relevant content for your ideal prospects.

You may also consider Facebook advertising that shows content as a sponsored advert on the newsfeeds of individuals who follow businesses similar to your own or match a targeted audience definition.

You can also consider posting directly onto other newsfeeds, but ensure the post is relevant and provides added value; otherwise, it will simply annoy people or even be deleted. For example, posting a comment or content on the Facebook page of local radio stations.

17   Get at least shortlisted for awards

A nomination, being shortlisted and of course winning the award contribute as a strong endorsement of your business. Most sectors now have some sort of awards, which are organised by recognised leaders, so from my experience such recognition is invaluable.

If a prospect sees that you have been nominated or won an award, there is respectful trust in this recognition that can outweigh any content you also write.

Ask your contacts, customers or a friend to nominate you for an award. For some awards you can even nominate yourself! Such action helps to gain external recognition and further credibility for your product or service.

Read the entry details carefully and understand what the judges will be looking out for in your submission, then personalise your nomination to blow your own trumpet and tick those boxes one by one.

When you have been shortlisted, tell everyone. When you win, tell them again.

18 Understand your statistics

Marketing is quite often referred to as a numbers game. Test and measure, understand what works, know what you have to spend to acquire a customer, appreciate your return on investment or know the key numbers such as the web page referrals resulting from a specific campaign.

You can then go further and identify the results. For example, from a certain number of hits on a specific web page, you know on average you will obtain a specific number of orders. Knowing this information from small tests will give you an indication how a much bigger roll out of that campaign will perform for you.

Reviewing your website analytics and understanding how your online communication performs is a key part of knowing your statistics.

Using Google Analytics, or similar, you are able to review the information in depth to know such things as which pages people stay on, how long for, how they enter your website, what device they are using to browse, do they exit where you want them to (e.g. the contact us page) or are specific pages simply not being visited. In addition, don't forget the analytics tools offered by the social media platforms.

19 You never know who knows who

So be proactive and ask!

Today, set yourself the goal of asking someone you do not already know what it is that they do. You may be pleasantly surprised by the link you can make. In reality, you may also be surprised how small our business communities really are.

Perhaps you are at a social event or watching the children's swimming lessons or similar activities and notice other people also just watching. Who are those other friends or the other parents? Look to introduce yourself, find out and see if there are opportunities to explore.

20 Hold customer review meetings

One of the most effective steps for growing a business is to find a way to sell more to the existing customer with whom you already have a trusted relationship.

Look to have regular review meetings with your customers to check on the relationship, further understand their expectations and explore further cross-selling opportunities. Position the reviews as a customer service type meeting, but have an agenda that you want to cover and link the conversation to areas of opportunity that you want to explore.

In addition, by simply spending time with the customer in this way you often find they volunteer information you were not expecting and this can lead to an opportunity.

21 What are the papers saying?

Gather information that you can use in your approach to a prospect. When the information you gain is used correctly, it can demonstrate empathy and an understanding that is appreciated by the prospect.

Read printed and online articles that cover news about the people who match your ideal customer profile, that actually mention your target customers and make a reference to the services you offer, such as job adverts. Then use this content as a reason to contact your prospects by making a relevant reference to the publication. For example, I have just read in … that the sector has seen … or congratulations on your award for …

22 Know your upsell opportunities

What else can you offer your customers?

Quite often, we are so delighted that we got a sale that we miss the glaring opportunity to sell more to the customer whilst they are in buying mode.

You will have witnessed or heard the famous McDonalds saying, 'Would you like fries with that?' Another example of an upsell offering is Amazon. When you are checking out, you receive a recommendation for a further purchase based on your previous purchases or search history.

When your customers are buying from you, what is your primary upsell opportunity and how can you link this in with another opportunity for your customer to make a further purchase from you? The upsell offer could be another of your products or services, or it may be offered by an affiliate for which you will receive a commission fee.

23 Create specific and relevant landing pages

Ideally, for each of your marketing campaigns, you want to drive traffic to a specific web page. This way, you meet the expectations of the person visiting the page, reducing the 'bounce rate', and can also provide specific relevant content to build on the interest they have already shown.

Look to create a specific landing page that is for your target customers as much as for the sales message and content that you want to provide. For example, if you sell widgets and want to sell widgets to hotels, create a web page with words focused on this expertise, utilising those key words and covering the benefits for your target customer.

You could have this page as part of your existing website, but if you have an effective website and you do not want to clutter the site with additional pages, then consider setting up a stand-alone web page with a specific domain for this marketing campaign, known as a landing page or 'squeeze page'. For example, www.widgets-for-hotels.com.

From your landing page you can then use links to take the prospect to your other web-based content once they have engaged with your initial content. As an additional bonus, if the traffic on your main website is seen to be coming from another domain, then this will also appear as a valuable inbound link for the organic search ranking of your main site.

24 Hold an expertise seminar

Demonstrate and share your expertise. This removes an unknown quantity for the prospect making a decision whether to trust what your marketing messages are saying and make a commitment to buy from you.

Look to deliver a seminar, either face to face or online, to share your expertise, knowledge and your personality.

You should have a headline title that grabs the attention of your prospects and highlights a problem they will be experiencing today that you can solve.

You have a catchment market when you organise such events, as you know the attendees have an interest in the content you are offering, which of course by coincidence is related to what your product or service can do for them. At the end of the seminar, have an offer that further engages the attendees to have further one-to-one contact with you. For example, a free review or sample.

25 Offer an expert hotline

Can you offer a telephone hotline, forum, chatbot or perhaps email support for your ideal customers?

What are their concerns, pain or problems that such a hotline would solve and be resourceful for them? For example, you are an accountant who specialises in manufacturing and one of your team is an expert in VAT schemes. So, how about setting up and publicising a VAT hotline for the manufacturing sector?

26 Signage on your vehicle

Do you have a vehicle? Well, you have another proactive opportunity!

You never know who may see your vehicle as you drive between customers and suppliers or you are simply parked at your home or office. Signage on your vehicle can be as simple as having the back window etched, magnet signs or perhaps full vinyl coverage with your brand message.

Whatever signage you choose, you should ensure the message and contact details are clearly displayed and very easy to read. It needs to be easily seen and easily captured. You may consider a QR code, so someone with a smartphone app can simply scan the coding image and pull up your contact information for later reference rather than trying to remember them or write them down.

27 Get your banners out and about

For a reasonable price, you can create a banner that can be displayed near roundabouts or in locations where the traffic queues or near locations popular for your target market to visit.

For example, you offer a children's holiday play scheme, so a banner near a primary school is a great location for you. Or you offer a service for owners with units on an industrial estate, so the entrance to that location is perfect.

Don't spend too much on the banner, as they may be removed, but only after they have been seen!

Ensure they make a strong visual impact and have a simple clear message that can be quickly seen and absorbed.

Banners are also very flexible tools. Unlike placing an advert in a magazine, you can move it if you initially choose the wrong location, so you can put them in a location for, say, a week and, after a week, when your prospect has seen it a few times, you can then pick it up and move it to another location.

28 Volunteer your expertise

Volunteering is another way to demonstrate your expertise, not only to those involved but also by mentioning the support as a case study.

Carefully select a committee or charity where you can volunteer your time and skill. Most committees, whether they are for your favourite local charity, the school governors or the chamber of commerce, will have other businesspeople attending. This is a great opportunity to share your expertise and build trust in you, your product and service. Remember to build the relationships with a purpose and ask for referrals.

When volunteering, ensure you do something you love and do not commit too much time that then highjacks your earning potential.

29 Build your lists and develop a contact calendar

During the year, how many touch points are you going to have with your customers and prospects to fuel your sales funnel?

Continually look to build your email or social following lists at every touch point. Create funnels that capture email addresses to build your list.

Then look to have a contact plan. Create a process or a structure that becomes a habit in your business and presents a reason for contacting your network. Schedule the touches, know why you are contacting and develop the relationship proactively with purpose.

30 Ask for feedback from your ideal customers

Information is invaluable, especially when your ideal customers tell you what they want, need or expect.

Run a survey with your ideal customers and prospects to ask them directly for feedback about your business or proposition. This is a simple, less direct exercise to remind your customers how fantastic you are and gives you the opportunity to explore new opportunities with those who are not yet buying from you.

Find out what your customers and prospects are thinking, raise awareness and interest in cross-sale opportunities and don't forget to ask for referrals. Ask questions, seek feedback, request votes and gather useful information for your future proactive marketing plans.

Bringing the business to the attention of your targeted prospects is likely to generate interest as you are no longer the best kept secret to them.

As part of the survey, ask your customers if they would refer you, which I am sure will be a yes response. Then later in another question ask for that specific referral.

31 Develop your email footer

If you are sending emails without an email footer, then in my opinion you are missing an opportunity.

Look to have an email footer that carries your key links and contact information: your contact telephone number, links to your website and links to your social media. You may include your strap line or consider an image of yourself but make it professional and eye catching.

Email footers come in all shapes and sizes from embedded images to simply a name and website written at the bottom of the email text. Be mindful that many email readers and platforms are no longer automatically downloading images and an embedded image-based footer may not get shown.

Consider links to an offer or a specific page on your website rather than simply the home page, especially when prospecting.

32 Use a branded promotional gift

A giveaway gift is a great tool to continually remind your prospects about you and your business in the future.

Too often, giveaways are simply placed in the bin or put away in a drawer, so ensure your giveaway is going to be used again and ideally on a regular basis. Consider something that the recipient has to make a conscious decision to use. Perhaps going to a draw of pens and picking out yours is not as powerful as finding your branded USB stick holding their key data.

Sometimes, you pay a little extra for the more useable product, but surely that is the purpose; otherwise, if it is never used then isn't it a waste of your money?

Giveaways are great for attracting interest at exhibitions and events.

33 Establish joint ventures

Joint ventures give you the opportunity to access the customer base of another business. A good joint venture will also add value to your offering and attract additional interest in your business.

Look to build relationships with other business owners who operate businesses that are also touching your ideal customers. Create an agreement to work together for referrals, events or by offering a packaged offering. Such collaborations can extend your reach and build your reputation. For example, bookkeepers and accountancy practices are a natural link but what is in it for both parties to engage in a joint venture and be of benefit to a prospect or your existing customers? Is it simply for raising awareness of each other's business to basically generate more leads by referral? Could the customer have a seamless experience and pay one fee and, in the year, have their bookkeeping undertaken by one person and the year-end compliance by another?

34 Truly target a handful of prospects

Quite often, I see business owners with the best intentions for their marketing campaign but who do not deliver because they have over committed to what is realistically achievable.

Perhaps a target list of 1,000 prospects or even 100 is too many for your business to manage. Not only the time for completing the actual marketing activity but also managing the lead enquiries and delivering the promise to a number of new customers at the same time.

Quite often with a large list, a business owner or even a marketing colleague will start well but the quality of the marketing activity will dwindle as time goes by. For example, they may have the list of 1,000 names and actually get the mailing completed to all 1,000 prospects. However, they only have the time or true inclination to call 25 per cent of them, and then never complete a second follow-up of the communication. It is better to truly undertake a great campaign with a small number than a poor campaign with a large number.

You could create a list of 100 or 1,000 prospects and approach in manageable chunks or create a 'wish list' of your most preferred 20 prospects that you'd love to work with.

Try focusing on five ideal prospects at a time to kick-start a relationship with each and every one of them. If you get knocked back by the five, then you can build another list with the lessons you learned. If you have a list of 100, then you may be demotivated in contacting any of the rest.

To maximise any list, look to implement various proactive personal touch points such as a telephone call, go and knock on the door, offer a free appointment, give something away like a sample, write a physical letter, send an email, send a LinkedIn InMail, tweet or use another social media message to engage.

35 Offer a free taster

When prospects can test the offering, it gives them assurances that they will experience the promises made.

This works effectively in the car sales market. You see a car you like, you go and test drive it, fall in love with the car and make the purchase. If you offer a product, can you offer a free, no obligation trial like a test drive? For example, software companies quite often give free periods to try out the package.

If you offer a service, can you proactively offer a free, no obligation meeting for 30 minutes or for whatever you consider is enough time for you to share your expertise and demonstrate your passion for what you do?

During the taster you should be aiming for the prospects to get to know, like and trust you and your business, which they will need to do before they buy.

36 Establish an affiliate programme

Do you have a product or service someone else can sell or simply promote on your behalf?

Consider this as a way of passing on some of your marketing activity to another party. Establish a programme that enables others to sell or promote your product or service on your behalf, and you then simply pay them a commission on the basis of a sale or perhaps receipt of a qualified 'hot' lead.

The commission you pay is your financial investment in your marketing instead of increasing your marketing spend in other areas.

For example, a business finance broker may share their commission fee, or an influencer may take a cut per sale for their promotion on a product.

To consider the level of commission to be paid, reflect on the lifetime value to you of a new customer. For example, a commission on a single initial purchase may not be attractive enough to provide a motivational reason for someone to market your business effectively. However, a commission based on a potential lifetime value will be much greater and desirable.

37 Re-connect with lost opportunities

Make contact with leads that were not converted previously.

Quite often, if someone does not buy at the time, we forget about those opportunities and move on. However, they demonstrated a need at the time but chose another solution. It is likely they still have the same need, but possibly now realise they chose the wrong solution or are willing to look again.

Even if they are happy with the solution they chose, you again are positioning yourself as the back-up option should circumstances change in the future. Don't give up on opportunities even when you did not sell to them the first time.

38 Put in the leg work with door-to-door deliveries

If you have a business that targets home-based customers, then a door-to-door leaflet drop can be effective.

You could just go for a walk and post in any door as your product is suitable for all homeowners. But what if you are a tree surgeon? Would you be best going to villages and posting through doors of householders with trees on their property? If you provide accountancy services for the 'white van man', then walk the local housing estates looking for properties with the vans on their driveway at night or on Sundays. You will have a better outcome if you have profiled your ideal customer and know where they are likely to live.

39 Sponsor with a purpose in mind

Is there a group or an activity that attracts your ideal customers? If so, can you increase your profile with them by sponsoring their interest?

For example, your target audience may be local professionals and they may all enjoy rugby, so sponsoring the local rugby team or a match day could give you the profile opportunity.

You may be thinking 'people won't see my advert on the shirt', but how can you utilise the relationship to get closer to your ideal target? What press coverage can you obtain with the support you have offered and how else can you leverage the relationship?

Be mindful of the level of investment when sponsoring versus the likely return and look to get as much as you can included in the sponsorship package. For example, you may sponsor the rugby team shirts, but can you get an advertising board around the pitch, some hospitality opportunities at future games or other aspects that won't cost them too much to include?

In addition, some prospects simply like a person or business that is also seen to be giving something.

40 Let your customers create your business name

This is an easy way to indirectly raise awareness of a new business or a new product or service.

If you do not already have a business name or you need a name for a new product or service, then create a competition with your followers and ask them to suggest a name for you.

This activity gives you the opportunity to describe your business and its unique selling points, which they obviously need to know to be able to suggest an appropriate name.

This can also create press coverage for you by offering the competition to their readers to generate more entries or by covering the story of the winner and the announcement of the chosen name.

In addition, ensure that each entry form captures the name and contact details of your entrant. This then immediately starts to build a list of potential customers for you because those who have entered tend to have a genuine interest.

41 Create a comparison guide

Could you produce a comparison guide to compare your products and services to a competitor or another resource? This is a common practice for SaaS products comparing their features and benefits with their direct competitors. If you are an external bookkeeper, could you show how your service and the amount you charge compare to employing someone 'in house' with a pension contribution, National Insurance, sick pay and holiday pay contributions? If you sell a photocopier to small businesses who usually buy the cheap £50 printers, then how does your toner cartridge and package compare to the cost of running those cheap printers the prospects usually buy? How many more pages does the cartridge print? What is the lifetime of your product in comparison?

Make the comparison, use infographics or content to demonstrate and share this with your ideal prospects online, by mail or face to face.

42 Take a good look at technological advancements

What is new right now that you could perhaps bring into your business and help you market yourself from a new innovative angle?

The good thing about being early on a new idea is yes being seen as innovative, but also it is usually cheaper as you are presenting a new angle for the supplier to also explore.

So let's look at two examples.

First drones, which we now see used for taking images at high level for surveying purposes, used by estate agents for showing large estates and even for delivering beer to festivalgoers!

Then there was Google Street view, which has engaged many people over recent years to support their navigation, but this was then brought inside buildings to give a 360-degree internal view for potential visitors to explore before actually leaving their home.

If you are first with these types of innovative approaches in your business, then you will stand out from the crowd and create a unique selling point for yourself in the meantime.

43 Advertise on your own packaging

Do you mail something to your customers or prospects? You may send a product by courier, you perhaps mail a catalogue or send an invoice by post, or you sell items that have to be safely packaged to transport.

Consider placing an advert on the external packaging or envelope. Yes, it may be seen by others during its delivery to your customer but, on receipt, it is seen by your customer who is already in buying mode and potentially attracted to your further offer.

This could be a sticker on the packaging or specially printed stationery items.

44 Send a text message

Are you embracing the technology that is literally at your fingertips?

Text messages are especially useful for those who prefer to communicate via their smartphone or social media rather than email. However, such proactive communications can also be a pleasant experience for many people as they feel personal provided it's not felt intrusive.

There is software available that enables you to send a text message en masse to many prospects or customers at the same time. However, you can take the philosophy and set up a text message for an individual or to a small group.

The key is knowing what to text. What is not considered intrusive? Do your customers or prospects want a sales message by text, or should the message be making an offer or directing them to your website?

Even businesses like your dentist are using text messages now, so how are you utilising this marketing method? Could you be texting a service message like a delivery or collection time, a meeting confirmation, sending a discount coupon or linking an offer to a visitor of your premises that you have just seen 'check in' on your Facebook page?

45 Ask for glowing testimonials

Testimonials and ideally video testimonials are fantastic for validating your marketing messages.

Be proactive in asking for testimonials rather than just hoping someone will like you enough and have a quiet day to write one for you. If you are not proactive, it is unlikely you have received a testimonial in the last three months.

What can you do today to proactively ask for a testimonial?

Look to identify who you ideally want a testimonial from and then simply ask. You could email or write a letter, but it is recommended to phone or ask face to face, thereby making it more difficult for them to say no and giving you the opportunity to position the quality of the testimonial you are looking for.

So why a glowing testimonial? Well, if you are going to take the time and sometimes uncomfortable effort to ask for a testimonial, then you want one that is a glowing reference of you and one that you will share with everyone else immediately.

You may even feel able to guide your customer with the content you would like to see in the testimonial. Quite often, if we do not take control during the request, then we may receive a nice testimonial but perhaps one that prospects read and say, 'So what, I would have expected that to be the situation,' thereby making no impact and potentially even a negative thought in your sales meetings.

If they hesitate due to the time or they may not be sure what to write, then take the problem away and offer to write the testimonial for your customer to then transfer onto their headed paper and sign.

On receipt of a testimonial, can you then ask for a referral? You could use a line such as 'Thank you for your kind testimonial. You obviously like what we do for you. Do you have any contacts in your industry, in which you know we specialise, that you would be able to refer me to such as ABC Limited in XYZ town?'

Once you have testimonials, use them! For example, print them on good quality paper and produce an appealing testimonials folder. You can also share them on your website as a PDF download in full or by using snippets within your page content. You may share them on social media if they were given to you via another platform.

Testimonials are a proof to prospects that you can deliver on your promise. They are great tools in your marketing mix to demonstrate that others also think you have a great business, and they are saying it rather than you having to find a way to sell yourself.

46 Offer yourself as a speaker

With speaking engagements, you have the opportunity to share your expertise, knowledge and skill or to demonstrate your product, but you also receive an indirect endorsement from the event organiser. You are introduced to their group as being a trusted resource for the subject you are talking about, so seen as 'the expert'.

Look to contact your local networking groups or the groups where your ideal customers may meet (e.g. your local Rotary meetings) and offer yourself as a speaker at their events.

Quite often, the organisers are looking for speakers to fill their programme, but look to approach them with an interesting topic and a title that is a gripping as per your best headline.

Yes, you want to attract their interest, but they will want to feel confident that by using your promotional messages it will help them to attract attendees to their event.

The objective with your messaging and your speaker bio has to be how to get others talking about you and your reputation. Well, choose your area of expertise, the topic you would be most comfortable speaking about, then generate a presentation and eye-catching title around this area. For example, you are an accountant who can talk about corporation tax. Would the audience want to know about the percentages paid to HMRC or more about the top 10 tips to save you paying corporation tax to the taxman?

Always have a handout and feedback form for your speaker events. For example, a handout that makes an offer or entices the attendees to your website. A feedback form is good to utilise for collecting views, but also take the opportunity to ask if they would like a no obligation follow-up meeting or to take up an offer such as a free download.

47 Create a credibility document

This is a document that simply focuses on demonstrating your credibility and trust positioning.

It may be a PowerPoint slide or a word document. It could be a printed postcard or a leaflet. Ideally, one page but if you plan to use printed versions then go with two pages so as to not waste the space on the back!

Your document should do exactly what it says in the title and that is to build your credibility. What would your audience want to see that builds their trust in you? For example, testimonials, your guarantee, review rating scores, the logos of similar businesses that trust you or your accreditations or award-winning badges. If you are a small team or a one-person business, then consider adding a picture of you or the team to personalise the credibility statements.

Such a well-written document will give you a distinctive identity, have a customer-centric proposition, communicate in a consistent manner and oozes credibility that works to control your prospects' perception of you and your business.

48 Send great email communications more regularly

There is money in your list.

Provided that your customers and prospects use email, email marketing is possibly the easiest way of communicating with them all at the same time on a regular basis and keeping you and your business at the forefront of their mind.

Your communications by email could be a regular newsletter, a promotional offer or with a purpose to build your relationship by sharing something of value.

If it's for a newsletter, please ensure your target audience would read emails and would not perhaps prefer an old traditional printed version. Your newsletter is a marketing tool to share your market knowledge and expertise so that you are continuing to build relationships of trust. These relationships will then buy from you or refer you to others.

You may have one newsletter for all your contacts or consider having a different version for different groups or segments of your list such as customers, prospects or potential referrers.

Your articles should aim to engage your readers with great content to build the relationship and trust in you and your business. There is no harm in the inclusion of sales messages, but more subtle references linked to your articles seem to work better than a direct sales message when in the newsletter form.

You can also use email marketing to send out promotions and more direct sales messages. Be mindful around what you send so that you do not encourage an unsubscribe action by those people you have engaged with your newsletter because they were unexpectedly sold to. However, don't worry about the odd 'unsubscribe' as this is just list cleansing!

49 Have great signage at your premises

Are you the best kept secret in your neighbourhood?

If you have premises or even work from a home office, do you have signage that is attractive, clear and encourages someone passing your door to stop and read further? If not, then are you not missing an opportunity?

Now I appreciate some business owners do not want people to know that they are based in a certain location for security or possible other purposes but, if there is no reason to hide, then don't.

Do your signs say what you do and what action they have to undertake if they are interested in finding out more? Many signs above a door quote the business name and telephone number, but few say come in and meet us! Envisage that your prospect is stood next to your premises. Do you want them to come in now or leave having possibly written down your telephone number and then call you at a later point? Of course it will depend on how accessible your premises are, if you can have visitors and if your premises are staffed at all times. If you can encourage them to walk in whilst their interest is engaged, then do everything you can to invite them in.

When it comes to telling them what you do, put yourself in their shoes. Quite often, you see signs simply with the business name. For example, saying ABC Accountants, but where is the sign saying we save you tax, we save you your hard-earned cash or we help you grow your business?

50 Make new referral contacts today

Is your word of mouth or referral marketing not generating the leads you desire because you perhaps have the wrong contacts in your network?

You should be working your network of contacts to take them from a 'nice to know you' contact, that you possibly speak to at most events you attend, to an 'advocate' of your business, who is referring to you regularly.

If you do not have enough contacts moving towards becoming an advocate, then sometimes you have to stop and draw a line in the sand and review your ideal referrer.

Fifteen ways to track your marketing is working

'How do I know?!'

This is the most common response when a business owner is asked if their marketing investment has the desired return on investment.

Do you know whether when you spend £x that you get £x+ from a marketing activity?

We all have limited resources for our marketing in terms of time and money, so how do we ensure we have a return on our investment?

Tracking the success of your marketing efforts is crucial for understanding the impact of your strategies and for making informed decisions moving forward.

To help, here's a list of 15 different ways to track the success of your marketing campaigns:

1. Call to action (button, form, sign up, payment).
2. Google/website analytics.
3. QR codes/NFC tags.
4. Vanity URL/designated domain.
5. Unique landing pages.
6. Call tracking numbers.
7. Voucher/discount coupon codes.
8. Google Ads tracking.

9   Social media reporting including hashtag tracking.
10 Referral partner codes.
11 CRM sales tracking.
12 Heat mapping tools.
13 Email marketing metrics.
14 Beacon technology (shops, events).
15 Ask them!

When you ask people 'How did you hear about us?', ensure you drill down to get the most useful response. The common response is that I found you on Google, but was that from an organic search, a paid advert or after being directed there by a leaflet, advert or referral?

These specific tracking methods can provide valuable insights into customer behaviour and campaign performance, allowing for more targeted and effective marketing strategies. It also ensures you are spending your marketing budget in the right places.

The key to successful marketing tracking is not just in the tools themselves, but in how you interpret and use the data they provide. Regularly review and analyse your data to understand what's working, what isn't, and how you can improve your marketing strategies accordingly.

Remember this

Test and measure what you do

A characteristic of individual entrepreneurs that I personally consider to have been successful (e.g. created a business that operates without them, whilst generating wealth for their family) is that they are near obsessive about great marketing activities and obtaining positive results from their marketing investment.

To know they have great marketing activities that work, they test and measure and have the results and statistics that tell them what works, what works best and if they make £x investment what the likely return will be in terms of turnover and profit.

You should be testing what works, learning from each of your campaigns by measuring the results and then tweaking, if necessary, before repeating the process. It is a continuous cycle of improvement again and again.

Contacting those elusive prospects

Are they really elusive or have you not found the way or given them enough of a reason to want to be contacted?

One frustration business owners find is the difficulty in speaking with the senior decision maker responsible for buying your product or service.

This has never been an easy task as decision makers do not make themselves easy to access, as they know they will be the target of constant cold callers. However, they are still open to contact from the right people, in the right way, with a solution to their pain, problem or fear.

Many will have gate keepers who will field so many of these contact attempts and are aware of techniques such as being friendly or commanding or even contacting outside expected hours.

It would be easy to say, 'I can't contact them so let's go for another', but we can't do that every time unless we have a vast pool of target prospects. Additionally, you may have already spent considerable time on researching that contact, so why give up at the first hurdle?

How do we find the contact details of those prospects that we just can't crack by telephone?

Have you used technology to establish the availability of such information? For example, try a Google search or AI tools and see what you find! With social networking, industry forums, directories and sites like LinkedIn, the prospects' contact information may simply appear if you dig beyond the obvious first response. Perhaps they have been a speaker or acted as part of a committee where they have provided their contact details as they are then only too willing to receive contact? Or perhaps the marketing team of the target business have put out a PR story providing the information you desire?

Have you researched the website of the prospect business? Do they offer a search box or are the details you seek in the 'about us' section? Again, areas where the mindset changes and they want to share their details. Is there a directory set up in the site map of the website?

Do you need to mine a little deeper to get to the person you want? For example, on LinkedIn, who are they connected with? At networking events, who do they link with or are seen speaking with? Who may they know, who could introduce you? How about a search utilising information recorded at Companies House? It is unlikely to give you direct contact information, but you may establish their professional relationships such as the bank or accountants who you may also know and are able to approach for an introduction.

These are just some ideas to help you find those desired contact details. Be creative with your thoughts and consider the information that you have available that may link to what you are seeking.

Often, finding the contact details can be the easy part, but when you then make contact how do you increase your chances of them wanting to speak with you? Highlight their pain, problem, fear, want, need and desire and look to share the benefits and solutions offered by your product or service. If you can correctly identify this and communicate in a timely manner, then there is little reason why they would not be interested in speaking to you.

I wish I knew this before I started my first business

You are always marketing, and it starts from day one or from today

Don't wait until your offering or your tools such as your website are 'perfect' before you start to get the word out to your chosen marketplace. Start today and constantly build your audience. Build your lists, build your pipeline, and build your brand profile (both your personal brand and that of the business). Share your stories, share your progress using case studies and share your 'go to' knowledge, all of which will help you gain trust and respect and as a result see you pull your prospects towards you. Our product development should be aligned with our market development; otherwise, there is the risk that you take an offering to market that not enough people want. It is common for businesses to not start, or pause, their marketing as they are unsure which tactics or latest 'shiny tool' they should be using. In my view, know what works and why, then invest say 80 per cent of your resources in that marketing and 20 per cent testing others. We all have limited resources, in terms of our time and money, so use them wisely.

Key points

- Establish what it is that you really do.
- Do you have a strategic plan as well as the tactical considerations?
- Who are you trying to reach and win as customers?
- What marketing channels or tactics will you need to use to pull your prospects towards you?
- How will you hook their interest and capture their attention?
- Are you clear how much you need to spend with your marketing?
- How will you track your marketing and measure if it is working?

Additional resources

Books
Weinberg, G. and Mares, J. (2015) *Traction – How Any Startup Can Achieve Explosive Customer Growth*. Portfolio.
Botterill, N. (2021) *The Entrepreneurs Marketing & Sales System*. Entrepreneurs Circle.
Kennedy, D. S. (2011) *The Ultimate Marketing Plan*. Adams Media.

CHAPTER 6
HOW TO BOOST SALES

Attracting prospective customers is not easy, so the aim of this chapter is to help you convert as many website visitors, or enquiries, as possible to paying customers.

What is a sale?

A sale is defined as the exchange of a commodity for money; the action of selling something.

Sales are activities related to selling or the number of goods sold in a given targeted time period.

Marketing will create the leads. Sales is to follow up the lead, build the relationship and close by obtaining a commitment to buy.

Your sales opportunities will be maximised with a good sales process, and you should look to consider:

1. Your introduction and positioning of the reason for a meeting and thanking the prospect for the opportunity.
2. An opening benefit statement considering the prospect's pain, problem and fear, which takes control of the conversation and captures the interest to want to take the next step to know more.
3. Establish the need or want with a series of questions (open, closed, probing, alternative, assumptive, leading, paraphrasing). Ask questions that lead the prospect to the point where they realise that they have a need.
4. Re-confirm the need or want by summarising your understanding and getting the prospect to acknowledge the need.
5. Meet the need/want by matching with the benefits of your solution.
6. Summarise the benefits and bring in the prospect's goals where possible.

7 Close and ask for the sale (assumptive, alternative, summary, fear, what if, direct).

8 Look for the buying signals.

Sales are made simpler with effective communication. Remember communication is not just the words you use. Too often people think of the perfect script and not how it will be presented. Research indicates that the tools of effective communication are based on the words (7 per cent), voice (38 per cent) and your body language (55 per cent).

Many factors are involved in the communication process which ultimately influences the final interpretation. You should recognise that different people receive information in different ways:

- visual (like to see it)
- auditory (like to hear it)
- kinaesthetic (like to feel it, do it).

Presenting your sales information in the way that best suits your prospect will influence decisions and make you more effective in dealing with people.

If you are fearful of sales, then reposition it. Consider that it is a process of helping someone to buy from you or some research to see if they would buy.

Finally, listen twice as often as you speak. Use silence to wait for the answer and don't answer for the prospect. Often, they will sell themselves.

Five crucial stages when building trust

In *The Trusted Advisor* by David H. Maister, Charles H. Green and Robert M. Galford, the process of building trust is detailed through five crucial stages, often referred to as the 'Trust Creation Process'.[1] These stages provide a structured framework for establishing and nurturing trust-based relationships.

---

[1] Maister, D. H., Green, C. H. and Galford, R. M. (2001) *The Trusted Advisor*. Touchstone.

The five stages are:

1. **Engagement:** the first stage involves engaging with the other party in a meaningful and genuine way. This includes active listening, showing empathy and demonstrating your willingness to understand their needs and concerns. Building trust starts with establishing a connection and signalling your commitment to their wellbeing.
2. **Listening:** effective listening is a cornerstone of trust-building. In this stage, focus on truly understanding the other person's perspective, objectives and challenges. By being attentive and asking clarifying questions, you demonstrate that their thoughts and feelings are valued.
3. **Framing:** once you have a clear understanding of their situation, collaborate to define the specific challenges or issues they are facing. Articulating their problems accurately shows that you comprehend their circumstances and are invested in finding the best possible solutions.
4. **Envisioning:** in this stage, you work together to envision a future state where the challenges have been overcome and goals have been achieved. Discuss the desired outcomes and potential opportunities, showing your commitment to helping them achieve their aspirations.
5. **Commitment:** the final stage involves jointly committing to a course of action to address the identified challenges and achieve the envisioned future. This commitment is not just about the solution itself but also about your dedication to supporting them throughout the process. This stage solidifies trust by demonstrating that you are genuinely invested in their success.

These five stages create a roadmap for building trust that is based on active engagement, empathy and collaborative problem solving. Following this process helps establish a strong foundation of trust, positioning you as a trusted adviser who is dedicated to the wellbeing and success of those you serve.

> **Remember this**
>
> **Reframe 'selling'**
>
> Too often, we don't try to sell as we are afraid of being rejected or don't want to be considered a salesperson. This impacts our mindset and our execution.
>
> In business we have to sell! We are in fact selling every day.
>
> You have a solution to their want or need, so surely you have a duty to make them aware of what you have to offer and explore their desire to purchase?
>
> How can you encourage your prospect to buy from you without the need of selling?

How to make the most of your sales opportunities

For many people their sales success is influenced by their mindset. There are two things abundantly clear around the marketing and sales mindset:

1. You are helping people to make a purchase – you are not selling.
2. Sales and marketing are not magic, they are planned processes.

Many business owners don't like picking up the phone because of a fear of being perceived as a 'salesperson' and being rejected. It is also perhaps related to the fact that many people don't like being targeted themselves by strong sales messages or tactics and therefore don't want to come across the same way.

To help make the most of your sales opportunities, follow these six steps that allow you to make the most of being helpful and not salesy:

1. Introduction.
2. Open with a benefit.
3. Establish the need.
4. Reconfirm the need.
5. Meet the need with a benefit.
6. Close.

Introductions – getting them right

You have between three and seven seconds to make a first impression. And only one opportunity to make it.

Choose a time for your conversation that works for you. If you're better in the mornings, try to avoid afternoons; you don't have to take the first time slot your prospect offers you!

It's best to begin by identifying yourself, especially if you haven't met or spoken in person before, and perhaps you're following up on a lead from a website or social media enquiry.

Look to thank the person, not for their time, but for the opportunity to share your product or service and explore how you might work together.

Finally, after each introduction, reflect on how it went. What could you have done better? What needs to change? Was your body language positive or was it communicating something you didn't intend?

Don't forget your listening skills because, if you don't actively listen to your prospect, you simply won't be able to progress the conversation.

Active listening means your conversation could go in any direction, which is why you need to be able to maintain control of your sales opportunity and steer it back in the direction you want it to go, without displaying any of these *bad* listening traits:

- Giving advice instead of asking more questions.
- Interrupting.
- Avoiding answering questions.
- Jumping to conclusions.
- Filling short silences to avoid awkwardness.

A good listener will make notes, make positive sounds and use body language such as nodding. They will allow pauses in the conversation for the other person to absorb and process what's been said, and a good salesperson will be non-judgemental about the end of the conversation, so you remain in active listening mode.

The aim of asking questions is to lead your sales prospect to the point where they realise on their own terms, that they have a need for your product or service.

The more your questioning prompts them to say 'yes', the more naturally positive the sales meeting will be.

Questioning softeners you can use to make your questions less direct and more friendly: Can I just ask, by the way, incidentally …

You should also use different types of questions as appropriate:

- **Open questions:** a way of eliciting conversation rather than a yes/no response.
- **Probing questions:** digging deeper.
- **Assumptive:** making a clear assumption so that your prospect can give you a yes or no response. This way you're learning – would I be right in saying …?
- **Leading questions:** you tend to know the answer you'll get, but you're leading them to clarify it so you can progress.
- **Alternatives:** OK, I understand, but how about, or what if?
- **Paraphrasing:** this is how to demonstrate that you have listened and are repeating the answer in the form of a question in your own words.

Think about how to structure your sales opportunity around these types of questions. Perhaps you'd use lots of open questions to begin with, move onto probing questions like, 'Can you give more specific details on …?' and then assumptive questions such as 'So, if this happens, then that is the result?' and finally present an alternative like 'Are you therefore looking to get X or Y from this solution?'

Look to convert the features of your solution into benefits that impact your prospect.

It's all too easy to go into a sales meeting with a list of features that make your product or service sound great. But your prospect isn't interested in the features, or is already aware of them, and now wants to know how those features will benefit them. I always use the example of the iPod: '1,000 songs in your pocket' says it all. It's slim, it's lightweight, it has a great capacity, but none of those things is quickly translated into the best thing about it – no more bulky Disc/Walkman with cassette tapes or CDs to carry around, you now have 1,000 songs in your pocket.

Here are some steps you can follow to best convert the features of your product or service into benefits:

- What we do is/the great feature is ...
- So that ...
- Which means that ...

For example, 'The great feature of this vacuum cleaner is the 60-metre power cord, so that it can reach all the rooms in your house, which means you don't have to move the lead to different plug sockets, to clean more easily and in less time.'

Objections can come at any point during your sales opportunity meeting. Expect objections so consider how to overcome them in advance.

Most solutions only have a handful of objections. Think about the five most common objections that could come up for your product or service and where in the sales opportunity they might come up so you can prepare a response in advance. Just like your pricing structure, be ready to respond at the drop of a hat.

Remember, a quick response to an objection deepens the trust in you. Here are some common objections to work from:

- Price.
- Somebody already does it for me.
- I have a regular supplier/provider already.
- I'm also speaking to other providers.
- You don't have what I need.

One of the main reasons people don't 'win' a sale is because they haven't asked for the sale, they haven't asked for the business or 'closed' the sale. Look to consider your strong closing technique.

The techniques for closing a sales opportunity are almost as varied as the questioning techniques we looked at above.

- **Assumptive:** making the assumption that they want to buy and discussing how the contract is produced or the payment method.
- **Alternative:** so, shall we say X or Y?

- **Summary**: summarising the conversation that has led to the end result of purchase.
- **Fear**: limited time offers, or even, 'you'll continue to experience the problems you told me about earlier'.
- **What if/So if**: leading your sales prospect to come up with the fear factor themselves.
- **Direct**: how many would you like? From our discussion, this is the best solution for you. Would you like to sign today?
- **Soft**: if you were going to ask for our support, which level would suit you best?

And it is imperative that you finish the close with a clear follow-up procedure to tell your sales prospect what happens next.

Remember this

Respond in a timely manner or communicate after a perceived delay

I am continually surprised and often disappointed by business owners who could not return a telephone call, acknowledge an email or stick to a meeting commitment.

Surely, it is common sense in business to do these things efficiently?

It is also about relationships and appreciating another individual's time and commitment, as they are likely to be waiting on a return communication from you.

Your reputation or the acquisition of new business may be reliant on your ability to communicate efficiently. How many times have you heard the story of a tradesperson saying they will call round to give a quote and then never show? Or say they will produce a quote for you, and it takes two weeks or more?

This is often due to the fact that some people are too distant from their own customers' expectations. What is a perceived delay for your customer? If they email you today, are they expecting a reply in 48 hours or is a week acceptable to them? Knowing this helps you meet those expectations and of course manage your own time, which as an entrepreneur are both critical.

The 'What, Why and So' sales technique and how to use it

The 'What, Why and So' sales technique is a persuasive selling approach that focuses on understanding the customer's needs and pain points before offering a solution to address those specific concerns. It's a simple yet effective way to connect with potential customers and demonstrate how a product or service can benefit them.

With this three-stage approach, your prospect often leans forward and is more interested to hear about your ideas.

1. Explore the 'What' to identify the person's pain, problem, fear, want, need or desire.
2. Establish 'Why' it is important for them to overcome something or to obtain their 'What'.
3. Reply with the 'So' that shares how your solution to the 'What' provides their 'Why'.

Identify the 'What' by asking open-ended questions to understand the person's needs, challenges and goals. This phase is all about active listening so you can gather information but importantly understand their emotion and motivations to start connecting the dots to find solutions. For example:

- What is it you're trying to achieve?
- What challenges are you currently facing?
- What features or qualities do you expect?

Acknowledge what has been shared, their concerns or needs (the 'What'). Empathise with their situation and clarify it with them to make sure you've got the right understanding. Let them know that you acknowledge their pain points and objectives. This step is crucial in building rapport and showing that you genuinely care about their concerns.

At this point, you are now uncovering the real 'Why' and confirming your understanding. For example:

- 'OK, so as I understand it, you're looking for X that can help you improve Y. Am I right?'
- 'So, just to clarify, it's important for you to find a solution that can [address a particular pain point], whilst [meeting a desire].'

This naturally leads to you receiving permission to present your solution.

Once you've identified the customer's needs and acknowledged their concerns, present your product or service as the ideal solution (the 'So'). Tailor your explanation, pitch your solution, to highlight how your offering directly addresses their specific requirements and provides value. Focus on the benefits rather than just the features. For example:

- 'This [product/service] is designed to streamline [specific process], which will help you achieve [desired outcome].
- 'So, with our [product/service], you can effectively [solve a particular challenge].'

The 'What, Why and So' technique is effective because it allows the opportunity for you to demonstrate your genuine interest in meeting customers' needs and that your product or service is not just a generic offering but a personalised solution to their unique problems.

And remember, they're not interested in you, and you don't have permission to tell them about yourself until you have established a deeper connection and they actually want to know more!

Ten tips for improving the dreaded sales call

Many business owners avoid making sales calls because they just don't like doing them, they feel awkward, they fear objections, they don't want to feel pushy ... The list goes on. You may not like getting sales calls, so don't want to make others feel the same way.

However, you needn't feel like that. If you follow these tips on how to improve the process, you'll become more comfortable with actually picking up the phone to make that dreaded sales call.

1 Warm calls, not cold ones

Making cold calls is a skilled art and takes someone with a good deal of resilience to conduct, especially in the early days of learning sales. You have to be prepared to make call number x after potentially receiving perceived rejections. So leave cold calls to the professionals and start with only select people who are either expecting your call, or who are already aware of your products/services.

They may have leaned towards you or interacted with a lead generation channel such as a lead magnet.

2 Go with clarity

It's unusual to get through to the person you need to speak to right away, so begin with asking, 'Who do I speak to regarding ...' When you do get to the right person, be clear on your reason for calling – do you want to arrange a one-to-one meeting, are you looking for an email address?

Consider making two calls! First, ask 'Who should I write to about X' and then call another time asking for that person.

3 Know your offering inside and out

If you can't confidently state your value, benefits, prices or expectations, your prospect won't feel confident talking to you.

4 Reframe the process in your mind

You're not making a sales call; you're making a service call. Your call is to offer support, solutions or opportunities. You're offering them an opportunity to buy. Also consider that you are doing them a disservice by not calling them to talk about something you know would be a solution to their pain, problem, fear, want, need or desire. This will change your mindset and you'll feel happier about making those calls.

5 Take your time

Break your call list down into easy to manage numbers – start with, say, 10 calls and take a break. That way, if you get a knock-back and start to feel negative about the exercise, you don't still have another 50 calls to make!

If you bail out of the calls you planned to make on a large list, you may not go back to them and potentially waste the large list compared to, say, the smaller number.

6 Prepare for objections

Quite often, you can predict the handful of objections you might hear. How would you respond to them? Remember, you may have to get past the 'gate-keeper' before you can speak to the decision maker, so being prepared makes you feel and sound more confident.

7 Make notes, not scripts

You can often tell when someone is checking off the points from a checklist or following a script. Rather than having a script, bullet point the main points you want to make on the call and work them into the conversation and its flow. Use prompts and remind yourself to not only hear but actually listen to the person you are calling rather than mechanically delivering messages.

8 Stand up and smile

Your energy and mood are easily transmitted down a phone line. If you adjust your energy by smiling and changing your posture, it will make the call go smoother. Perhaps you could have a visual reminder of your 'reason why' in your periphery to aid the smile.

9 Outsource or delegate the job

For a micro, early-stage small business, you are likely to be making these calls. That's OK, as you know your 'why', you have the passion for your offering, and you know it better than anyone else. However, as you scale, you may need to look for someone else to make the calls and perhaps open the doors for you by warming up the prospect and clarifying the call list.

10 Story tell, don't sell

Still thinking about using that call script? You'll have more success pulling people towards you with interest by sharing stories, anecdotes and case studies, rather than by mechanically following a sales script. Remember, people buy people, so be a real person, not a dreaded salesperson!

Overcoming price objections

Like many others, you may feel under pressure to drop your price when you face an 'objection' over how much you charge. You may think you need to discount your service or product in order to successfully close a sales opportunity.

Discounting is an option in response to a price objection but not the best. It immediately devalues your brand, your product, your service and your entire business. It even sets the tone for any future relationship. However, at times, it may be necessary to have a special offer, or even negotiate on price, but look to negotiate on terms at the same time or use the tactic of inflating the price to begin with, so that you can negotiate down to the price you deserve. If you find these tactics are needed every time you face a price objection, then you may need to reconsider your pricing structure, your target audience or the value package associated with your price.

Don't present your prices too early in the sales meeting. This gives you time to demonstrate the true value of your product or service.

Here are seven thoughts on how you can approach the right sales opportunities with a considered approach, so that the common objection around price doesn't arise as often.

1. **Approach your ideal customer**
   If you work with and approach your ideal client, the ones that are the best fit for your solution, they're less likely to be price-sensitive or price-driven.

2. **Ask powerful questions**
   Use your questioning to discover what's important to the buyer, not to you. Making the sales meeting about them defines the value from the customer's viewpoint, and not your own.

   Your questions can be formed through feedback you've received or from other sales discussions.

3. **Remove or reduce the risk to the buyer**
   For example, can you offer a guarantee or trial period to the buyer thereby removing the risk and making the buyer's decision easier?

4. **Do you have real clarity around your proposition and how it fits in the market space?**
   Being able to clearly define your proposition allows you to speak with confidence. As an example, this is the power of having a niche market as you know that market very well and you'll know that your solution fits. You'll also know your value to the people within that market space and be able to convey that value with confidence.

5. **Demonstrate your market knowledge every time you go into a sales opportunity**
   Position your business to your prospect by putting yourself in their shoes and use strong relevant benefit statements based on your understanding of how the market serves the customer.

6. **Know the likely objections you're going to face beyond price**
   Being able to predict your objections means you can instantly reply to any. This creates a greater balance of value that takes the attention away from just the cost.

   Rehearse your responses to all the common objections you're likely to face so you can instantly respond with credible confidence.

7. **Know that people are going to try and get the best price they can**
   Some sales prospects will always try and negotiate and drive down your price no matter how you try to overcome their objection. Have a reason why you have to hold a price rather than being in a position to offer a discount. Why? Because if you have this reason it creates empathy with your buyer, and they appreciate that that is the price. Therefore, they will consider that price against all the other value you've demonstrated.

   And remember, it's OK to walk away. If you value your product or service and have priced it fairly and competitively, whilst considering your audience, then don't let it be devalued. Someone who chooses on price is likely to also move away on price and is therefore, in many cases, not your ideal customer.

> ### Remember this
>
> Many objections are not a 'No thank you', but often an interest and a desire for clarification.

Using your sales process to improve your customer journey

Despite the customer journey appearing the same for everyone, as we look a little closer, you'll see that each customer has their own experience with you at each stage. So, what are *your* customers' journeys like with your business?

For example, you may have six steps in your journey that customers go through. If they go through steps one to three very smoothly, but at step four they lose interest, this identifies which part of your sales process needs tweaking. This could help you identify where additional, different or fewer touchpoints are required, such as emails, phone calls or a meeting or if the communication content needs development.

Considering the key touchpoints allows you to tap into what your customer is feeling at every step of their journey. This is essential for understanding what they need from you along the way.

Many people make decisions on an emotional level. Can you solve a problem? Do they care about your sustainability? How does your service make them feel?

Do you know what your customers are feeling at each step of their journey? Consider your customers' emotions and how they may change as they progress through the journey in terms of awareness, consideration, purchase, retention and loyalty.

Once you know what your customer is doing, their touchpoints with your business, and the emotion they're feeling, you can consider the best possible solution for them. The aim is to use your systems and processes to blend your touchpoints, so they form a natural flow of communication, guiding your customer from awareness to purchase and loyalty. You are considering how to move your relationship from social media, onto your website and onto a telephone call or in-person meeting. The smoother the journey, the more comfortable your customer will be when they arrive!

The hidden cost of selling to the wrong people or at the wrong margin

As an entrepreneur, securing sales is crucial. But have you ever considered the impact of selling to the wrong people or securing orders for your offering at the wrong margin? It's a trap that can lead to financial strain and operational chaos.

I've seen it happen with businesses celebrating sales without realising the true cost of these deals. Here's why selling to the wrong clients can lead to going broke:

1 **High maintenance:** the wrong clients often demand more time, resources and attention, draining your energy and inflating costs.
2 **Misalignment:** when clients don't align with your values and goals, it leads to friction, dissatisfaction and a tarnished reputation.
3 **Opportunity cost:** focusing on unfit clients means missing out on ideal customers who can drive sustainable growth.
4 **Cash flow issues:** late payments and endless negotiations with the wrong clients can cripple your cash flow.

It's vital to identify and target your ideal clients — those who resonate with your vision, appreciate your value and contribute to long-term success.

Additionally, I see businesses driving sales at a low margin without appreciating their numbers and driving their cash flow towards the point of being broke without realising it.

Selling at a low margin can seem like an attractive strategy to drive volume and capture market share quickly. However, this approach can be perilous for your business in the long run. When margins are too slim, it becomes challenging to cover operational costs, invest in growth and sustain profitability whilst having the financial return you deserve. The immediate influx of sales might look promising, but the hidden costs can erode your financial stability.

Low margins often lead to a vicious cycle of financial strain. As profits dwindle, there's less room to manoeuvre during tough times, leaving your business vulnerable to market fluctuations and unexpected expenses.

Here are a few strategies to ensure you're selling to the right people:

- **Define your ideal customer:** understand their needs, pain points and how your solution fits. They are also those that are willing to pay for your offering at the 'right' margin.
- **Qualify leads:** implement a qualification process to ensure potential clients are a good fit.
- **Focus on relationships:** build strong, meaningful connections with clients who align with your business ethos.

Selling to the right people not only enhances profitability but also ensures a harmonious and rewarding business journey.

I wish I knew this before I started my first business

Balance the hustle with your self-care

Your business will thrive when you prioritise your wellbeing. You can only best run a healthy business when you are a healthy leader. We often think it won't happen to us, but burnout is very real, and it can creep up on us once that stress pot is filled more than the energy pot.

Like many other business owners, you may find it lonely at the top, so have good people around you. These may include your advisers, your supporters, those that listen, and those that help, but one key lesson for me was that, when you need help, please make sure you ask for it.

We don't miss appointments with prospects or customers, so ensure you put the same value to your health and wellbeing by making time, even appointments, so that you keep your personal battery recharged.

Key points

- How will your customer get to know, like and trust you?
- Are you ready to overcome the common objections to your offering?
- How does the relationship evolve as the customer progresses their journey with you?

Additional resources

Books
Belfort, J. (2017) *The Way of the Wolf*. Gallery Books.
Carnegie, D. (1998) *How to Win Friends and Influence People*. Pocket Books.

Podcasts
The GaryVee Audio Experience hosted by Gary Vaynerchuk

CHAPTER 7
HOW TO MAXIMISE PROFIT AND PRICE RIGHT

Let's assume you now have the business up and running. This chapter looks at the ways to maximise your profits and how to price and position your offering.

Seven systemised steps for growing your business revenue and profits

The most critical numbers in most businesses are related to your revenue and profitability.

The marginal gains philosophy demonstrates the benefit of working on all the elements of your business at the same time, demonstrating how you could improve each area by a small percentage to give you a greater cumulative effect to your bottom line.

Seven steps to consider are:

1 **Number of leads** – is your marketing strategy, and the chosen tactics that you have considered to pull your prospects towards you, actually working? How can you generate more leads?
2 **Conversion rate** – how can you continually improve your sales process for greater proposal to acceptance success? Or basket to completion?
3 **Number of sales** – whilst your prospect is in buying mode, are you maximising the cross-sale opportunities? Could you sell more, package more at this initial stage?
4 **Value of sales** – what is your pricing strategy to maximise the value of each sale? Are you pricing effectively? How are you packing or presenting your products or services? Could you increase your prices and average order value?

5. **Profit margin** – are you proactively reviewing and managing your costs to maximise your return on investment? Are you able to reduce your direct costs or those costs to resource your delivery and improve your margin?
6. **Repurchase rate, the number of times they return to buy** – encourage your customers to buy more often. How are you encouraging repeat business or other sales income from your existing customer base?
7. **Increase lifetime value** – what are you doing to retain your hard-earned customers for longer?

Consider how you could improve each of these seven areas in a systemised way so that the activity becomes a habit in your business and not just a one-off exercise.

Use the table below to review your numbers, with 10 per cent uplift on all seven areas and see the possible cumulative impact:

Per year	Existing numbers	Plus 10%
Number of leads		
Conversion rate		
Number of sales		
Value of sales		
Profit margin		
Times they return to buy		
Retained number of years		
Total		

Here's an example:

Per year	Existing numbers	Plus 10%
Number of leads	100	110
Conversion rate	50%	55%
Number of sales	1	1.1
Value of sales	£1,000	£1,100
Profit margin	50%	55%
Times they return to buy	1	1.1
Retained number of years	1	1.1
Total	£25,000	£48.718
		a 94% increase!

Let's look at the seven steps a little further. What could you do?

1. **Increase the number of leads.** Do you have a marketing plan? How effective is your marketing? How are most of your existing leads generated? What resources are required to obtain the level of leads you need for the financial forecast? How can you change or improve the number of enquiries you receive?

2. **Improve your sales conversion rate.** What is your target conversion rate? How clear is your unique selling point when you are in a sales meeting? Test different approaches that maximise the conversion of those leads generated to actual sales. Know why you do not convert leads to sales.

3. **Increase the average number of transactions (sales) a customer makes at first instance.** Can you make additional cross-sales to your client base? What can you do to help the customer purchase from you more regularly? What offers can you make to encourage additional purchases? What packages can you create to encourage additional purchases? Is there something you can sell direct or for a commission that links with your product or service?

4. **Raise the average value of each transaction.** Review your pricing policy and look at opportunities to increase your prices. Can you offer above your desired price to allow for negotiation or to receive a premium? Can you package your products or services together to increase the average order value? How will you retain the demand in your product or service, as when demand falls it is likely the price expectation will also fall?

5. **Improve the profit margin.** Review your resourcing and look at cost savings available. Can you cut your costs by removing an expense or negotiating or changing suppliers? How can you increase your productivity?

6. **Increase the average number of transactions (sales) a customer makes in a year.** How will you encourage your customers to buy again? Is there a natural timeline to when they would be buying again and will they need a reminder? Can you make an offer at first purchase that encourages the repeat transaction?

7. **Extend the average number of years that a customer buys from you.** What is your retention policy to increase the buying lifetime of a client? Are you communicating? Are you listening? Do you know your client, their wants and demands after they have bought?

> **Remember this**
>
> **The marginal gains philosophy**
>
> Adding a 5 per cent increase in all areas does not just return a 5 per cent increase in your bottom line. The cumulative effect provides a greater return on investment.

Gross profit margin – know it, maintain it

Gross profit (GP) measures the money your goods or services earned after subtracting the total costs to produce and sell them.

The formula to calculate your GP is the total revenue minus the cost of goods sold.

The gross profit ratio is an important financial measurement that evaluates profitability. Organisations can calculate the gross profit margin to understand how efficiently costs generate sales.

The gross profit margin is often shown as a percentage:

$$\text{Gross profit} \div \text{Net sales revenue} \times 100$$

As an example of a gross profit margin calculation, let's say your service business makes £20,000 on a contract or per month. It costs you £8,000 to provide those services. Your gross profit is £12,000. Your gross profit margin is 60 per cent.

Do you know your current gross profit margin? Do you have a target gross profit margin that you wish to achieve and maintain?

Is this margin sufficient to cover the overheads of your business based on the volume you are selling or need to sell?

Unless you are deliberately giving away margin as part of a price offer to increase your sales, it is important to keep an eye on and even retain your gross profit margin.

For example, you have a sales drive and increase revenue but have not kept an eye on the costs to deliver that increase. Therefore, you subsequently spend more on people, expenses, direct marketing, etc. The related cost of sales is higher than you have spent before. Your margin has reduced. Have you possibly left profit on the table?

Maintaining a healthy gross profit margin is vital for several reasons:

1 **Business sustainability:** your gross profit margin reflects the core profitability of your business. It shows how effectively you are managing your production costs relative to your sales revenue. A strong gross profit margin ensures that you have sufficient funds to cover operating expenses, invest in growth opportunities and withstand market fluctuations.

2 **Cash flow management:** consistent gross profit margins contribute to stable cash flow. This stability allows you to meet your financial obligations, such as paying suppliers, employees and other operational costs, without compromising the financial health of your business.

3 **Investment and growth:** retaining a solid gross profit margin means more capital is available for reinvestment into the business. This can include expanding your product lines, entering new markets or investing in marketing and technology. Growth is crucial for staying competitive and meeting long-term business goals.

4 **Pricing strategy:** understanding and maintaining your gross profit margin helps in setting the right pricing strategy. It allows you to price your products or services competitively whilst ensuring that you are not undercutting your profitability. This balance is key to attracting customers whilst sustaining your business.

5 **Financial health indicator:** gross profit margin is a key indicator of your business's financial health and efficiency. Investors, lenders and stakeholders often look at this metric to assess the viability and stability of your business. A healthy margin can make your business more attractive for investment and financing opportunities.

6 **Benchmarking and performance analysis:** by monitoring your gross profit margin, you can benchmark your performance against industry standards and competitors. This analysis helps identify areas where you can improve operational efficiency, reduce costs or adjust pricing strategies to enhance profitability.

How to increase the profit margins in your business

Increasing profit margins is a crucial goal for any business. Here are some strategies that can help boost your profit margins effectively:

Some will improve your gross profit margin and others will help improve your 'bottom line' net profit.

By implementing a combination of these strategies, you can work to improve your profit margins over time. The key is to carefully analyse your specific business situation and focus on the approaches that will have the biggest impact for your company.

1. **Evaluate and reduce costs where possible:**
   - Audit your fixed costs and expenses and cut unnecessary expenses like unused subscriptions or services.
   - Address inefficiencies, streamline operations and automate processes to reduce labour costs.
   - Negotiate better rates with the supply chain.
2. **Strategically raise prices:**
   - Conduct market research to determine optimal pricing.
   - Add features or value to justify higher prices.
   - Focus on differentiating your products/services from those of competitors.
3. **Improve your product/service mix:**
   - Focus on promoting and selling higher-margin products.
   - Discontinue or de-emphasise low-margin offerings.
   - Increase your average order value through upselling and cross-selling.
4. **Enhance customer retention:**
   - Implement loyalty programmes to encourage repeat business.
   - Provide excellent customer service to reduce churn.
   - Communicate the value and ROI customers receive.
5. **Optimise your stock management:**
   - Improve inventory visibility to avoid markdowns.
   - Stock the right amount of fast-moving items.
   - Reduce excess inventory of slow-moving products.

6 **Differentiate your brand:**
   - Focus on your unique value proposition.
   - Build brand loyalty to reduce price sensitivity.
   - Emphasise quality and service over competing solely on price.
7 **Increase average order value:**
   - Offer volume discounts to encourage larger purchases.
   - Bundle and package complementary products.
   - Set minimum order values.

> **Remember this**
>
> Your gross profit target should allow for paying your fixed costs/overheads, provide you with the profit return you deserve and allow for an element of free cash to reinvest in the business.

The basis of pricing

Pricing a product or service can be one of the biggest challenges for a start-up business owner, and therefore the price is often set based on what the competitors are charging.

There are many factors to setting a price. Supply vs demand, the costs associated, the market and competitor positioning, ethical considerations of your buyer, your target audience and the perceived value, to name a few.

Let's start with a look at your offering.

Take a piece of paper and draw three columns. The first column is the service or product, the second column is the benefit to your customer or your prospect, and the third column is the scope of the service that you're offering.

For example, if I was going to do the social media for someone that would be the name of the product as the service, the second aspect would be the benefits for the customer outsourcing that to me to do that for them and third, I'd have the scope of service. This may be in terms of a content plan, giving them some ideas, putting the posts together, designing the artwork, etc.

Service/Product	Benefit	Scope

Once we've got those three columns, we can then think about a price per service.

The price will be based on the value to the customer (column two) and the scope of the service (column three) in terms of what it is that you're delivering and how. You can then look at that offering and establish the value offered, and then consider the specific costs to you in terms of delivering that service.

Now that you have a base price, perhaps a minimum charge, you may want to flex this with a price based on the size of the organisation you are supporting or the complexity of the requirement. For example, if you were writing a blog for somebody, would it be that you would go back for two adjustments of that blog or would you be solely responsible for writing the blog or would you just be reviewing the blog? Whilst considering the scope, what are the options for the customer? Can you flex the scope to suit the need and therefore have a menu of options with different pricing levels to suit?

You can now take this base pricing and build the numbers into your financial forecast. You can make sure that your capacity can deliver your desired revenues, at the identified margin and result in the income that you desire, based on that pricing model.

If it does, then you can start to think about how you then present those prices in terms of your positioning. Do you present them as a package? Do you offer your prices as menu choices? Is the value clear to attract buyers for the prices you are presenting?

Once you have taken a price to market, keep testing it. Can you increase the price to improve your average order value? How does that impact your sales conversion rate?

Setting your price

There is often a range of prices that you can charge in your market, but the objective is usually to set prices at a level that meets the market demand and provides the highest possible profits. For example, you could sell a few at the highest possible price, but selling higher volume at the optimum price may bring you more profits.

Pricing decisions are critical for your business. What you charge will affect how many sales you make, determine the profit achieved and usually whether your business can survive.

Many new businesses price their business by calculating their costs and adding a margin that provides for their desired lifestyle. Others price their business lower than their competitors in the belief it will open doors and buy market share. Neither of these take into account the customer or the market opportunity for your product or service.

As a good guide, you must be aware of what your competitors are charging, so you should do some research, but this should not be the sole basis of your chosen level. When reviewing a competitor's price, consider your price and offering against their price, performance, availability, appearance, quality, service, packaging and image.

Pricing is also a marketing issue

Your pricing level will impact on the potential customers' perception. Simply setting a low price is not the answer. If you are too cheap, they may believe quality is poor or you are desperate for business. In addition, with incorrect pricing at the start-up stage, especially if it is too low, it is more difficult to amend that price in the future. Customers will pay for quality and service, hence why the motor vehicles in demand are not always the cheapest available. However, if you charge too much, then they may simply choose your competitor without considering the difference of your offer.

If you plan to charge a higher price than your competitors, then you need to answer the following possible questions from your prospect:

- Does the product have a genuine advantage?
- Are you in a niche market and able to control your price?
- Do you offer a real unique benefit that customers will pay for?
- Are your customers motivated to pay a premium price?
- Are the non-price benefits, like service and the added value you provide, clear to the potential customer (e.g. after-sales care)?

Service businesses that charge an hourly rate will usually calculate a minimum price based on the number of hours the fee earners can work (allowing for holiday and sick pay) and based on the desired return for that period.

Use your market research to identify what your product or service is worth to the customer, what they value and the price level they are prepared to pay.

Your price should take into consideration:

- the profit forecast and related volume of sales predicted
- the production costs, both fixed and variable costs, variable costs being those that change as you sell different volumes
- your delivery costs
- a perception of value or how unique the offering is.

- How price-sensitive your customers are likely to be.
- Your payment terms. For example, you may have a lower price if getting paid earlier so that you have the cash to manage your business.
- Your desired profit margin. Simply, your reward.

Once you have decided on a price, this will help you continue to build your financial forecast, based on the expected volume of sales. You will then establish if you have to charge more to have a profitable business or if the idea will simply not work financially for you.

When you have a set price, you can continue to test the market or adjust to external factors with pricing tactics such as:

- **Discounting.** Perhaps to capture a large order or to motivate a customer purchase at certain times.
- **Special offers or promotions.** These are great for turning old product to cash or focusing on a specific product.
- **Odd value pricing.** This is when you sell at £9.99 instead of £10.
- **Loss leaders.** When you sell something cheaply to generate interest in your other products or services.
- **Skimming.** A tactic of selling a unique product at a high price until all likely customers have purchased. Then consider a price reduction.
- **Penetration.** When you start at a low price for market share or to sell high volume. Once you have the market, you then increase prices. I mention this last as this is seen as a risky strategy for a new start-up.

There will be two limitations to the price you set. The minimum price level and the constraints. The minimum price will be based on your overall costs and forecasted sales volume because selling below this price will make you a loss, unless of course you have a long-term deliberate strategy for this pricing strategy. Many of the constraints are legal constraints, which may govern the market price of your product or service. However, one big constraint on your pricing potential may be you! Remember you are not your customer, so what you are willing to pay may not be what your customer is willing to pay.

Don't get fixated on price

When you buy something, is price the driver? Do you always try to get the best price? Do you always negotiate your suppliers down to the cheapest price?

Do you move supplier or provider, despite the relationship, because you can get it cheaper elsewhere?

Do you get annoyed when someone won't pay what you're worth, your price?

Are you one who negotiates because they aren't worth it, but you expect everyone to pay your ask?

If so, I suspect your mindset may result in you being fixated on price and this fixation may mean you will miss things.

Of course, getting the right price for the right service or provision is a key decision to running a lean business and maximising your profit.

Primarily, when you just think that price is the driver, you will miss the other reasons why people don't buy from you. You will be so fixated on price that you'll be thinking people don't buy from you because of price when often it's because they've not seen your value. You'll end up reducing your price when that was not the deciding factor and therefore unnecessarily lose profit.

> **Remember this**
>
> *Your* price does not have to be the price your competitors charge or less!

What is your time really worth?

This question has two lines of thinking. First, are you using your time as you want to and what is the financial connection to your time that links to your pricing considerations?

If your business sells time, such as a service business, consultancy, etc., then the answer to this question will also help you consider your pricing.

Any serious entrepreneurial journey has clarity. A clear why, purpose, direction and one that influences the utilisation of your resources including your time and money. This clarity ensures you value your own time first, and that influences how you are then prepared to account for this in your pricing.

Here's a little test for you, plus the three ways to understand what you truly value.

Ask yourself what is important to you, what you value most, what your business means for you.

Give it three weeks and review the following to see if you are committed to those things or whether they are just a pipe dream. Are you delivering or just talking the talk?

1. What does your diary say about how you spent your time? (More importantly, reflect on how you spent the time not allocated in your diary!)
2. What have you spent your hard-earned money on? (Review your business and personal expenditure.)
3. Review your interruptions and establish how easily you were distracted and what caught the attention of your valuable time.

Then reflect on your findings of the three questions and whether they mirror what you say you value.

The route of this question is to figure out how you could be spending your time and looking at how you or other people value your time. When you have a quantitative value of your time, hour by hour, it can drive some very important decisions in your business, and in your personal life, whilst influencing what you need to charge.

It's true that all time is not created equal and how you value it differs. Time spent with family and loved ones is completely different from the time you spend creating compelling presentations to convert leads into sales. But you can't do everything all at once!

Time vs cash

We all have an instinctive awareness of the value of our time. How many times have you said, 'It's not worth going all that way,' or weighed up whether to pay for shipping or spend your own time making a collection? Or maybe you've recently bought extortionate concert tickets and justified it as an experience of a lifetime.

You make decisions like these all the time without really knowing how your time compares to the cash value of it. And that's why it is important to figure out what your time is really worth, to better inform your decisions.

This time/worth calculation will help you spend your time effectively, ensure you're charging your true worth and your clients or customers respect your true worth.

1. Write down the amount of time you spend actually working (x).
2. Write down the amount of money you earn during that time (y).
3. Divide y by x and you get your hourly value.

It seems obvious really, but let's say you're a freelancer charging £50/hour, over a working year of 50 hours/week you are earning and, say, 44 weeks a year. Are you actually earning £110,000 a year? That's the value – the price, but what is your worth?

Perhaps a more accurate way of calculating your time's worth would be to compare what the market will pay. How much are other companies like you charging? What could you expect to be paid if you were employed, rather than self-employed? Do you have overheads to cover, training and specialist skills? Are you positioning yourself as a 'budget-friendly' or 'high-end' provider?

> **I wish I knew this before I started my first business**
>
> **Ideas are easy, shiny things are attractive, but the right execution is what it's all about**
>
> You may have a brilliant idea, but it means nothing without the discipline to execute what is required to make it real and bring it to life. You may have a new idea, but have you executed and tested the ideas from before? Do you need to execute it now or should it be parked for later?
>
> I encourage you to consider your vision, mission and purpose. Identify your high pay-off activities and focus on the proactive activity that influences your 'success drivers'. Yes, be creative, be innovative, but avoid looking for new ideas every minute. Also be wary of those new shiny things, as they are most often distractions and not the 'golden bullet' we hope for.
>
> It is common for entrepreneurs, who are trying to get the revenue engine going, to find things pretty repetitive and even boring. Not boring in the sense of you don't have anything to do, but just that we do a lot of the same thing every day and that's why people chase shiny objects, without actually realising that they were already on the right path to success if they gave it more time and are patient.

Key points

- How will you price and position your offering?
- What is the value of your time and what are you worth?

Additional resources

Books
Ries, R. (2011) *The Lean Startup*. Crown Currency.

Podcasts
www.impactpricing.com/podcast/.

Websites
www.kolenda.io/guides/pricing.

CHAPTER 8
HOW TO BUILD THE RIGHT TEAM

You may just want a lifestyle business that you can operate on your own but, if you want a business that is not reliant on you, then this chapter will help you consider when to hire, who to hire, how and what should be considered.

Will I need to employ people?

When starting a business or when you later want to expand, you will need to consider how to best resource the planned workload. Your considerations could include reorganisation, outsourcing, hiring temporary staff, obtaining training for yourself and any existing staff or recruiting new employees.

Before you look to hire people and the committed costs involved, you should understand whether you really need to recruit and if this matches the objectives of the business.

Recruitment should not be an unplanned decision just because the current workload suggests a need. You should consider if the current work is going to be consistent over a period of time, profitable enough for the recruitment you are planning and, if you were to take on people, would the requirement be part or full time? If or when you look to hire people, you need to make sure that you attract the right people and that they do what you recruited them to do in delivering your planned objectives.

Most successful entrepreneurs will acknowledge how key it is to have a reliable and skilled team around you. When considering your people requirements you need to look at what skills your business needs and plan how best to bring them into the team.

What is your skill gap? What skills do you need to improve your business? These will be role-specific skills such as marketing, finance, production, etc. but also consider how important the person-specific skills are to your business such as the ability to build relationships, a positive attitude, pressure management, their commitment to the business, etc.

Planning what people your business needs involves deciding whether you should employ staff, planning how to get the right people, considering how you are going to train them and how you will get the best return on your investment from them.

An employee can be defined as a full-time or part-time worker, a casual worker or a director.

Employing people has risks, costs and responsibility. At the start-up stage, if you cannot identify or sometimes afford the right person, first consider outsourcing activities that are not core to your business.

In summary, to maximise any recruitment and the return on the investment, look to:

- work out what skills and people you need
- decide which ways of hiring extra resources best suit the business
- review the advantages and disadvantages of employing people, if this is a consideration
- plan how you will find the right people
- understand how you will decide who to employ
- know the value of the role to the business to help decide a remuneration level
- know the detail of any role and how to communicate your expectation so that they deliver the intended result
- create an induction plan for all new recruits showing the role in detail, covering the legal requirements, your company philosophy and your expectations
- decide on a training plan for the people you employ.

When is the right time to hire my first employee?

There is not one answer that fits all when it comes to hiring your first employee and for most it is a big decision.

It is likely that, in the early stages of your business, you become the heart, soul and head of the business and your customers have an excellent relationship with you. The numbers may add up, the level of work needs more resources, but you may not feel wholly confident that another person can replicate that passion and dedication, or that you can nurture someone to become that person.

As a start-up who has grown, seemingly to the place where you can expand and take on an employee, it's nerve-wracking to think that you will be handing over the reputation of your business to someone else. What if they turn out to be a flop? What if you feel exposed as an inexperienced leader? What if you can't generate enough work for them?

First of all, relax. You're not alone.

It's been on your mind from the moment your business was conceived, whether subliminally or as an identified goal for the future, but there is always that stomach-churning moment when you ask yourself the big question: 'Is this the right time?'

Change your perspective.

One successful tactic is to look at your problem from another angle. In this instance, we can turn the question on its head and ask, 'Do I know when I shouldn't hire someone?'

Are you desperate for an extra pair of hands?

Decisions that will affect the future of your business, your clients' relationships with you or your cash flow should never be made under high stress. If you have more work than you can manage, there are other short-term measures you can take to alleviate the desperation so you can continue to deliver your promise to your customers. This allows you to get an objective view on your readiness to employ.

Is it clear what duties can be delegated?

Everything about you and your business will be unfamiliar to a new starter, no matter what their experience is. It might be unreasonable to expect them to be on the same level as you in the first few weeks and so the type of work you can ask them to do may need to be smaller, simpler tasks, with longer deadlines. That way it's easier for you to plan a defined set of responsibilities and expectations for them and allow time to review their work before it is committed. Which leads me to ask ...

Do you have time to commit to nurturing?

Your new employee will need handholding and guidance in the first few weeks so, if you don't have time to support them, or you don't have confidence in leaving them to manage themselves for a while, then you may not be ready to hire.

Getting strategic

There is a way to recognise that moment when the decision to hire is the right thing to do.

Write down all the indicators that would give you confidence to hire that person. For example, the level of work you have in progress, or in your pipeline, your cash flow and reserves or the capacity of your existing team/yourself. Once this feels more comfortable than uncomfortable, you have a factual basis on which to make your decision. It's a great way of linking your gut feeling with the facts.

You may have a defined role for them in mind, you have the time for guidance and training, and you're not overpromising your customers. Here are a few strategic questions to double check it's the right time to hire an employee:

- Will the work they do generate income?
- Will the work they do save the business money?
- Does the new person bring a new skill set to your business?

In the early days of business, making money is often more important than saving it, so if your expenditure for an employee outweighs the income they will generate, you may need to look at what other values they will bring. What additional skills do they have, do they have an established network of contacts and how can they fortify your products or services?

These points fall into your 'impact measures', considering what your business needs are, what you want and expect from your candidate, in addition to the traditional job description and person specification. Together, these provide you with a sound framework for communicating your expectations at the interview and also measuring those early days in terms of performance, without bringing emotion into the relationship.

What you need to do right now

The process of hiring your first employee can be overwhelming, so ask others how they found the same process themselves and find a recruitment strategy that works for you. Then create an action plan with clear steps to follow as you take the journey from no employees to your first.

Recruitment – building your team of talent

One of the biggest challenges for businesses looking to start, scale and grow is recruitment. The attraction of talent can be tough but not impossible if you know who you want and for what impact.

When you take on people either as employees or as an outsourced resource, you should first identify your specific requirements and plan how to fill your vacancy to ensure you get the best person for the role.

During any recruitment process, you must treat all candidates fairly and avoid any discrimination in terms of areas such as their sex, race, age, sexual orientation, religion or belief, or because they have a disability.

First, build a picture of the perfect person to work with you, to meet the needs of the business and match your values. How much will be down to their skill or how important is their character and attitude?

The common place to start is to prepare a job description and person specification. This would include your essential and desirable requirements. A job description can be useful for understanding the scope of the work, how best to advertise, and for clarification with applicants who will have to do the job. They are also useful later when you are reviewing the performance of your recruit.

As a minimum, a job description should include:

- details on the position, including the job title and to whom they would report
- the job's location

- a summary of the role's objectives
- a list of the main duties or tasks of the person.

Before you start searching for potential employees, it's essential to define the type of candidate you want to attract. This begins with understanding the specific skills, experience and personality traits that would make someone successful in the role.

A person specification is useful to help you describe who you want and what you will look for in the candidate. It is usual to include the knowledge, experience and skills you would like them to have, separating those that are essential for the job from those that are desirable. Also include any values that you expect to be aligned to you or your business. Creating a detailed candidate persona, similar to a customer persona in marketing, will help you focus your efforts and ensure that you're reaching out to the right people.

Consider the following questions when defining your ideal candidate:

- What skills and qualifications are non-negotiable for this role?
- What experience level are you looking for?
- What cultural fit and personality traits are important to your company?
- What are the long-term career goals of your ideal candidate?

You should also be clear about what you are offering the person. Is it a full- or part-time position, permanent or temporary role, what working conditions will you provide, and what terms and conditions will you offer such as a contract overview including, pay scales, holiday, sick pay, etc? This way, there are no surprises or disappointments that can lead to the right person leaving the business in the short term.

Also consider an 'impact statement'. This extends the job description beyond what they will be doing to include the expected impact that they will have. Consider what return on investment you want for recruiting in this role. How would you later measure the return on investment? For example, if you are hiring a sales person, then have their targets in mind, such as their sales target. Then you can also share this in the interview process to sound out their confidence in achieving those objectives.

Once you know who you want and what you can offer them, you now need to go and find the right person. Finding the right team members is crucial to the growth and success of your business. Like attracting customers it's again time to sell your business, sell your vision.

In essence, recruiting is very much like marketing, both require a well-defined strategy, precise targeting and choosing the right channels to reach your desired audience.

Just as with your marketing, you need to understand your target audience and have a clear understanding of the person you want to attract and where to find them. Then you can sell them your business, in this case as the place to work.

Where do your ideal candidates hang out?

Just like your different customer segments frequent different platforms, your potential employees are likely to be found in specific places depending on their industry, experience level and interests. Identifying these 'hangouts' will help you focus your recruitment efforts on the channels where your ideal candidates are most active.

An important point here is to reflect on where the ideal candidate who is *not* looking for a new job is hanging out, as I suspect you'd like to attract them also.

The most common options to help you find suitable people are advertising the vacancy, using a recruitment agency or approaching the job centre. Advertising can be undertaken in printed copy such as newspapers or magazines or online. If you opt for printed adverts, then choose publications that are likely to be read by your targeted person.

To decide on the best method, you need to consider where your ideal person is right now and what they will be doing, watching or reading. For example, if your ideal candidate is likely to be in employment and busy working for someone else, then perhaps they need to be head hunted, as it is unlikely they are reading the job vacancies in your local newspaper. So, an agency with a database of candidates to suit your ideal profile would be beneficial. Although agencies are considered to be more expensive, you have to consider this against how much you want to be involved in the process and the cost of your time. The right agency will help you source candidates, attract their interest and review the CVs.

Here are some common platforms and approaches for finding talent:

1 **Online job boards and marketplaces**
    - LinkedIn: the go-to platform for professional networking, LinkedIn is ideal for recruiting experienced professionals and specialists.

Use LinkedIn's advanced search tools and sponsored job postings to reach a targeted audience. Who are the movers and shakers in your sector? Can you attract them?

- Indeed and Glassdoor: these are excellent for reaching a broad audience across various industries. The detailed company profiles and employee reviews on Glassdoor can also help attract candidates who are aligned with your company culture.

- Industry-specific job boards: for niche roles, industry-specific job boards are invaluable. For example, GitHub Jobs for developers or Behance for creative professionals.

2 **Social media platforms**

- Facebook and Instagram: leveraging targeted ads and organic posts about your company culture can attract candidates who resonate with your brand's values. With paid ads you can serve a post to your target persona.

- X (formally known as Twitter): a great platform for engaging in industry-related conversations and identifying potential candidates through hashtags and mentions.

3 **Networking events and industry conferences**

- Attending and sponsoring industry events is a fantastic way to meet potential employees face to face. These events are also great for showcasing your company as a leader in your field, which can attract top talent.

- Consider hosting or participating in webinars, panels or workshops. These events can position your company as an authority and provide an opportunity to connect with highly engaged individuals.

- Does anyone in your network know your ideal candidate?

4 **Employee referrals**

- Your current employees are one of your best resources for finding new talent. Encourage them to refer candidates from their professional networks, and consider implementing a referral bonus programme to incentivise this. It is common for people to hang out with people similar to them, so this can be an effective recruitment strategy.

5 **Universities and colleges**
   - For entry-level positions or internships, partnering with universities and colleges can be highly effective. Attend job fairs, collaborate on projects, or offer guest lectures to connect with students and recent graduates.

What's in it for them?

Once you've identified where your potential employees are, the next step is crafting a compelling message that will attract them. Just as in marketing, your message should focus on what's in it for the candidate. Highlight what makes your company an attractive place to work, whether it's your company culture, growth opportunities or the impact they can make.

To many potential candidates you are the best kept secret, so you have to sell your business as the place they need to work and capture their interest to lean forward.

Share your mission, vision, purpose and values to attract potential candidates with your story and engage them with the desire to support your why. This will all help you to sell the business to them. Much like attracting a customer, you will need to sell your business and vision to the talent you wish to attract.

Make sure your job postings and recruitment materials are clear, concise and reflect your company's brand voice. Tailor your messaging to the platforms and channels you're using; for example, a job post on LinkedIn might be more formal, whilst a post on Instagram could be more casual and visually engaging.

Finding your potential employees is not just about posting a job and waiting for applications to roll in. It requires a strategic approach, similar to marketing, where you identify your target audience, find out where they spend their time, and share a message that pulls them towards you with interest.

Your search should encourage interested prospects to send you a completed application form, CV and references.

You could also ask them to send you a video answering the three questions you'd first ask at an interview. This is especially useful when shortlisting for customer-facing roles.

The next stage is to decide who you will shortlist and interview.

With an application form, which you have designed to gather the information you want, you now have a consistent method from which to compare your candidates' skills and experience.

The CV and references should confirm information stated on their application form such as facts like their last job to supporting claims made in the application about their ability.

Hopefully, you receive a number of applications that enables you to create a preferred shortlist and invite those to attend an interview. The best way to draw up a shortlist is to refer back to your job description and person specification and decide who meets more of the requirements you have documented.

At this stage, consider how you may assess the candidates beyond their application and CV. It is common practice to ask for a test or exercise to be completed or even completing personality profile assessments.

Next is the interview process

When it comes to the interviews of your shortlist, you should be consistent with your questions to all candidates and have a record of your discussion. The questions you ask should be planned in advance to draw out the additional information you desire. It is recommended to have a method for identifying your best candidate such as scoring the response to each question. This approach would also support your decision if ever challenged.

As well as interviewing, as part of the process you may ask the candidates to undertake a form of test. This could be practical tests, psychometric tests or assessment centres that are generally used for senior appointments, but can be used for any role.

Your objective from the interview and any testing is to find the right person with the competence and ability to do the job, who suits the business and can become the right person.

Once you've decided on the candidates that you wish to hire, then it is time to make a formal offer to them. This is often undertaken by telephone for a quick response or by email or letter.

What's your role?

From day one, understand the roles you are doing and which hat you are wearing at what time. This mindful approach will help you to clearly identify what you enjoy, what you are good at and where you add most value for your business.

There will be a point in your business journey when you will have to ask yourself 'What is my role?' Too often, a business owner will stay involved in everything and often continue meddling when they don't need to be involved. Trust the talent you have hired, give direction and get out of their way.

Some business owners automatically position themselves at the top of the organisation as the managing director or CEO just because they are the owner. However, is that the best for the business? Would it be better to hire a leader in this role and utilise your own skills elsewhere in the business?

Your role may be linked to a specific task in the business, especially in the early days. Your role may be strategic and leading the business. A good question to keep in mind and to ask yourself (or those close to you) is: 'What would I hire myself to do and pay myself what I want to earn from the business?'

When reflecting on your roles within your business, take a moment to examine how reliant those tasks are on you and whether you really need to do them yourself to get the task completed to the same standard.

Another good question to consider when reflecting on your role is: 'How will I exit this business?' The reflection on this question will help you consider the structure and resources you need to make that happen and therefore where you place yourself in the interim.

A good way to identify your best role and your future people requirements is to draw out your ideal organisational chart. What roles do you need in your business and where do they fit together? An organisational chart is a visual representation of your structure, including job titles, roles and reporting relationships. It is typically created using boxes and lines to show how different departments or teams fit together and who reports to whom.

To help you consider your best role in the business, map your current responsibilities into one of these boxes to help identify what you can or should let go of.

Only I can do this	I must/need to do this
I want to do this	This can be done by delegation/automation or not at all

How do I move from working 'in' the business to working 'on' the business?

This may not feel like a consideration for a start-up business, but for sure it is one that often needs to be made earlier than it often is.

If you stay working 'in' the business too long then that may bring constraints to the business and make it harder to unwrap in the long term.

As covered by Michael E. Gerber in his book *The E-Myth*, your journey as a business owner should consider how you move from a technician (doing the business), to being the manager, to then investor of resources into your business.

Often, it is a challenge of letting go or it is related to the management of profits for reinvestment in future resources such as systems or people.

It's a case of navigating the transition from operational involvement to strategic leadership in the business.

The entrepreneurial journey often involves a pivotal shift: moving from working 'in' your business, where you're caught up in day-to-day operations, often firefighting and being the bottleneck, to working 'on' your business, where you focus on growth and strategy. This shift is crucial for sustainable business development, scaling and, most importantly, your enjoyment and personal fulfilment.

Here are some thoughts to help you master the shift:

First, let's be clear on the difference:

- **Working 'in' the business:** this typically involves handling daily tasks, solving immediate problems, and being deeply involved in the operational aspects. Quite often working on tasks that appear urgent and important.
- **Working 'on' the business:** here, the focus is on strategic planning, growth opportunities, long-term goals, marketing plans and system improvements. These are those tasks that are so often put to one side until you have time (which you rarely have!) and are perceived as also important but not urgent, but they are!

The shift to working 'on' the business is essential for many reasons, but here are the top three:

1 **Sustainability:** working 'on' the business ensures long-term growth and survival.
2 **Personal growth:** it allows for more personal development and strategic thinking.
3 **Scalability:** focusing on the bigger picture makes scaling the business more achievable.

Transitioning from working 'in' your business to working 'on' it is a gradual process that requires patience, planning and a mindset shift. Here's a step-by-step guide to help you make the shift:

1 **Delegation is key**
   Ask yourself where you add most value. What role you would do if you were employing yourself? Start by identifying the roles you don't have to undertake anymore. Identify tasks that can be delegated (e.g. those that distract or interrupt you from what you need to do). Look to invest in training your team to handle these tasks efficiently.

2 **Implement systems and processes**
   Map out your processes to establish what can be automated, delegated, outsourced in full or in part. Create standard operating procedures for routine tasks and utilise technology for automation where possible.

3 **Set clear goals and objectives**
   Define what success looks like in the long term and break down these goals into actionable steps.

4 **Regularly schedule strategic planning time**
   Dedicate specific time blocks for strategic planning. Use this time to review goals, purpose and progress, and adjust strategies.

5 **Schedule time for execution**
   Book time in your diary for working 'on' the business that you value as much as an appointment. Can you commit x minutes per day, week or month for execution of strategic activities?

6 **Build a strong team around you**
   Hire for skills that complement yours. Encourage new team members to first follow your systems (as that's the best way you've found to do it so far), and then utilise their creativity and innovation to improve them. Continually cultivate a culture of responsibility and ownership.

7 **Seek mentorship and coaching**
   Engage with mentors and business coaches to see the things you don't see or challenge you with the questions you don't know to ask. Gain insights and advice from the experience of others.

8 **Learn to let go**
   Focus your energy on areas where you add the most value – strategy and growth. Then find your way to trust your team to handle operational tasks. What needs to happen for this to happen?

9 **Measure and adjust**
   Regularly review business performance against your strategic goals. Have a set of KPIs that focus on activity and outcomes to easily measure performance. No grey areas! Reduce the gut feeling with data and fact to justify your investment! Be prepared to adjust your strategies based on these insights.

> ### Remember this
> ### What would your ideal team look like?
>
> Draw out an organisational chart that highlights the support you would need in all areas of your business. Also consider the structure of the team (e.g. reporting lines).
>
> All the roles may have your name on for now, but it will help you consider the resources you need in the future and the first roles to let go off!

Subcontractor vs employee – considering internal vs external

Choosing the right type of workforce is crucial for the success and growth of your company. Often, cash flow and timing seem to control the choices made by businesses, but are there other considerations?

When considering the expansion of your team, we are often faced with the decision between hiring subcontractors or employees. Both options have their own unique benefits and are suited to different business needs.

Let's look at the key differences and benefits of each.

Hiring a subcontractor	Hiring an employee
Flexibility and scalability: ● Project-based engagement: subcontractors are typically hired for specific projects or tasks, allowing businesses to scale their workforce up or down based on project demands. ● Specialised skills: they bring specialised expertise that might not be needed on a full-time basis, providing access to high-level skills without long-term commitment.	Stability and commitment: ● Consistent workforce: employees are more likely to be committed to the company's long-term goals, providing stability and consistency in the workforce. ● Company culture: full-time employees are integral to building and maintaining the company's culture, contributing to a cohesive and motivated team environment.

▶

Hiring a subcontractor	Hiring an employee
Cost-effectiveness: • No employment benefits: businesses do not have to pay for benefits such as health insurance, pension contributions, or holidays and sick pay, which reduces overall labour costs. • Reduced overheads: subcontractors often work remotely or use their own equipment, saving on office space and resources. • National insurance savings: provided the sub-contractor does not fall under the IR35 rules, you do not pay the Employers National Insurance percentage on their fee.	Control and availability: • Direct management: esmployers have more control over how employees perform their tasks, allowing for better alignment with company procedures and standards. • Full-time availability: employees are available during set working hours, ensuring their presence and participation in daily operations and long-term projects. Subcontractors may be balancing a number of jobs/clients at the same time.
Administrative simplicity: • Fewer legal obligations: hiring subcontractors involves fewer regulatory and administrative responsibilities compared to employees, such as tax withholdings and compliance with employment laws. • Easier termination: ending a subcontractor's contract is generally simpler and less risky than terminating an employee, avoiding potential legal complications.	Development and loyalty: • Skill development: investing in employees through training and development can enhance their skills, loyalty and productivity, benefiting the business in the long run. • Career growth: providing opportunities for career advancement can lead to higher employee satisfaction and retention, reducing turnover rates and associated costs.

The key differences:

- **Engagement type:** subcontractors are hired for specific projects or periods, whilst employees are hired for ongoing roles within the company.
- **Cost structure:** subcontractors usually invoice for their work, whereas employees receive a regular salary with additional employment benefits.
- **Legal obligations:** hiring employees entails adhering to employment laws and regulations, whereas subcontractors are generally responsible for their own taxes and legal obligations.
- **Control and integration:** employers have more control over employees' work processes and their integration into the company, whilst subcontractors maintain more autonomy over their methods and schedules.

Deciding between hiring a subcontractor and an employee depends on your business needs, financial considerations and the nature of the work. Assess your business goals and operational requirements to determine which option aligns best with your strategy in the short and long term.

> **Remember this**
>
> Your first hire does not have to be a full-time employee.
>
> Would your initial requirement be best covered by a part-time resource, subcontractor, virtual assistant, etc?
>
> Thinking this way helps you to build your resources as you scale the business.

You lead what you breed

Your leadership will have a profound impact on your team's behaviour.

'You lead what you breed' encapsulates a truth that many overlook: as a leader, your influence shapes the behaviour, attitudes and performance of your team. Leadership is not merely a position; it's a responsibility that extends beyond strategy and operations. It reaches into the very fabric of your organisation's culture and team dynamics.

The ripple effect of leadership

Imagine a stone thrown into a pond. The ripples expand outward, touching every part of the water's surface. Similarly, a leader's actions, decisions and demeanour ripple through the team, creating an environment that either supports growth and innovation or breeds discontent and stagnation.

You set the tone. Every action, word and even silence from a leader sets the tone for the team. Are you approachable and open to new ideas, or do you shut down suggestions and discourage dialogue? Your approach to leadership can either encourage a culture of collaboration or create an atmosphere of fear and rigidity. For instance, leaders who prioritise transparency and open communication often find that their teams are more engaged and proactive. Conversely, those who lead with an iron fist and secrecy may notice a decline in morale and an increase in staff turnover.

Your leadership will model the behaviour of others. Your team looks to you as a role model. If you demonstrate integrity, dedication and a positive attitude, your team is likely to mirror these qualities. On the other hand, if you exhibit inconsistency, negativity or a lack of commitment, expect to see these reflected in your team's behaviour.

Consider the impact of a leader who regularly acknowledges and rewards hard work. Such recognition can inspire team members to strive for excellence and build a culture of appreciation and motivation.

Leadership is also about creating an environment where continuous learning and development are valued. How will you encourage the development of your people? By investing in your team's growth, you not only enhance their skills but also demonstrate your commitment to their professional journey. This investment can cultivate loyalty and drive, creating a team that is not only capable but also dedicated.

Leaders who actively mentor and support their team members' career aspirations often see higher levels of job satisfaction and performance resulting in a greater return on investment. This signals that you care about their success, leading to increased engagement and a stronger, more cohesive team.

A leader who takes responsibility for their actions and decisions sets a powerful example. Accountability breeds accountability. When team members see that their leader owns up to mistakes and works to rectify them, they are more likely to adopt a similar approach. This culture of accountability can lead to improved problem solving and a more resilient team.

How will you build trust? Trust is the cornerstone of effective leadership. Without it, teams can struggle with communication, collaboration and cohesion. As a leader, building trust requires consistency, honesty and empathy.

The leadership style you adopt today will shape the team you have tomorrow.

Leaders who focus on cultivating a positive, supportive and dynamic work environment will likely see long-term success and sustainability. They breed teams that are not only high-performing but also resilient and adaptable in the face of challenges.

Remember that 'You lead what you breed'. The legacy of your leadership will be reflected in the behaviour, attitude and success of your team. Strive to be the leader who inspires, supports and guides with integrity and vision. The results will speak for themselves, not just in metrics and milestones, but in the thriving, motivated and engaged team that surrounds you.

Lead by example! Model the behaviour you want to see in your employees. Demonstrate a strong work ethic, ethical behaviours and a commitment to live by the values of your organisation.

Lead wisely and breed success.

Aligning your team for success

You get a great business idea, it works! You work really hard to develop your business and find you need to introduce a team of people to help you. *But*! As you build the team, you are not sure the team members are all working towards the same goal as you. You suspect they have their own agenda and may not be as passionate about the objectives as you.

To ensure the whole team is on the same path and pulling together to help you reach your goals, you need to understand what that team should look like and, importantly, how to create a positive environment and a business culture that cultivates true teamwork.

Your success will be defined by you but, if it is to have a business that operates without you, what would happen to your business today if you weren't around and what needs to happen to ensure it runs like clockwork without you in the future?

What is the right environment for excellent teamwork? Simply put, it is an environment where everyone understands the mission, vision, values and purpose of the business and are committed to delivering it.

1 **Your mission:** what are you going to do every day?
2 **Your vision:** the goal you're using your business to work towards.
3 **Your values:** the things that are important to you and define your attitude to your business, customers, suppliers and employees.
4 **Your purpose:** the big *why*!

When communicated and understood properly, they can be hugely valuable to aligning your team with your goal.

These four things are vital pieces of the puzzle and, by having clarity on them in your own mind, only serves to help your team understand them better. It will also give you the confidence to give your team ownership and autonomy because they've now got the framework within which they can operate.

How to roll out your mission, vision, values and purpose (MVVP)

Communicating these important factors in your business will eventually come naturally, once they are front of your mind. However, it is essential to lead by example when it comes to managing the environment and culture in your business. If you want your team to be aligned with your own MVVP you have to show them you are committed yourself. A boss who shows up late, looking dishevelled or unprepared is not someone you want to work hard for.

You may also display posters in the office, use your MVVP in your business tag line, email footers and social media platforms, or mention them every time you have a meeting with your team. Living by your mission, vision, values and purpose will soon highlight those who are aligned, and those who may need more understanding.

Ten ways to create a culture that attracts, retains and boosts productivity

There are some organisations with amazing cultures that they have no issue attracting the talent they desire and retaining them. On the other hand, there are many toxic cultures that can't easily attract people due to their reputation and they leak staff most weeks despite paying above average.

Creating a culture that attracts, retains and boosts productivity can be challenging and will need an investment of resources but here are some tips to help you achieve this:

1. Communicate a clear mission and set of values to your employees so they know what your organisation stands for and what you are working to achieve. Create a sense of purpose and belonging.
2. Pay your employees fairly and offer a competitive compensation *and* benefits package that reflects the value they bring to your organisation. Design a benefits package that ticks their box not yours!
3. Create a positive work environment where employees feel valued, respected and supported. Make sure your workplace is clean, organised and comfortable. Encourage employees to take breaks and socialise with each other.
4. To boost productivity and engagement, create and provide opportunities for your employees to learn and grow in their roles, such as training programmes, mentorship and coaching.
5. Lead an open and collaborative environment where employees feel comfortable sharing their ideas, opinions and feedback. Encourage teamwork and communication across the whole organisation.
6. Employees who feel empowered to make decisions are more likely to be engaged and productive. Give employees the authority to make decisions. Give them permission to fail.

7 Recognise, celebrate and reward employees who perform well, whether through bonuses, promotions or other forms of recognition. Recognise this in private and in public. This can help to boost morale and motivation.
8 Encourage work/life balance by providing flexible work arrangements. This can help to reduce stress and burnout.
9 Promote diversity and inclusion to support a more productive workforce. Make sure your organisation's culture is welcoming to people of all backgrounds.
10 When hiring new employees, look for candidates who share your company values and are a good cultural fit. This will help to ensure that everyone is aligned and working towards a common goal.

Remember this

The culture of your business starts and ends with you!

Considerations when becoming a manager for the first time

When your business has grown to the point when you're ready to take on new people, you essentially have two choices, become an employer or take on subcontractors.

It's important to note at this point that you do *not* need to become a limited company to employ staff, but you do need to register the change with His Majesty's Revenue & Customs (HMRC).

When your business is ready to hire internally or externally, you are likely to have systemised processes in place. They may be written down but most likely are just the best way you have found to do the thing you do. Now is the time to look at those processes and ensure they are ready to be shared with another person who is new to your business.

- Are there enough processes in place?
- Can they be easily followed by a fresh pair of eyes?
- Can the processes be modified by your employee or subcontractor?
- Are you available to train and guide your employee or subcontractor?
- How will you measure performance against the process?

If you don't have processes in place, you are now presented with the opportunity to not only write up the priority tasks but delegate some responsibility to your employee to complete the 'process file' or your standard operating procedures. It is a great opportunity to create and document your processes. You can verbally induct and train the new team member but ask them to write this up as a process. This also enables you to check their understanding!

Having your systems and procedures makes it very clear how you want the tasks to be completed in the first instance before inviting the innovation and creativity for further improvement.

When becoming a manager for the first time, here are some considerations whether you choose to employ or subcontract extra help:

- Register with HMRC as an employer (if employed resource).
- Decide whether you'll need an office, coworking space or remote conferencing communications.
- Decide what 'perks' can be offered and what career progression opportunities are available.
- Write up the job description, expectations and reward.
- How many hours and what length of contract can you offer?
- How much can you pay them?
- Write up the contract and get it checked with an HR professional for legality (or get it written by them).
- Get employer's liability insurance (for employees and labour-only subcontractors).
- Set up and manage a workplace pension scheme (for employees only).
- Provide guidelines on work culture.
- Engage with an HR professional to find out what workplace manuals and guides need to be written.
- Engage with your accountant for payroll and taxation advice.

The key difference when becoming a manager is that you are moving away from being the implementor and becoming responsible for the activities of another person in your business.

Another consideration is the type of manager you want to be. This may need exploration with a coach or friend, but how do you want to manage, what do you want to be known for as a manager and what is your identity? This will also include how you inspire your people, their performance and productivity.

Employment documentation and payroll

It is important that you meet the laws and regulations in your operating country around recruiting and employing staff.

The main considerations are employment law, contract law, health and safety and equal opportunities. As these laws are always being reviewed and updated, it is recommended that you seek the expertise of a qualified adviser in these areas.

You would need to ensure that all employees are:

- given a job offer with the job description
- provided with a contract of employment
- asked to read the staff handbook that includes the disciplinary and grievance procedures.

Even if you do not issue a written contract of employment, you are under a legal duty to provide most employees with a written statement of their main employment particulars within a period of time from starting their employment with you.

Depending on the size of your business or the role the employee is undertaking, it is likely you will have to share your written health and safety documentation, which will include your health and safety statement, risk assessments and safe systems at work.

It is recommended that all sub-contractors and outsourced resources are also aware of any health and safety requirements.

As a business, you will be required to operate a payroll.

The first consideration is whether you have the skill, expertise and desire to run the payroll function. If not, then consider outsourcing this to your accountant or a specialist provider.

There are many rules and regulations that apply, especially if your payroll includes sick pay, maternity leave, bonus calculations, deductions such as pensions and a mix of pay rates.

You may also consider a software package to calculate the payroll for you, but you should not simply rely on the software as the expert, as any software is only as good as the user or information provided.

When running a payroll there are also payments and returns that are required to be made within certain deadlines.

This section primarily references the requirements for a business based in the UK. As a reminder, we recommend that you always seek guidance from local professional advisers to understand your local laws and policies wherever you are located.

Inducting your team into the business

It is recommended to give all your new starters an induction. All inductions should be structured so that the messages and information are consistent. A professionally organised and delivered induction is your new employees' first impression of you and your organisation. A good induction will help to retain your new employees in those early months. An induction is the initial activity to welcome your new employee before any formal training plan is started.

An induction helps your employees to understand the business and where they fit in, get motivated to do their best, become productive earlier, understand the job more effectively, understand any health and safety obligations and acknowledge the culture of the business.

An induction can last a few hours to a few months depending on the business and the role. It can be delivered in groups (with care) or most often on a one-to-one basis. The content of an induction should be planned to ensure that interest and concentration are maintained. It is bad practice to just push the new employee around the business to the next person who has some time to show them something else.

The main areas to cover in an induction include:

- Any administration such as pension scheme, handbooks, uniforms, etc.
- Any clarification in the terms and conditions of employment especially the working hours, breaks, sickness and disciplinary and grievance procedures.
- The provision of health and safety information including the business' health and safety policy and fire safety procedures.
- A tour of the premises.
- An introduction to colleagues, especially the owners, line manager, human resources manager and health and safety officer.

- An introduction to the job.
- If their job involves the use or operation of machinery or equipment, you must ensure that they are properly trained, that they understand any associated risks, and that they have the appropriate safety equipment.

Either you or your human resources manager should also ensure that you have all the required paperwork to add the new employee to the payroll immediately as you do not want to leave it until it is too late and you cannot pay them at the first attempt.

Training and development

Training should be an integral part of your business strategy, planning and staff development. It establishes you have a culture of continuous improvement in your business.

Maximising the skills of your staff will help your business success. By providing timely and effective training, you will benefit from your employees' full potential and this will help improve your business performance.

When considering the training requirements of your team, we can break this into three areas:

1. What the business is required to undertake to meet its legal obligations.
2. What training is required to enable the business to operate effectively.
3. What is required to develop the skills and knowledge of your individual employees.

Meeting your legal obligations may include health and safety training or the training of first aiders and fire marshals. If you are a food business, you will need a food hygiene certificate.

The training required to operate effectively will include vehicle, equipment or machinery training. It will also include internal training covering the business systems and standard operations that exist, but this is personal to your business.

A training need is identified when there is a gap in the existing skills and knowledge of your employee. The best way to assess an individual's training requirement is to identify their skill gap with a training needs analysis.

Information to help identify the training need is usually gathered from other employees' comments, management observation, customer feedback or by admission of the employee themselves.

To avoid any discrimination, we suggest you undertake such an analysis for all your employees on an ongoing basis and ensure that all employees can have access to the training you provide, if relevant to them.

Before implementing any training programme in your business, it is important to find the training method that will suit both your business and your employees. You should consider the pros and cons for each type of training before deciding which type to use in your business. The popular options for training staff include taking time to train someone yourself, sending staff on courses, distance learning, work-based training qualifications or getting someone in to run an inhouse course.

Once you have decided upon the training requirements of your team, it is advisable to complete a training plan for the business, which then provides you with an ongoing reference document. This training plan will cover the training requirements of all your team, the expected delivery dates for effective absence planning and will also record when the training has been undertaken. A good training plan is a useful resource to the business as it will identify any trends in the business that highlight areas for greater focus either at the induction stage or ongoing. It is recommended that each employee should have a personal training record, which also includes copies of any certification evidence.

> **Remember this**
>
> Get it right the first time.
>
> No, not the person you hire, as you may have to go through some poor hires until you get the best ones. But do get the documentation, induction and training right, as that will save you pain in the long run.

People management

Managing the performance of your team will be an important part of helping you reach your business objectives.

If your recruitment has been planned and effective, if you have a good training plan, if your vision and goals have been communicated to the team and everyone is clear what action needs to be undertaken to achieve those business objectives, then, in basic terms, it is down to individual and collective performance if the objective is met or not.

The process of effective performance management starts with effective communication. Have you effectively communicated to the employees your expectations of them? Do they know how they contribute to the business? And have you clearly advised them of their specific responsibilities in relation to their role?

You should have a culture in your business that has the opportunity for the members of your team to raise their concerns, difficulties or training requirements.

An effective tool to encourage this two-way communication is regular appraisals or performance reviews, even casual conversations. At these meetings, it is good practice to review the job description as a conversation between the employee and manager. Together, review the role step by step together with a summary of the individual's performance.

The conversation must cover three matters. Are they delivering the expectations and meeting the key performance indicators associated with their role? Are they still engaged and driving to deliver the purpose? What support do they need to help them deliver what you need from them?

If there is an underperformance, the reason should be identified and explored to determine a valid reason and, if so, together you should establish the action required to improve. This is an opportunity for you, or the manager, to coach the employee, identify a training need or discuss actions that need to be taken to improve their performance.

A difficult conversation may be needed but is easy to avoid. If such a conversation is needed, then plan it, book it and do it. When such conversations are avoided, the problem often escalates and can be much more difficult to resolve.

For any new employees, it is recommended to include a probationary period in the terms of employment so that, if the performance does not improve, it is much easier to dismiss that employee during this period.

For established employees, you should not be afraid to use your disciplinary procedures, including meetings, warnings and dismissals.

On a day-to-day basis, the performance of your team can be managed with quality-control methods. Having standards, processes and expectations to be adhered to can quickly highlight any underperformance.

A simple management resource is a scoring system. Score each employee/worker against a framework and score between 1 and 5, 1 and 10, etc. Do this periodically, and without reference to the last, so as to highlight reductions and help you consider why.

Such a good scoring resource is the 'Skill vs Will Matrix' as developed by Paul Hersey and Ken Blanchard, who created the Situational Leadership Model in the 1970s. This matrix is a tool that helps you and your managers to assess an employee's performance by evaluating their Skill (an employee's competency to do the role) vs Will (the employee's motivation). The tool helps to identify if they need more support in developing their skills or supporting their motivation. When someone starts with you, then hopefully their motivation, their will is high, but they perhaps need some development or internal training to develop their competency, so their skill is mid to low. With support and training, they then have high will and high skill but, as is often seen, an individual loses interest, gets bored in the role and, despite maintaining the skill, their will slips backwards. Again, regularly scoring your employees on this matrix will highlight areas for discussion or focus.

> ## I wish I knew this before I started my first business
>
> Expect failure … it is part of the journey.
>
> Setbacks are your best teachers, but don't let them stifle your momentum. Consider how you can learn, pivot and keep moving forward, and look at every outcome as a lesson.
>
> Whether positive or negative, every result teaches you something valuable.
>
> Each time you execute an activity, you will get a result. It may not be the outcome you wanted, but every outcome presents a lesson. Is it something to repeat, something to tweak or something to avoid for now? I encourage you to embrace setbacks as they are really steps forward in disguise.

Key points

- What would be the trigger points that prompt you to hire your first employee?
- What does your organisational chart look like and what is your role in the ideal structure?
- As a leader, what will be the culture associated with your organisation?
- How will you attract, recruit and retain the talent you need for your organisation?
- What training and development do you need before you become a manager?

Additional resources

Books
Erikson, T. (2019) *Surrounded by Idiots*. St. Martin's Essentials.

CHAPTER 9
HOW TO EXCEED YOUR CUSTOMERS' EXPECTATIONS

You may have experienced this yourself when buying from others. Quite often, the customer is taken for granted, especially during the after-purchase experience.

In this chapter, we will consider your customer journey, feedback and the delivery of your promise to ensure you remain customer centric at essential moments if not always.

Put the customer experience at the core of your business

Will your business be customer centric and, if not, why not?

Customer service is the support you offer your customers, both before and after they buy, and then use your products or services, with the objective of ensuring they have an easy and enjoyable experience at every touch point with you.

It is often a direct one-on-one interaction between a consumer making a purchase and a representative of the company that is selling it. However, a customer's experience may be related to the useability of any digital platform. It is an interaction and experience that often highly influences the decision to purchase, even when the potential buyer knows that they want to buy.

Good customer service will help you to:

- build your customer loyalty
- increase the total spend by each customer

- retain your customer for longer and increase the lifetime value of your customer relationships
- encourage your customer to buy from you more often
- generate positive word-of-mouth about your business
- gain competitive advantage.

Good customer service often relates to the provision of timely, attentive, engaged service to a customer, and making sure their needs and expectations are met in a manner that reflects positively on the business and its brand.

You may argue that the outcome of good customer service is a sale that does not result in a return, complaint or negative comment, or a repeat order or recommendation.

If your service is not experienced positively by the customer in the first instance, then there is often an opportunity to recover the relationship. For example, effective complaint handling by your returns team.

Good customer service may come naturally to some people, and others may develop these skills with good training. Remove people who obviously can't or don't want to offer such an experience from such positions.

The skills and characteristics often needed include:

- listening
- patience and calmness
- attentiveness
- integrity
- trustworthiness
- communication
- product knowledge
- persuasion
- empathy and compassion
- body language
- courtesy
- consistency
- proactiveness.

Good customer service is a cycle. Your business delivers a level of service that impacts your customers and reflects in how your team feel. So keep it positive!

Customer service is often a series of planned and systemised activities in your business that ensures that your product or service delivers high levels of satisfaction and exceeds the expectations of your customer.

It is far too easy to get this wrong by not listening to your customers and doing what you think they want.

Your activities should be before, during and after a purchase. It is just as important to consider your service delivery whether you sell a product or if you offer a service.

You should consider every time a customer touches your business and then consider what you have to do to ensure that the customer experience is exceptional every single time. Every time a customer interacts with your business you have the opportunity to improve your reputation with them.

Not one service will fit all. A positive experience will be more important to some customers than others. Can you segment your customers and identify possible different expectations for different customer groups?

It may also be that the service experience is expected at different stages of their journey with you. For example, on placing the order it may be a different expectation than when they receive the delivery. Or when they want to complain!

Excellent service delivery can be more important in some businesses than others and will vary according to your industry. For example, online businesses will not need the face-to-face positive contact, but will need order efficiency, after-sales care, complaint handling and effective delivery channels. Or as a retailer you will have the face-to-face contact expectation, but how good are the telephone manners of your staff if a customer calls before visiting and what is the returns policy?

Customer service will be more important in some employees' roles than others; however, every role in the business should have a customer service focus. It is obvious to us that we should train receptionists, sales staff and any role meeting the customer in customer service. However, what about the person who cleans the floors, arranges the distribution of goods on time, manages the website or cooks the most fantastic meal? Without them your customer service and reputation will suffer.

Customers will pay more or return more often if they receive a level of service that meets or exceeds their expectations.

When you ask business owners what makes them stand out from their competition, quite often, we hear that it is due to a better customer service. However, why is your service better? Because it is not just a question of being more polite as some businesses think!

Keeping the thinking at a high-level 'great customer service' then many businesses will promote their great service in their marketing, but then not delivering the promise will create a big disappointment for the customer. Therefore, know what really creates your 'great'.

A positive customer service experience can change the entire perception a customer has of your business. There will be many factors that will impact on the customer experience including value for money, professionalism, friendliness, expertise, accessibility, need satisfaction and your communication style. However, for you to deliver exceptional customer service, you need to know and really understand your customers' expectations.

As a business, we all collate data about our customer, sometimes without even considering it. For example: what did they order? What did they order with it? What is different from last time? What else did they ask for? Where are they based? How do they prefer to buy from you?

You can also instigate direct feedback from your customers and learn what further improvements are needed. By asking for feedback, obtaining the completion of a feedback form, by holding customer forum meetings or by simply listening when they are with you, you will continue to capture vital information.

It is all good collecting information about what your customers want from you, but it is the action you take with this information that will stand you apart from your competitors.

With any outcome or lessons from your data, review your current activity and systems to establish what needs to change. Consider giving the responsibility of exceptional customer service to one of your team, so it is always on your meeting agendas, discussions and, more importantly, the day-to-day thoughts of your team. An important part of this responsibility for customer service is to establish some form of measurement. To have some management information that can help you measure the satisfaction of your customers. For example, are they buying more, how many complaints or comment cards have you received, what are your order and delivery times, how many times did your account manager speak to the customer in the last month, etc?

Day-to-day activity such as the telephone manner or face-to-face experience may be difficult to measure but, from time to time, you should check the delivery is as expected. You could do this with observation or by using mystery shopping techniques where someone pretends to be a customer of your business.

This is a good technique for seeing what your competitors are doing and benchmarking your business against their service delivery standard.

If you are a business heavily reliant on telephone orders or contact, then you should consider telecommunications that allow you to listen to calls or record conversations.

Looking after your existing customers will be a key part of your business. They have already chosen you above your competitors and will therefore continue to do so with the right experience. Much research indicates that it is cheaper to retain a customer than recruit a new one!

From time-to-time, customers will not be happy and will make a complaint either verbally or in a written form. Please take these seriously as they may be speaking for many other customers who will not complain and just simply not buy from you again.

Your business should have a system for managing any complaint. First, what you do on receipt of a complaint, such as listening and the initial comments you make. Then how quickly will you respond to the complaint, such as a written response within 24 hours and a resolution within 7 days. You should also know your options to rectify the situation for your customer such as repair, refund, replace or repeat order.

If you manage a complaint well and to the customer's expectations, then there is every chance you will retain them as a customer.

The two best ways to help and encourage your team to deliver exceptional customer service is from training and reward.

In terms of training, I believe that you need to communicate your goals and standards, your expectations, take the opportunity to advise of any feedback, provide details of the systems in the business that deliver great customer service but, more importantly, try to get your team to feel the experience for themselves. Asking them to put themselves in the customer's shoes and consider the expectations of the customer and the different touch points with your business will usually bring visible results.

Where possible, try to involve your team in creating the standard, as this will create greater ownership.

One area of specific focus for any customer service training should be in effective communication skills.

Customer service is everyone's responsibility. You should lead by example, have a commitment to excellence and demonstrate a customer-focused approach.

Building your customer relationship

Whatever relationship we are in, albeit personal or in business, much centres around effective communication, so how do you keep in contact with your customers and maintain your relationship?

Too often, the relationship with the customer is taken for granted once they have parted with their hard-earned money. However, the customer journey continues from that moment to the after-sale experience, to loyalty and advocacy.

Put yourself in your customer's shoes. How would you feel if you were no longer 'important' once you've bought your product or service? I suspect not delighted! So, how can you ensure that does not happen in your business?

It is good practice to map out your customer's most likely journey. How do they build a relationship with you that encourages them to buy? After the sale, how does the relationship continue as they receive delivery of your product or service? How do you keep them close? How do you continue to communicate with them and, if applicable, ensure they buy again? What can you do to make them an advocate and encourage a recommendation, review or referral to another customer?

The relationship changes over time with our customers. When they were a prospect in the awareness stage, they did not know you and would have likely started their engagement from a sceptical position. They got to like, but now know, you and you became an option as a solution or desire. Over time, during the consideration stage, they warmed to your offering and began to like and trust you. That relationship grew to a point that they were happy to buy from you. Now that a transaction has been made, the relationship builds further, as the ultimate trust has been shown by the customer spending money! You won't be personal friends, but the relationship builds and to a point that they may buy again or recommend you to others.

What can you do to influence this experience and how the relationship is built with your customer?

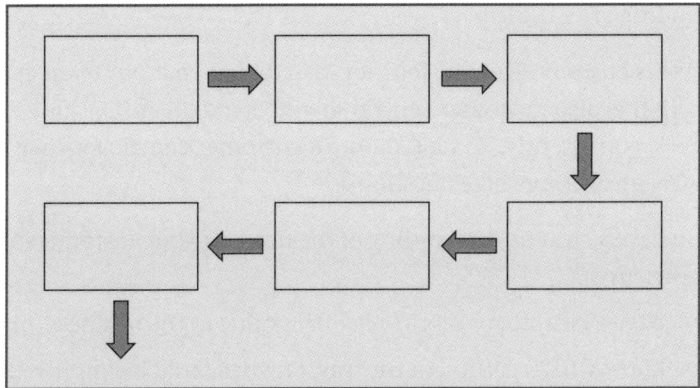

Delivering consistent excellence through a customer-centric experience

Gaining customers is one thing, but to be predictably profitable, you must be delivering excellence at every step of the customer journey.

'Please make me feel special' – what every customer of every business is secretly saying every time they interact.

When did the standard become great?

Have you recently been to a shop or restaurant and genuinely thought *'That was great service, they were really helpful'?* When, in fact, what they have done was deliver the basic standards. Sadly, we've become so used to poor service.

Now, how would your customers behave if they felt they were consistently served with higher-than-average standards and constantly wowed? What would the impact be on your bottom line, on you and on your team?

One risk of growing a business is that it can become focused on internal processes, which of course are important, but not more important than the customer journey and how your customers feel when interacting with your business. It's easy to forget the fact that we should be fixated on the customer's experience, and that in turn defines our processes.

A customer-centric experience produces excellent delivery.

Some business owners may freely admit to understanding the customer journey as that of a prospect to lead to a customer. However, customer-centric experiences mean providing a consistent and defined journey throughout our business, including after the sale.

Defining this customer-centric journey also means that our team can follow a process that is also customer centric so you can deliver the same excellent experiences, consistently. To help define a customer-centric journey for your business, try answering these questions:

1. Do you have a clear understanding of the needs of your customers and prospects (insights)?
2. Do you have a clear focus on the resulting value to the business (impact)?
3. Do you know what's getting in the way, or what could be improved to meet the needs of your customers (issues/opportunities)?
4. Have you or can you design solutions that deliver both customer and organisational value (innovate)?

The reason defining a customer-centric journey is important is because it can provide you with a 'road map', a visual illustration of your customers' pains, needs and perceptions throughout their interaction with you, all on one sheet of paper.

With the answers to the above four questions in mind, take a look at the three key actions to help you deliver excellence to your customers in a consistent, predictable, profitable and routine manner.

1. **Map your customer journey**
   Create an initial map that focuses on areas like your current customer types, what characterises your brand and the personality behind it, the attitudes and emotions that your customers experience, and backend support. Can you research reviews and social media comments to find out more about what people say about your brand?

Then consider and build in the desired transformation that you'd like to see, for example for your customers to refer you more often.

2. **Test it on your last five customers**
   Look at the real 'moments that matter' for your customers and what the impact would be if you increased referral rates or reduced refund rates, for example. Examine the impact of processes such as billing, processing refunds, sending invoices, etc.

3. **Final review and sign-off**
   Collaborate with your team on the final review and define a period of time to measure the results. It's worth designing a monitoring method to evaluate the changes you've implemented.

By defining a customer-centric journey, you will be able to understand your customer better and begin delivering excellence with ease. It should also help you effortlessly communicate an excellent customer experience to your team, your prospects and your referral partners alike.

Seven ways to improve customer experience and grow revenue

A good customer experience is one that may lead to referrals and advocacy.

Customer experience is more than customer service. Service implies the direct contact you or one of your departments has with a customer, whereas experience is what helps the customer form an opinion of you possibly without ever making a purchase or speaking with you.

Here are seven particular ways you could improve customer experience that will inevitably improve revenue.

A clear and easy to navigate your website

A website is vital as a place for people to learn more about your services and products, prices and processes in their own time. It's a tool for converting viewers into buyers and one-time purchasers into repeat customers. It's a content management system that contains high-value information and advice at no cost, so it's imperative that your website is easy to navigate and has a clear 'journey' for your customer to follow.

Your web designer or marketing strategist may be able to help you decipher your customer's website journey from Google Analytics and, once you know how people are using your website currently, you can look for unnecessary button clicks or pages that can be removed or improved. What action can you take to improve the user experience?

Welcoming and useful social media content

Social media may be the first experience your customer has of your brand, especially if they're responding to a recommendation from a group or a friend, or if you've sponsored content through ads. Is your content welcoming, useful, engaging? Is it projecting your brand voice appropriately?

Bear in mind, organic social media is less likely to convert your viewer into a buyer when compared to a website. Therefore, consider how you may turn the visitor to your social media platform to a website visitor. You can try quizzes, free downloads or offering a solution following a quick questionnaire to do this or simply by asking them to read the latest new article! Just don't forget to make it easy for them to act.

Social media is great for creating emotional connections with your audience.

Make social media advertising personal and seamless

Or you could use social media ads to convert your viewers into buyers. If you do this, be sure to enhance the customer experience by personalising the ads through a solid buyer persona, targeting and relevant content. And always write a specific landing page that is hosted on your website, to make this part of the journey seamless.

Ask for customer feedback

Don't be scared to ask for feedback! Yes, sometimes you'll get less than favourable responses, but this is how we learn and improve, and that's the aim here. There are many ways you can gather feedback. Depending on the size of your business and customer base, you could outsource to a telemarketing company, use an online form or call or email them directly.

Identify where improvements can be made on the customer journey

Having received feedback from your customers about their experience of your business, you must act to make improvements, or you risk the exercise becoming a task that wasted your resources and telling your customers that you didn't really care after all.

With continual customer experience improvement, comes better and more customer reviews.

Identify training needs for yourself or your employees

Can you identify the strengths and areas for development within your team? Now we're talking customer service; presentation, attitude, openness to listen and positive body language.

Ask your customers again!

Having asked them what improvements could be made to their experience, and followed up by acting on those recommendations, it's now time to find out if your investment has paid off.

This is a key action, as the customer relationship changes at different parts of the customer journey, as do their expectations and their requirements.

Customer experience is more than service; it encompasses the entirety of the customer journey, from awareness to advocacy and their emotional connection. There are multiple points along the customer journey at which you can stop and analyse the experience to see how continual improvements can be made.

> ### Remember this
>
> #### Build your reviews
>
> Encourage happy customers to leave you a review that will help influence the buying decision of others.
>
> Take them directly to the review page by using the link of your review site (e.g. Google, Trustpilot, etc). Add the link on your email footer. Put a QR code on your invoices or thank you to your customers.

Aim for operational excellence

Aiming for operational excellence is a key strategy for ensuring the efficiency, effectiveness and overall health of your business processes whilst meeting and exceeding your customers' expectations.

Operational excellence isn't just a goal; it's a mindset that involves constantly looking for ways to improve your business processes and deliver the best possible experience and value for your customers.

Here are some tips to help you achieve this:

1 **Standardise processes:** develop standardised procedures for all your operations. This helps to maintain consistency, reduce errors and makes it easier to train new staff. Document these processes clearly and ensure they are accessible to all relevant team members.

2 **Implement continuous improvement:** adopt a mindset of continuous improvement, such as the Kaizen approach. Regularly review and refine your processes to increase efficiency, reduce waste and improve quality.

3 **Invest in technology and automation:** utilise technology to automate repetitive and time-consuming tasks. Consider automation before you delegate or outsource. This not only increases efficiency but also allows your team to focus on more strategic, value-added activities.

4 **Focus on quality management:** implement quality management systems like Six Sigma or Total Quality Management (TQM) to enhance the quality of your products or services and reduce defects.

5 **Train and empower employees:** invest in training your employees to ensure they have the necessary skills and knowledge. Empower them to take ownership of their tasks and encourage them to contribute ideas for process improvements.

6 **Measure and analyse performance:** establish key performance indicators (KPIs) to measure the efficiency and effectiveness of your operations. Regularly analyse these metrics, as part of a scorecard, to identify areas for improvement.

7 **Culture of excellence:** encourage a company culture that values excellence, efficiency and accountability. Recognise and reward teams and individuals who contribute significantly to operational improvements.

8 **Enhance communication and collaboration:** promote open communication and collaboration within and across teams. Ensure that everyone understands their role in the larger operational process and how they contribute to the company's objectives.

9. **Optimise supply chain management:** streamline your supply chain to reduce costs and improve reliability. Build strong relationships with suppliers and consider practices like just-in-time inventory to reduce waste.
10. **Embrace change management:** as you implement changes in pursuit of operational excellence, manage these changes effectively to ensure smooth transitions and buy-in from all stakeholders.

How do I create systems and processes for my business?

With good systems and processes, you are able to build your business so that it may run independently of you and generate the income you need, without you working every hour.

A business system or process is an activity or set of activities that will accomplish a specific organisational goal.

There are many reasons for having systemised processes in your business. Here are a few:

1. Put your team in charge.
2. Free up your time – and give your life back.
3. Step back and work 'on' the business.
4. Test new ideas – and improve everything around you.
5. Do everything the best way.
6. Help induct new people to get up to speed quickly.
7. Replicate and grow.
8. Minimise costs due to manual errors and inefficiency.
9. Attract a buyer.
10. Streamline your communications.
11. Induct people more quickly and with a structure.
12. Drive accountability in your business.
13. Improve the ability to scale more quickly.
14. Increase the value of your business.

So, how do you consider what systems to create and then how do you go about creating them?

First, think of a business as a series of systems and each system has a role, a purpose within that business; otherwise, it should not be there. Then consider that each system in your business has an objective and that the key is to measure how effective each system is at achieving its objective.

Systems can be created with six key steps:

1. List the systems – leadership, operational, marketing, customer, people, finance, administration.
2. Classify the systems – a core or support system?
3. Map each system – identify what steps are required to best deliver the process. Look to establish how the process would flow in the most efficient and effective way.
4. Analyse each system – Is it efficient? Is there any waste? What is its likely impact?
5. Document each system and allocate responsibility.
6. Implement each system – notify and train the team, gather feedback.

When building your systems, start with the end in mind

First, think about the output. What are you looking to achieve by creating this system? What impact will it make? Then consider the processes and various elements needed to deliver that outcome. Once you know the core element of the system, what inputs do you need and who from? It may be data from your internal team or information from an external provision such as the customer or your suppliers.

Map out your business and prioritise which systems to tackle first

Start by building out your process map. A process map is a way to show what steps are required to transform inputs to outputs. It is a means by which we can identify the relationships between the resources we have, the tasks they perform and the dependencies between tasks. This will help you to clarify how all parts of your business come together to deliver your operational excellence. When listing out your systems for the various areas of your business, give each a score based on how complete the system is at this time. For prioritising, then also consider how important the systemisation of that part of the business is against others. This will give you a good idea of where to start. However, there may be a natural flow. For example, the marketing system may need to come before the sales system before the delivery system.

Now it's time to create your standard operating procedures

Consider what you already have in place and the tools that you currently use, to then establish any gaps in the process, skills or knowledge. Each of your systems may have many steps and various types. These may be made up of:

- step-by-step processes
- instructions
- standard letters
- scripts
- checklists
- forms
- templates
- agendas
- workflows
- software
- videos.

Also consider what can be automated. Many tasks can now be automated with the assistance of some fantastic apps and software. Consider your steps and which could be automated and which still need that critical human intervention or delivery.

Implement your systems with good training

You may feel that the hard graft has been completed and the system is now finally ready to roll out. However, a poor implementation plan or bad training can waste all that hard work. With training, everyone, from your most experienced to your newest people, should be able to carry out the tasks and deliver the system without you or your intervention at any point. Systemisation of your business gives empowerment to your team encouraging them to take responsibility and authority for delivery. You can then manage your people to their ability to follow a system and use their personality and innovation to improve it.

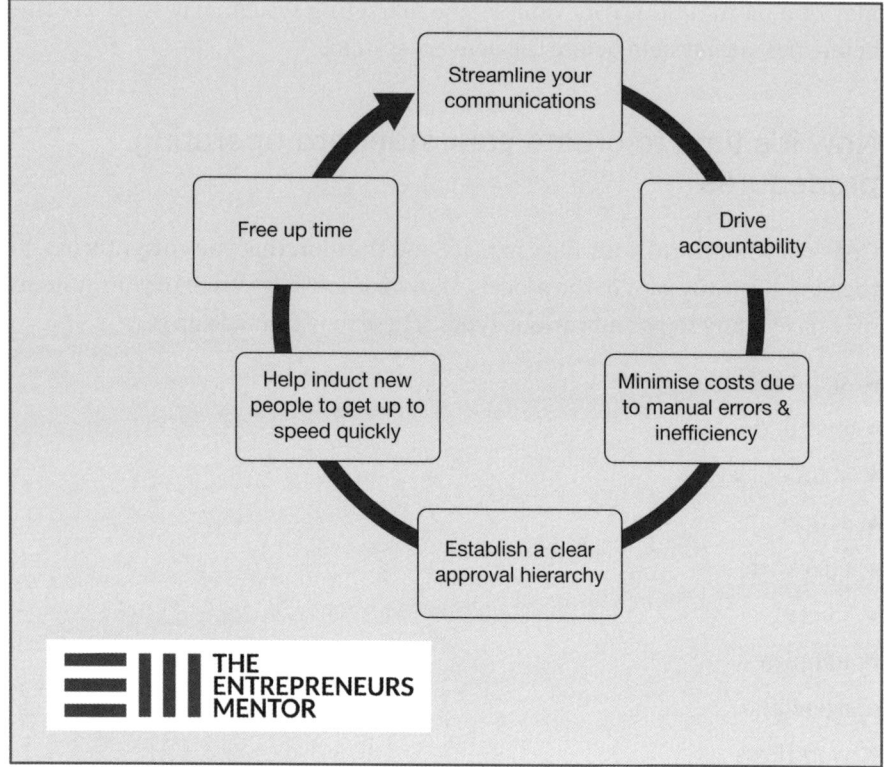

Figure 9.1 Some benefits of creating a process

Ask a member of the team to create the system and related processes

Asking someone else to create the system is of course great for your own time management! However, it can also help with your training of your people. For example, you show them how it is done including all the elements you would put into a system. Then ask them to write up their notes in a structured manner to suit your operations manual. You then of course have the system written up for you, but you also check that person's understanding and the quality of your training!

Build your business so that it has the appropriate systems in place to generate the income you need, without you working 24/7 and generate a higher valuation as it works independently of you.

> **Remember this**
>
> When creating systems in your business, work backwards.
>
> What are you trying to achieve as an outcome?
>
> What is the process to best deliver this?
>
> What is needed as an input to ensure you do that?

Utilising the 80/20 rule

This is a rule that can transform every aspect of your life.

The 80/20 rule, also known as the Pareto Principle, is a concept that suggests a disproportionate relationship between inputs and outputs, causes and effects, or effort and results.

The 80/20 rule can be applied to many aspects of life. The most common reference is that 80 per cent of the results come from just 20 per cent of the effort.

In many countries, you hear it referenced that roughly 20 per cent of the population controls 80 per cent of the wealth.

In business I'm sure you will relate to:

Income: 80 per cent generated from 20 per cent of your customers.

Marketing: 80 per cent of our results comes from 20 per cent of our resources.

Staff issues: 80 per cent of the problems are generated by 20 per cent of your team.

Service: 20 per cent of customers often generate 80 per cent of complaints.

Profits: 80 per cent of a company's profits often come from 20 per cent of its customers.

Product range: 20 per cent of your products typically generate 80 per cent of their revenue.

Sales people: 20 per cent of your sales team will usually produce 80 per cent of total sales.

Analytics: 20 per cent of a website's pages usually generate 80 per cent of its traffic.

But it's more than just work or productivity; this principle can shape every part of life:

> Time management: 20 per cent of your time is likely spent on activities that generate 80 per cent of your productivity.
>
> Wealth: 80 per cent habits, 20 per cent maths.
>
> Happiness: 80 per cent purpose, 20 per cent fun.
>
> Health: 80 per cent eating, 20 per cent exercising.
>
> Communication: 80 per cent listening, 20 per cent speaking.
>
> Achieving: 80 per cent doing, 20 per cent dreaming.
>
> Social grouping: 20 per cent of the people do 80 per cent of the talking.

Too often, people are focused on the 20 per cent factors, often because they are shouting the loudest or falsely appearing more important.

Avoid the quick-gratification moments of looking at the 20 per cent, but identify that your true success and fulfilment will come from the quiet, consistent 80 per cent. It's the habits, purpose, listening and doing that build wealth, happiness, health, relationships and achievements.

The 80/20 rule isn't about ignoring the 20 per cent; it's about recognising that the 80 per cent, the habits, persistence, giving and understanding, is what truly drives us forward.

By understanding and applying these principles, you can make more informed decisions, improve efficiency and achieve better results with targeted efforts.

Here are the key principles of the 80/20 rule:

1. **Disproportionate distribution**
   The core idea is that roughly 80 per cent of effects come from 20 per cent of causes. This ratio isn't exact but illustrates a significant imbalance in many situations.

2. **Focus on high-impact factors**
   It encourages identifying and prioritising the vital few (20 per cent) that produce the majority (80 per cent) of results.

3. **Efficiency and prioritisation**
   By focusing on the most impactful 20 per cent, you can achieve better results with less effort and fewer resources.

4 **Wide applicability**
   The principle applies across various fields, including business, economics, time management and personal productivity.

5 **Not a mathematical law**
   While often expressed as 80/20, the exact ratio can vary. The key is recognising the imbalance, not the specific numbers.

6 **Scalability**
   The principle can be applied recursively within the top 20 per cent; there may be another 80/20 split.

7 **Resource allocation**
   It suggests allocating resources more heavily to the areas that produce the most significant outcomes.

8 **Identifying leverage points**
   Helps in finding the most effective areas to intervene or improve in a system or process.

9 **Simplification**
   Allows for simplifying complex situations by focusing on the most critical factors.

10 **Continuous improvement**
   Encourages ongoing analysis to identify and capitalise on the most productive elements in any system or process.

So, what will you focus on today, the 80 per cent or the 20 per cent?

How to improve your business with technology

When technology is introduced, the common reaction is fear, uncertainty and doubt. How will it create change? Will it really work?

Some people are early adopters and others wait for the version x.1 to start using it with the improvements made.

Technology can significantly enhance business operations and drive growth through various means.

By leveraging these technological advancements, businesses can enhance their efficiency, improve customer relations, and achieve sustainable growth:

- **Faster, more comprehensive communication**
  Technology enables faster and more efficient communication within and outside the organisation. Tools like email, instant messaging apps (Slack, Asana) and video conferencing platforms (Zoom, Skype, Teams) facilitate seamless communication, regardless of geographical barriers.

- **New communication technologies**
  Emerging technologies such as virtual presence tools and enhanced cloud services allow for real-time collaboration and communication, which can improve productivity and decision-making processes.

- **Resource management and efficiency**
  Technology helps streamline resource management and operational efficiency. Automation tools and productivity software can replace laborious paper-based processes, reduce costs and improve overall efficiency.

- **Project management software**
  Investing in project management software helps track business development, manage multiple projects and coordinate remote or hybrid work environments effectively.

- **Integrated business management systems**
  An integrated business management system can streamline various business functions such as accounting, billing and project management, making operations more efficient and less time-consuming.

- **Customer relationship management (CRM) software**
  CRM systems help businesses manage customer relationships more effectively by tracking customer interactions, sales and feedback. This data can be used to tailor marketing campaigns and improve customer service.

- **Cloud services**
  Increased use of 'the Cloud' (Cloud services) offers scalable and cost-effective solutions for data storage and collaboration. They enable businesses to grow without the need for expensive server upgrades and facilitate remote work by allowing access to data from anywhere.

- **Cybersecurity – enhanced security measures**
  With the rise in cyber threats, robust cybersecurity measures are essential. Regular updates, employee training and limiting access to sensitive data can help protect business assets and customer information.

- **Digital marketing and online presence**
  A strong digital presence, including a well-optimised website and active social media channels, is crucial for reaching a wider audience and building brand loyalty. Digital marketing strategies like email marketing and pay-per-click advertising can drive business growth.
- **Real-time data and analytics**
  Financial management platforms and digital marketing analytics provide real-time data that helps businesses make informed decisions, optimise strategies and improve ROI.
- **Labour cost savings**
  Automation and machine learning technologies can perform repetitive tasks, reducing the need for manual labour and allowing employees to focus on more strategic activities. This leads to significant labour cost savings.
- **Low up-front costs**
  Many cloud-based platforms and applications have low initial costs and do not require ongoing maintenance, making them ideal for start-ups and small businesses.

Gather feedback for your business

Feedback is a powerful tool that can significantly benefit your business.

In time, I hope you are not running your business on a day-to-day basis and you will have freed yourself from the weeds. You will have built systems, processes and a pool of talent, working within a values-led culture, that delivers your mission, vision and purpose.

Therefore, feedback is a great way to establish if the activities are being executed as you expect and are having the impact you desire with those that engage with you.

Feedback is essential in helping you scale, grow and enjoy the success you define for your business. Feedback enables you to remain competitive, adapt to changing market trends, acknowledge your customer expectations and build relationships with your customers as they build their loyalty to become advocates of your business.

Too often, the areas for development can be dismissed as 'well that's only one person's view' when many times that one person is speaking on behalf of others. Then the cynical say that feedback is only provided by those who are 'super happy' or those who are 'very upset' and you will hear nothing from those in between. However, that's because the request for feedback is irregular, even a one off or not requested at the right time or in the right way. Is your feedback systemised or asked for when you remember or when you need it?

For some, often feedback makes us feel good and it pats the entrepreneurial ego, but in these moments quite often the benefits are missed.

These are the benefits of feedback that are often not considered:

1 **Increased engagement with your customers**
   It involves and interacts with your customers in a way that they feel valued and considered. This builds the relationship and then deeper levels of feedback later. Our customers then feel engaged and able to easily raise anything they feel we need to know before they are even asked!

2 **Enhanced customer retention**
   Keeping in touch with your customers and their feelings will lead to a reduction in your churn. A customer who gives good feedback this month

is unlikely to leave the next. If you have negative feedback, now you know and can fix it. Otherwise, they often leave and you never knew! When a customer feels heard and valued, they often become loyal.

3. **Development of your product or service**
   When you hear what works and what does not, this is valuable insight to help you continually shape an offering that your customers want and need. By not just hearing, but actually listening to the feedback, you can make improvements that build a wider level of satisfaction across your customer base. The feedback helps you tailor your offerings.

4. **Identification of new opportunities**
   Ultimately, this is information to act upon that keeps you ahead of your competitors. Feedback will often highlight what you may not have noticed yourself or give you an insight into any unmet needs or expectations in the eyes of your buyers.

5. **Improvement of your customer experience**
   By listening to what could be better, you can identify what improvements can be made to your customers' journey. Such continuous improvements will result in few complaints and a happier, more engaged, customer.

6. **Help to make better decisions**
   Feedback provides valuable data that can inform your strategic decisions. By understanding your customer needs and preferences, you can mitigate risks associated with launching new products or services.

7. **Increased employee engagement**
   Positive feedback boosts morale and motivates your employees to perform at their best with the confidence that they are doing the right things for the customer. The best employees take constructive feedback for their own development by helping them identify areas for improvement and grow professionally.

Remember this

Feedback is part of the loop

You take your value out to market using the marketing channels that utilise where your customers hang out. As you build relationships with your customers they give you feedback. Formally or informally. Invited or uninvited. However, all feedback is good feedback as it helps you to improve the delivery of your promise or better understand the value you are offering.

Assess the risks to your business

Navigating the landscape of business risks is a critical aspect of entrepreneurship. Understanding potential risks and preparing strategies to manage them ensure the sustainability and growth of your business.

A regular risk assessment of your business is advisable. If you identify a risk, then consider its likelihood and, if it were to come to fruition, what would be the consequence. If it is highly likely with a high consequence, then you need to look at the options to mitigate that risk immediately.

Risk management is not a one-time task but an ongoing process that requires vigilance and adaptability. By identifying, assessing and mitigating risks, you can navigate uncertainties and steer your business towards long-term success and stability.

Here are some thoughts to help you to consider your process of identifying, assessing and mitigating risks in your business environment.

Identifying your business risks

- **Market risks:** changes in customer preferences, market trends and competition.
- **Financial risks:** cashflow challenges, credit risks and investment uncertainties.
- **Operational risks:** supply chain disruptions, internal process failures and technology breakdowns.
- **Compliance risks:** legal and regulatory changes affecting your industry.
- **Strategic risks:** decisions about business direction, partnerships and expansion.
- **Reputational risks:** public perception and brand image issues.
- **Environmental risks:** natural disasters and environmental changes impacting operations.

Assessing the impact and likelihood of risks

- **Risk matrix:** utilise a risk matrix to evaluate the likelihood and consequential impact of identified risks.

- **Prioritisation:** focus on risks with high probability and high impact.
- **Regular reviews:** continually reassess risks, as their impact and likelihood can change over time.

		Outcome				
		Negligible 1	Minimal 2	Average 3	Severe 4	Substantial 5
Probability	5 - Very Likely	5	10	15	20	25
	4 - Probable	4	8	12	16	20
	3 - Average	3	6	9	12	15
	2 - Doubtful	2	4	6	8	10
	1 - Rare	1	2	3	4	5

Degree of risk		
Substantial	21	25
Severe	16	20
Average	11	15
Minimal	6	10
Negligible	1	5

Developing a risk mitigation plan

- **Risk avoidance:** eliminate activities that pose too high a risk.
- **Risk reduction:** implement strategies to minimise the impact or likelihood of risks.
- **Risk transfer:** share the risk burden (e.g. insurance, outsourcing).
- **Risk acceptance:** acknowledge and prepare for the risks that can't be mitigated.

Creating a risk management culture

- **Training and awareness:** ensure all team members understand potential risks and management strategies. Educate all team members with the mindset of looking for risks.
- **Open communication:** develop an environment where employees can report risks or uncertainties with confidence of no repercussion.
- **Continuous learning:** learn from past incidents and adapt your risk management strategies accordingly.

> ### I wish I knew this before I started my first business
>
> #### Know what you 'really do' and how you solve your prospects' pain, problem, fear, want, need or desire
>
> Many businesses are set up by technicians, so the owner focuses on the technical aspect of their offering and hence their marketing or sales is led with features rather than benefits. What is your 'value proposition'? How do you differentiate? What are your unique selling points? How do you engage the interest and emotion of your audience and prospects?
>
> It is very likely that your prospect is not looking to buy what you think you do! Establish what you really do.
>
> An example of this is a website designer. They offer websites, but their customers seriously do not want a website. They want an outcome. If they could achieve that outcome, such as more leads or automations, then they wouldn't want a website!
>
> I encourage you to have relationships with your business, that constantly feed back to you what you 'really do' and what you solve, so that the promotion of your business is maximised.

Key points

- How centric will your customers be in your business?
- Have you planned your customer journey and how you will interact to maintain and build your relationships?
- What does operational excellence look like in your business?
- Which systems and processes are critical to establish for your business?
- How will you gather feedback for your business?
- What risks have you identified for your business?

Additional resources

Books

Blanchard, K. and Bowles, S. (1993) *Raving Fans: A Revolutionary Approach to Customer Service*. William Morrow.
Heath, C. and Heath, D. (2017) *The Power of Moments*. Simon & Schuster.
Hill, V. (2012) *Fans! Not Customers: How to Create Growth Companies in a No Growth World*. IPS - Profile Books.
Jenyn, D. (2020) *SYSTEMology: Create Time, Reduce Errors and Scale Your Profits with Proven Business Systems*. Systemology.

Podcasts

Amazing Business Radio with Shep Hyken.
Business Processes Simplified Podcast.

Websites

www.cxnetwork.com.
www.opexsociety.org.

CHAPTER 10
SCALING YOUR START-UP FOR GROWTH

Once the foundation of your new business has been formed and you've started, then the next phase for your business will be to scale. How will you level up and take your business to the next stage?

In this chapter, we will consider how to grow your business further and be ready to embrace the growth opportunities that come your way.

> **Remember this**
>
> **One step at a time**
>
> Start first.
>
> Then scale.
>
> Before you grow.

What is a growth opportunity?

A growth opportunity refers to any situation or initiative that allows a business to expand its operations, increase revenue, enhance its market presence or improve profitability. These opportunities can arise from various sources, including market trends, technological advancements and changes in consumer behaviour.

A growth opportunity often exists for your business when:

- there is a new or big market
- your solution relieves human pain
- you have the right or new skills in the team
- you have a competitive advantage.

In the ever-changing world of business, growth opportunities are the catalysts that propel a company forward. These opportunities, when seized, can lead to developments, expansion, innovation and long-term success. Growth opportunities are vital for the sustainability and success of any business. Identifying, evaluating and effectively capitalising on these opportunities can set a business on a path to higher profitability, market leadership and long-term success.

Types of growth opportunities:

- **Market expansion:** entering new markets or demographics (e.g. expanding a product line to cater to a different age group).
- **Product or service innovation:** developing new products or enhancing existing ones (e.g. introducing an eco-friendly version of a popular product).
- **Strategic partnerships:** collaborating with other businesses for mutual benefit (e.g. partnering with a tech company to offer digital solutions).
- **Operational efficiency:** improving internal processes to reduce costs and increase productivity (e.g. implementing automation in manufacturing).
- **Acquisitions and mergers:** joining with or acquiring other companies to expand capabilities (e.g. merging with a competitor to dominate a market niche).

Identifying growth opportunities involves market research, analysing internal data and staying attuned to industry trends. It's crucial to assess the feasibility, risks and potential return on investment (ROI) of each opportunity.

Strategies to capitalise on growth opportunities:

- **Strategic planning:** developing a clear plan aligning with the business's long-term goals.
- **Resource allocation:** ensuring the necessary resources (capital, personnel, technology) are in place.
- **Risk management:** assessing and mitigating potential risks associated with the opportunity.

When following growth opportunities, ensure you balance the pursuit of growth with maintaining current operations.

> **Remember this**
>
> As you look to embrace a growth opportunity, then be mindful of the need to adapt to changes and unexpected outcomes as you are likely to be entering an area of the unknown for your business.

Are you ready to grow?

Too often, a business wanting to grow has a weak foundation, has no strategy and no clear action steps to make this happen. Additionally, the initial start-up period was unplanned with the growth in mind, so the business is now difficult to scale with its existing model and use of resources.

Often, the business owner is the bottleneck in the business that stifles growth because nothing gets done without them wanting control, doing it or approving it.

As always, cash flow should be a focus and ensure you have a good grasp on your numbers. You will need funds for the reinvestment in your growth plans but will want to ensure that this does not impact on the business you have already established.

At this stage of the business journey, it is common to see the business owner struggling with all or some of the following:

- The development of a strategy and plan, which provides confidence that the growth desired will maximise the opportunities.
- A lack of confidence to actually make it happen or a feeling of being overwhelmed with the potential actions needed.
- Not understanding the real numbers in the business, which drive the growth and make those numbers work for the future success.
- Finding it difficult to find and hire the right people who can help achieve the growth consistently across all areas of the business.

Look to create a plan, a step-by-step system, which is not overwhelming but has clear actions that you can implement quickly to scale and effectively grow your business.

- **Analyse** – initially review where you are now and identify the appropriate steps that are relevant for your business.

- **Strategy** – develop a clear strategy to know your key objectives, who you want to work with, the offering you are going to make to attract them, and create your vision and goals. Have a concise plan and clarity that you can share with your people, customers and suppliers.
- **Win more customers** – build on your existing activities and develop an effective marketing strategy to establish how you are going to proactively attract more of your ideal customers and generate a bigger income.
- **Financials** – know your finances, understand how the planned growth will impact your cash flow, and know the real numbers that drive your business growth.
- **People** – create a system for attracting, recruiting, managing, developing and retaining the best people to work in your business and help you deliver the success you desire.
- **Systems and processes** – establish a business build with operational excellence, which gets things right the first time every time. Use systems and automation to create efficiencies in both time and money.
- **Resources** – ensure you have the time to make it happen or do you need support and expertise in your business to help you grow?

What are the three best ways to grow your revenue and ultimately your business?

1. Increase the number of clients.
2. Increase the average transaction value.
3. Increase the number of times they purchase.

There are many activities you can execute to increase all three outcomes. Consider the activities that you execute that influence these outcomes. Here are some thoughts to get you started, as starting is the difficult bit!

Increase the number of clients

- **Leverage personalised outreach:** understand that your clients seek a personal touch. Craft personalised emails or messages that resonate with their specific needs and challenges.

- **Optimise your online presence for local SEO and pixels:** your clients are likely to be searching for solutions locally. Ensure your website and social media profiles are optimised with local keywords and phrases. Have your pixels embedded to remarket to those people who visited your online presence but were not ready to buy.
- **Network especially at niche-specific events:** attend and even speak at events where your target clients are likely to be. This positions you as an authority in your field and puts you directly in front of potential clients or those who know them.
- **Offer value-driven content:** create and share content that addresses the specific pain points and aspirations of your target clients. Make sure the content is actionable and demonstrates your expertise and understanding of their unique challenges.
- **Referral programme with incentives:** encourage your satisfied clients or network to refer others by offering them something of value in return. Word-of-mouth recommendation is powerful, especially when it comes from a trusted source within their own network.

Increase the average transaction value

- **Bundle services into packages:** create tiered service packages that cater to varying needs and budgets. Encourage clients to opt for premium packages by highlighting the comprehensive benefits and long-term value.
- **Implement upselling techniques:** train your team to identify opportunities to offer advanced services or add-ons that complement the client's current selection. This should be done by understanding and aligning with the client's goals, ensuring the upsell is seen as a value addition rather than just an extra cost.
- **Offer exclusive memberships or retainer agreements:** develop exclusive membership programmes or retainer services that provide ongoing support, advice or premium content. This approach suits clients who value consistent, high-quality service and are willing to pay for the convenience and assurance it brings.

- **Create a loyalty programme:** reward repeat business with a loyalty programme. Offer discounts, special access to events or resources, or other perks that incentivise larger or more frequent purchases. This not only increases transaction value but also builds a long-term relationship.
- **Provide customised solutions with a consultative approach:** use a consultative approach to deeply understand each client's unique needs and offer customised solutions. Everyone prefers services that are specifically tailored to their challenges, and they are often willing to invest more.

Increase the number of times they purchase (the lifetime value)

- **Develop a subscription model:** introduce a subscription service for your offerings. This ensures regular engagement and recurring revenue. Tailor the subscription tiers to various needs and budgets, encouraging clients to remain connected with your services on an ongoing basis.
- **Implement a customer loyalty programme:** create a loyalty programme that rewards clients for repeat business. Offer incentives like discounts, exclusive access or additional services after a certain number of purchases. This not only encourages repeat business but also fosters a sense of belonging and appreciation.
- **Regularly update service offerings:** continuously evolve and update your services to meet the changing needs of your clients. Keep clients engaged and interested by introducing new aspects to your services or by improving existing ones.
- **Engage with personalised communication:** maintain regular, personalised communication with clients. Use email marketing, social media or direct contact to keep them informed about new services, updates and special offers. Make your clients feel valued and keep your services top of mind.
- **Offer exclusive deals or early access:** provide existing clients with exclusive deals or early access to new services. This not only makes them feel privileged but also encourages them to take advantage of these offers before they're available to the general public, thus increasing their purchase frequency.

> **Remember this**
>
> **Continually focus on four key steps to grow**
>
> You can be successful focusing on one area, but most truly great entrepreneurial success stories that I have researched all focused on the cumulative effect of working on a number of improvements at the same time.
>
> Whichever successful entrepreneur you choose to read about, it is very likely that they have focused on these top four steps at the same time and made them a habit in the business:
>
> - First, increase the number of customers.
> - Second, increase the average sale value.
> - Third, increase the frequency that the customer buys from you.
> - And last, improve the gross and net profit margins.
>
> Consider every day how you can build on each of these key areas in your business.

Plan to exit your business, starting today

To clarify the term, 'exit your business', it is how you intend to wrap up your involvement and step away. It also includes what you want to gain from doing so, which may include limiting your losses, as much as receiving a pay-out as your pension.

Start with the end in mind. Think strategically about an exit plan at the very early stages of your business. The earlier you can plan for major change, the better it is for guiding your business decisions. Planning to exit your business is a major change often considered too late. The clever part is to have a vision and plan for your exit. Build the business that brings the plan to life and makes the objective real but keep your eyes open to maximise any opportunity that may arise along the way.

Let's look at some of the practical considerations of exiting a business.

What option you take will somewhat depend on the goals you set yourself when you started your business. Which of these sound like your potential options?

Sell the business and walk away

This option may result in a lump sum, but it also leaves you without a regular income from your years of involvement. Part of your plan should be to know the sum you want and how you ensure your business will be valued that way by the buyer. There are different ways to sell your interest in the business. For example, selling to someone you know (family, your team or externally), merging, selling on the open market, or selling shares as an initial public offering (IPO). Essentially, you're selling your value, which may be a database, processes, your intellectual property (IP), staff expertise, products and services. If your goal when you started your business was to have a succession of businesses, then that lump sum may be how you begin your next. Often it is the case that running the business is also the owners' love or hobby so, if you don't plan another business, what will you do next, and will the desired sum be enough for you? If you plan to walk away on the day you want to go, ensure you create the business with a plan that allows you to do this. It can otherwise be commonplace to stay involved for a period of time, but you then have to watch someone else run the business. Could you do that?

Close the business and cease all trading

Often seen as the easiest. Sometimes, the only option is a liquidation or the cessation of a trading business. Once again, you are without an income for the future, and this time you may be without a lump sum unless there are surplus assets you can cash in over your liabilities. However, you may be happier this way having created your wealth in the past resulting in a comfortable pension or cash reserve. This option also requires the consideration of staff and stakeholders, and how to deal with them.

Retire but remain as a member of the board

With this option, you retain an income, shares and maybe major decision-making powers, but you cease working for the most part. Here, you do risk letting go of operational control and delaying the reward of that lump sum when you sell. However, if your goal was to bring family members into the business, this could be a good option for you.

The best time to plan your exit is now.

Whether that looks like selling up and taking the profits, staying on the board, or simply wrapping it up, there must be a strategy in place to ensure you maximise on the years of hard work and effort you put into it.

A question for now: can you take time away from your business now and comfortably leave it in the hands of a reliable team? What happens when you do take time away? If not, what needs to happen to make that a possibility as your exit will be easier or increase the valuation when the time to exit comes?

Here are some considerations to prepare your business for your exit:

1 Your roles within your business. Take a moment to examine how reliant those tasks are on you to get them completed to the same standards.
2 Your team. Can you delegate, train or recruit team members to step into your various roles? Are they ready to run the business without you?
3 Your stakeholders. Who are they, what are their expectations from you now, and the business following your exit?
4 Your systems and processes. Are they reliable? Working like clockwork? Followed? Automated where possible, humanised when needed?
5 Your expectations for the business and your goals as an entrepreneur. How close are you to achieving them?
6 How long do/did you intend to stay within the business?
7 Are you looking for a new opportunity, or are you looking to stop working?
8 If applicable, what is the business valuation and what influences that valuation? Are the contributing factors secure and steady? (For example revenue, profit margins, EBITDA, customers contracted, etc.)
9 If applicable, who is your potential buyer/s? Why would they be interested? How do you attract them to your business?
10 How would you structure the exit? How would it impact your personal tax position?

Growing your business

Growing a business is a journey that requires strategic planning, innovation and adaptability. Whether you're a start-up or an established enterprise, implementing the right strategies can significantly accelerate your growth. Here's a breakdown of actionable strategies to help your business thrive:

- **Understand your market**
Growth starts with knowing your audience. Understanding your customer needs, preferences and pain points allows you to tailor your offerings effectively. Conduct market research to identify trends, customer behaviour and

gaps in the market. Use surveys, interviews and feedback forms to gather insights directly from your customers. Analyse competitors to understand what's working for them and where they fall short.

- **Focus on your value proposition**
Your value proposition is what sets your business apart. Clearly defining it will attract your ideal customers. Identify what makes your product or service unique. Communicate your value proposition consistently across all marketing channels. Deliver on your promises to build trust and loyalty.

- **Leverage digital marketing**
A strong online presence is essential for reaching a broader audience in today's digital-first world. Optimise your website for user experience (UX) and search engines (SEO). Use social media platforms to engage with your audience and promote your offerings. Invest in paid ads, email marketing and content marketing to drive traffic and conversions.

- **Strengthen your sales process**
A streamlined sales process ensures you convert leads into loyal customers. Train your sales team to focus on consultative selling, listening to customer needs and offering solutions. Implement a customer relationship management (CRM) system to track leads and automate follow-ups. Continuously refine your sales pitch based on feedback and results.

- **Expand your offerings**
Diversifying your product or service line can open up new revenue streams. Introduce complementary products or services that align with your existing offerings. Bundle products or services to increase their perceived value. Test new offerings on a small scale before a full launch to minimise risk.

- **Build strategic partnerships**
Partnerships can help you access new audiences, resources and expertise. Collaborate with businesses that complement your own (e.g. a web designer partnering with a copywriter). Establish referral programmes to encourage other businesses to recommend your services. Co-market products or services to reach a broader audience.

- **Optimise operations and processes**
Efficient operations reduce costs, improve productivity and enhance customer satisfaction. Streamline workflows by automating repetitive tasks. Regularly

evaluate and refine your processes to eliminate inefficiencies. Invest in training and tools to empower your team to work more effectively.

- **Invest in customer retention**
Retaining customers is more cost-effective than acquiring new ones, and loyal customers can become brand advocates. Provide exceptional customer service at every touchpoint. Offer loyalty programmes or exclusive perks for repeat customers. Collect and act on feedback to continuously improve your offerings.

- **Scale smartly**
Rapid growth without the necessary infrastructure can lead to operational challenges. Ensure your systems, processes and team are scalable. Gradually expand into new markets or demographics. Maintain financial stability by monitoring cash flow and managing resources wisely.

- **Monitor performance and adjust**
Measuring results ensures you're focusing on strategies that work. Use key performance indicators (KPIs) to track progress toward your goals. Analyse data regularly to identify trends, successes and areas for improvement. Be flexible and willing to pivot your strategies based on insights.

Growing your business is a dynamic process that requires both strategic thinking and execution. By understanding your market, delivering value, leveraging technology and continuously optimising your approach, you can set the foundation for sustainable growth. Remember, success doesn't happen overnight. Commit to the journey, and the results will follow.

If you're unsure where to start, consider working with a business coach or consultant to create a tailored growth strategy for your business.

The Ansoff Matrix is a strategic planning tool used by businesses to identify and evaluate growth opportunities. It provides a structured approach to assessing potential strategies for market and product expansion, helping businesses make informed decisions. Consider using the Ansoff Matrix when you are:

- **planning for growth:** to evaluate where and how to grow your business
- **launching new products or services:** to assess the best market or approach
- **entering new markets:** to determine feasibility and risks
- **strategic reviews:** to explore alternatives for expanding your business.

By using the Ansoff Matrix, you gain a clearer picture of your growth options, enabling data-driven decisions that align with your business goals and risk tolerance.

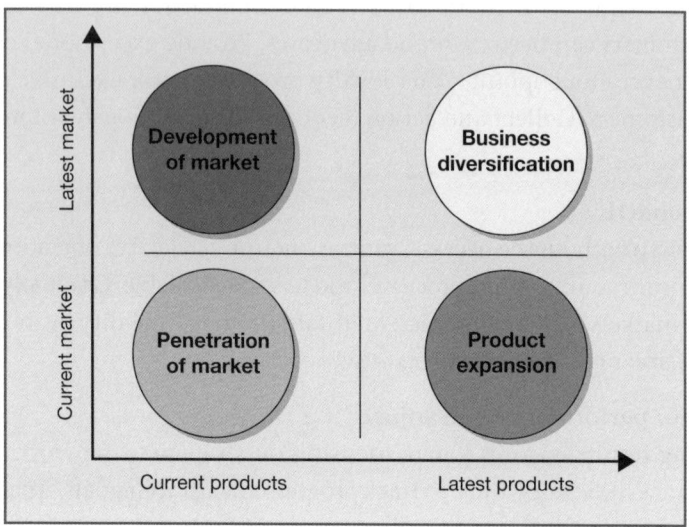

Figure 10.1 The Ansoff Matrix

Ten proven strategies to grow your business

In the ever-evolving business landscape, growth is not just a goal; it's a necessity for survival and success. Whether you're running a small start-up or a well-established enterprise, finding effective ways to grow your business is crucial.

Here are ten proven strategies that can help you expand your business and strengthen its position in the market.

1 **Understand your customers**
   Growth starts with understanding who your customers are and what they need. Use customer feedback to shape your products and services to better meet the needs of your target market. Surveys, social media listening and customer interviews can be invaluable tools in this process.

2 **Invest in digital marketing**
   In today's digital age, having a robust online presence is vital. Invest in digital marketing strategies such as search engine optimisation (SEO),

content marketing, social media advertising and email marketing. These tools not only increase your visibility but also help you reach a broader audience.

3 **Expand your product or service line**
Diversification can be a key driver for growth. Consider expanding your product or service line to attract new customers. However, make sure that these additions align with your core business and add real value to your customers.

4 **Focus on customer service**
Exceptional customer service can set you apart from competitors. Satisfied customers are more likely to return and refer others. Implement a customer service policy that emphasises speed, efficiency and, above all, a personal touch.

5 **Leverage social media**
Social media platforms are powerful tools for business growth. They allow you to engage directly with your customers, build brand loyalty and market your products or services to a large audience. Regular engaging posts and interactions can drive traffic and sales.

6 **Explore new markets**
Expanding into new markets can significantly increase your customer base. This could mean targeting different geographic areas, different demographics or even going international. However, make sure you understand the new market dynamics and customer preferences.

7 **Form strategic partnerships**
Collaborating with complementary businesses can open up new growth opportunities. Partnerships can provide access to new customer bases, shared resources and increased brand exposure. Choose partners that align with your business values and goals.

8 **Invest in your team**
Your employees are your biggest asset when it comes to growing your business. Investing in training and development can improve their skills and efficiency, leading to better business performance. Also, a motivated and skilled team is crucial for innovation and customer satisfaction.

9 **Utilise data and analytics**
   Data-driven decision making is key in today's business environment. Use data and analytics to understand market trends, customer behaviour and your business performance. This information can guide your growth strategies and help you make informed decisions.

10 **Stay flexible and adapt**
   The business world is constantly changing, and flexibility is crucial for growth. Be willing to adapt your strategies in response to market changes, customer feedback and internal business performance. Staying agile allows you to capitalise on opportunities and navigate challenges effectively.

Growing a business is a multifaceted endeavour that requires a combination of strategic planning, customer understanding and the willingness to adapt. By employing these 10 strategies, you can set your business on a path to sustainable growth and success. Remember, growth is a journey, not a destination, and continuous effort and adaptation are key to achieving your business goals.

How to create a 90-day plan to scale your business

One of the elements of planning the development of your business is placing a time-bound restriction by when you should see the results you are working towards.

The power of small steps should not be underestimated. With a smaller step there is less to get in the way and trip you up, plus you celebrate wins or achievements on a more regular basis that will fuel your motivation.

Ninety days is long enough for goals to be achievable and impactful, but short enough that success and reward is not too far in the distant future. Occasionally, businesses may fail if the people responsible for building them are too focused on the end goal and not paying the proper attention to the steps along the way.

Ninety-day plans are also flexible and adaptable enough that we can pivot or diversify with relatively short notice, something that most of us have learned the necessity of in recent years.

Making a 90-day plan

Sit down with your team or adviser and make at least an annual plan that highlights where you want your business to be in a year's time, why that goal is important and what activities you need to undertake to get you there. Yes, your ultimate goal timeline, to match your vision, may be longer, but clearly knowing where you need to be in 12 months will help keep you on the trajectory you desire.

Part of making this annual plan is so that you can visualise your end goal, but also so you can break down your 365-day marathon into shorter manageable 90-day 'sprints'.

1. Gather your numbers – any previous analytics you have from past plans and any reviews or debriefs that explain how your business scaled or didn't over the last year, 6 months or 90 days.
2. Find time away from your day-to-day duties in your business – a change of location removes distractions and aids creative thinking.
3. Look at your vision for the year and break it down into four stages – what can you do in each three-month sprint to help you get there?
4. Set a growth vision for the next 90 days. Apply the SMART goal principles of goal planning, especially make it realistic and achievable. Is there one theme you can work on, one priority?
5. Clarify your reason why the next 90 days are important, and find a way to communicate this to others essential to your success.
6. Plan for the obstacles that could interrupt or risk your achievement. You can refer to your previous analytics to help with this. The better you can prepare for obstacles, the smaller the chance they'll actually crop up.
7. Decide on the activities for the next 90 days that will bring you the biggest gains, get you closer to the next sprint and give you the highest pay-offs. Can you do them? Do you need to look at software, automation, delegation or outsourcing to help you?
8. Block out time in your calendar to work on the activities that will scale your business. Give yourself permission to stop working *in* your business so you can work *on* it. Perhaps even create some intentions or affirmations to help you move away from being busy.

9 Think about how you will track your progress and measure how successful your achievements have been in scaling your business. This way you can decide if your goals can be bigger, harder or if you can take more risks next time.

10 Be accountable to your plan – were you too ambitious or not ambitious enough? Did you change your habits of being busy, so you had time to scale your business? Were your intentions and vision clear and specific enough?

The A to Z to help you grow your business

From my experience and by observing what the more successful businesses do on a regular basis, I have identified a number of critical characteristics that I share in the format of an A to Z.

Attitude and appetite – I truly believe this is a key differentiator with those who actually make things happen. From experience, these entrepreneurs truly want to bring about the change that drives the business growth, have a strong reason why they want it to happen and have the positive outlook that makes even the largest obstacles appear small.

Budget/forecasts – how well do you know your financials? Not just the headlines such as turnover, profit, gross margin and the bottom line, but the drivers that make up your numbers. By knowing the success drivers for your business, you can build a meaningful budget for your business, apply some sensitivity analysis around those numbers and take more calculated risks with your plans.

Cash flow – cash is king. You may be profitable, but you will only grow and even sometimes survive if you have the cash. From your forecast, what is your proposed cashflow position? Do you need to make any plans? How can you collect the monies owed to you more quickly?

Determination – a positive attitude is a fantastic characteristic, but pair this with determination and you will see the success this can bring. The definition is the firmness of purpose, which for me means a positive that creates perseverance in spite of the obstacles. A positive attitude can be knocked, but determination is a quality that makes you continue in your pursuit of the goal.

Ethics and values – do you have a set of values that you work to each and every day? Are your decisions ethical? I am sure you have met another business owner who you feel has no ethics or has poor values. What did you think of them? Don't let others think the same of you, so consider your values and every day strive to deliver with these in mind and demonstrate they are part of your culture not just a set of words you thought of for your marketing purposes.

Friends and family – those close to us are so important whilst we are running our business. They are also often the easiest to forget about when we are busy or a customer is demanding our time and attention. Involve your friends and family in your thoughts, your success and also your difficulties, as I guarantee they are your most trusted resource.

Goals and objectives – do you have goals and objectives towards which you are proactively working? Do you write your goals down and plan how you are going to achieve them? Many sources publish statistics that demonstrate that if you write your goals down, not only will you be in a minority but also you have a better chance of achieving them. For me, the visibility, the reminder and the emotion attached to this drive your action. When I work with my clients around effective goal planning, the process of writing down the goals actually helps people to truly consider the pain of not achieving the goal and the potential delight of success. In addition, you can more easily see the solutions to potential obstacles before you dive into the planning steps, which quite often too many people jump straight into.

High pay-off activities – these are the truly important actions that you have to undertake to make things happen, to achieve your targets and ultimately succeed with your vision. For example, you want to grow by obtaining new customers. You want 20 new customers this year and, based on your conversion success, you need to have 30 face-to-face meetings that lead to you making a proposal. So your high pay-off activities are those actions you have to undertake to generate that number of meetings.

Immunity to criticism – one thing I can guarantee is, as you grow, succeed and deliver, you will attract criticism. It is out of jealousy that you have made things happen or it is perhaps an attempt to stop you appearing successful. None of that is truly important. However, how do you handle such comments either directly or indirectly? Does it make your blood boil or does it make you more determined? You have to be immune to such expected criticism, and the best way to build that immunity is to keep focused on your motivation and your strong reason why. If you have done something for a purpose, does it matter what others think in the long run?

Just do it – quite often, to avoid procrastination, the best thing to do is to just do it. However, ensure you have a good reason with a calculated risk before diving into an activity. That does not mean you spend days reviewing your spreadsheets, statistics, performance indicators, etc. Sometimes, what I call an entrepreneurial gut feeling is enough to take action. Too many times have I seen entrepreneurs delay action on an idea and lose the maximum opportunity. After all, whatever happens is only ever a learning opportunity. Provided it is not too expensive (hence the calculated risk), you can review the outcome, be honest with yourself and identify what has to be done differently next time. I have always said that every action has an outcome, whether it is the desired result or one from which we learn and don't repeat in the future.

Keep it simple – please do not overcomplicate your growth plans and thereby make it too difficult to achieve or too complex for your team to deliver. Keep it simple, not because we are all stupid but, when goals are specific, measurable, achievable and realistic, there is more chance they will be achieved in the desired time. Yes, when growing a business there are infrastructure and logistic considerations to be made, but primarily, if you generate more leads, convert more leads to sales, increase the value received per sale and deliver the promise to retain your customers for longer, then you will grow a business.

Leadership – first, consider who you lead. The obvious is your employees, but your team is much larger than this. Your team may include your subcontractors, your network and your trusted advisers. You may also be leading the perception of your customers. Good leaders create a vision that inspires people to do the right things in the pursuit of its achievement. Then motivate and inspire people to engage with the vision, whilst managing the delivery of the vision in a proactive way. Good leadership brings together those skills that are needed to get the right things done but also done right the first time.

Marketing – this is a particular passion of mine and I will simply break this into the three key areas: strategy, tactics and measurement. What is your marketing strategy? Consider who you want to attract, and develop your proposition to ensure that the business is positioned to engage the interest of your ideal prospect. You want your prospect to get to know, like and trust you to motivate their buying habits and decisions. Then consider the tactics you are going to use to attract them. Is it online or offline? Primarily, it is to ensure you are fishing in the right pond with the right tool to catch what you desire. Finally, you should be measuring your marketing; otherwise, how do you know that it is the best use of your resources in terms of time and money?

No – do you have the ability to say no? It is not always easy, but sometimes you have to be strong and refuse, decline or simply say no. It may be taking on a new customer that is not right for your business or considering an option that will impact on your work/life balance. Again, having a strong reason why will help with your effective decision making.

One – of anything is dangerous. It can work, but for most businesses having one customer, one supplier, one key employee, one product, one income source, one marketing activity, etc. can result in difficult times. Consider your 'ones' and how you can spread the risk.

Personalities and behavioural style – how well do you work with other people or have you considered whether your team can work together effectively and efficiently? I am an advocate of understanding the personalities around you and how you can work to the best of your ability with their behavioural style. They may be your team, they may be a supplier or a customer, but you can get better results from your relationships if these styles are known and understood. Do you need to give direction or perhaps give praise? Should your communication be verbal or written? You can profile people using many of the tools available, or quite often many of the core characteristics can be understood by allowing the individual to talk and simply listening.

Quality – how do you ensure that you deliver quality throughout your business? What is considered as 'excellence' with everything that you do? What impacts your service levels, those first impressions, your operational excellence, excellent recruitment or effective marketing? Every time someone touches your business, how do you ensure that you deliver a quality, memorable experience that gets them coming back for more, time and time again?

Return on investment – this is a key performance measure that I use in every business that I am involved with. However, this is not simply a question in relation to the actual money I have invested. Yes, you need to know the numbers relating to your ROI; however, also consider your return on your time and people investment. Quite often, these considerations identify trends that often reflect later in the financial elements of the business. How are you maximising your time, managing your time effectively and ensuring that you best use every second? If you don't use the next minute effectively then in 60 seconds it will be gone forever. Also, how are you managing the best return from your investment in your people? How well are your people managed, measured and developed? How are the best recruited and retained? Are they trained, following a proven system that is regularly tested, and do they know the return expected of them?

Systemise your processes – when you know what works, what works best and gets the results you desire, then systemise it. Then train and manage people to follow the system, ideally without deviation. Yes, you will want to always develop and improve your systems, but that is a different activity. Encouraging your people to follow the system without any deviation ensures that it is tested and proven to work or tweaked before it is released to the masses. When you see a system work and followed without interpretation, you will only see positive results.

Team – together everyone achieves more. Yes, it is a common phrase, but it is also so true. Your team starts with your employees but includes other internal and external resources. As mentioned earlier, your team may include your subcontractors, your network and your trusted advisers, but can even include your suppliers and customers. For example, your suppliers may play a key part in the delivery of your physical product or your service offering.

Unique – what is unique about you? What is your differentiator? Please do not rely on one of the common phrases 'I offer a better service', because this is often difficult to measure and does not simply mean you answer the phone more quickly or smile more often. You may be unique, a common characteristic of your team may be unique or perhaps the sector or vertical market is unique for your offering. Know what is unique about you and your business and communicate this at every opportunity as it helps to make you stand out from the crowd.

Vision and mission – what do you truly want to achieve with your business? Why are you truly in business? Where are you planning to take the business? What is your exit strategy? Without a vision or a mission statement, then how will you ever know when you have got there and how do you establish what needs to be undertaken to achieve it.?

Work/life balance – it is so often placed on the back burner as entrepreneurs strive to be the best they can be, deliver the best business model possible and meet all the customers' expectations. Yes, these are positive factors, but they are likely to lead to burn out if you are not focused on your work/life balance. For me, the important aspect of a work/life balance is knowing what you truly want and not just striving to achieve what others may define as a positive work/life balance. I know more than one entrepreneur who does not want such and it would have the opposite effect on them if they were not working. However, too often, I hear people say they don't want to work weekends or evenings but still do because they have no real reason not to work. So, if I gave you every night off, every weekend off and one day per week off, what would you do with the time? Spend it with your family, play a sport, participate in a hobby? When you know this, truly want this, then I can guarantee that you will normally ensure it happens.

Xplore, Xccelerate, Xpose – I could have said have the X Factor, as many do with this letter, but I am not sure even some of the judges on the actual show know what that means! So, I have taken a play on a few other words I think help your business growth. Explore the opportunities that are around you. Accelerate your action to ensure you deliver in good time and within expectations. Expose yourself more from a marketing perspective. Don't be the best kept secret and get out there, shout about your business and raise awareness with as many of your ideal prospects or referrers as possible.

Yes – this is the word you want to hear in your sales meetings. You want to be asking questions that gain a response of yes, yes, yes. Your marketing communication needs to generate the response, 'Yes, that's me. Yes, that's what I want now.'

Zest and ZZZZ – do you demonstrate positive energy? Do you have the energy that people want to engage with rather than avoid because you are a drain on theirs? Such energy creates a positive first impression with the people that you touch. And, finally, ensure you get some rest. Different people can work best with different amounts of rest, but know your body and know when you personally need to rest and recuperate. This may be by taking a break from an activity, committing to a regular break each day or ensuring you have enough hours of sleep each night.

> **I wish I knew this before I started my first business**
>
> **Know your real numbers**
>
> I was lucky. Before I started my businesses, my career and training had taught me what I needed to know about the numbers in my financial accounts. I understood the lines in my profit and loss account. I knew what expenditure was an expense, cost of sale or capital investment. I understood the elements of a balance sheet and what impacted my cash.
>
> However, what I learnt beyond the theory was the reality that those numbers in your accounts are all outcomes and are influenced by other numbers.
>
> For example, your turnover is likely to be influenced by the number of people you sell to, the number of times they buy and your average order value.
>
> For me, many things in business come back to a number. Of course, your financials, but what about your delivery times, your customer satisfaction ratings, your team happiness score and your service level agreements? So, I encourage you to know the 'real' numbers in your business plus the percentages (e.g. gross margin %), your ratios (e.g. costs-to-sales comparison across periods) and the trends that are related to your numbers.

Key points

- Have you considered how you would exit your business and by when?
- What levers will you be focusing on as you start your business and then grow?
- What do you need to execute in the first 90 days of your 'scale' period?

Additional resources

Books

Norbury, M. (2016) *I Don't Work Fridays*. Rethink Press.
Clear, J. (2018) *Atomic Habits*. New York: Penguin Random House.

CHAPTER 11
WHAT TO DO NEXT

Now it's time to turn your vision into reality.

Congratulations! You've reached the end of this book but, in many ways, your entrepreneurial journey is just beginning. We've covered a comprehensive range of topics, from the earliest stages of conceptualising your business idea to the critical strategies needed to sustain and grow your enterprise.

Throughout these pages, I hope you found the guidance, tools and inspiration to feel confident about the road ahead. Starting a business is a transformative experience, one that will test your resilience, push your boundaries and reward your efforts in ways you never imagined.

The journey of entrepreneurship is rarely a straight path, and challenges are an inevitable part of the process. However, every hurdle you overcome is a step closer to your vision.

By applying the principles and frameworks we've explored, you're equipped to navigate the unexpected with clarity and confidence.

Let's revisit some of the key considerations:

- **Lay the foundation:** success begins with thoughtful planning and clear goals. By addressing the initial considerations and crafting a solid plan, you've taken the essential first steps.
- **Focus on value:** at the core of any thriving business is a deep understanding of what you offer and how it solves your customers' problems.
- **Market with purpose:** your marketing, sales and profit strategies are what translate your vision into reality. Remember to adapt to your audience and measure your efforts to refine them continually.
- **Build relationships:** whether it's your team, your customers, or your network, investing in relationships is what will set you apart. People buy into people, not just products or services.
- **Exceed expectations:** exceptional businesses don't just meet customer needs, they anticipate and surpass them, turning clients into loyal advocates.

This book is not the end of your learning but the beginning. Keep seeking knowledge, testing your ideas and refining your approach. Remember that every entrepreneur faces challenges, but those who persist and adapt are the ones who succeed.

Above all, believe in yourself and your ability to create something meaningful.

Now, it's time to put what you've learned into action. Start small, stay focused, and never lose sight of your goals. The entrepreneurial spirit within you will fuel your journey, and the future you create will be a testament to your vision and determination.

Here's to your success, your growth and the incredible adventure ahead. Go out there and build the business you've always dreamed of, one step, one decision, one inspired action at a time.

Good luck and remember: the possibilities are limitless and you are in control.

INDEX

21/90 rule 22
80/20 rule 13, 98, 299–301
90-day plan 324–6

accessibility 286
accident book 118
accountability 270
accountants 52, 145
accounting records 140
acquisition cost 187
acquisitions and mergers 312
active listening 223
adaptability 5, 7
adaptation 40, 324
advertising 175, 194–5, 209, 259, 320
   online 179, 181
advocacy 288
affiliate programme 205–6
agendas 297
alignment with larger brands 191
Amazon 6, 199
annual accounts 146
annual form P9D/P11D 120
Ansoff Matrix 321–2
appetite 326
Apple 6
application form 261, 262
appraisals 279
artificial intelligence (AI) 120
Asana 302
assertiveness 19
asset finance 138, 140
assets 125–6
   current 126
   depreciation of 117
   fixed 125
assumptive questions 224
attention, attracting 175

attitude 326
audience, reaching 178–80
automation 28, 120, 174, 190, 294, 303
average cost per customer 134
average invoice value 134
average order value 134
average transaction value 314, 315–16
awards 196–7

background checks 112
balance sheet 125
balanced approach 40
bank account 53, 139, 143–5
banners 201
Behance 260
behavioural style 7, 329
benchmarking 241
big data analytics 120
big picture thinkers 89
Blanchard, Ken 280
blogs 179
body language 223
bonus calculations 275
bounce rate 199
brain 11–12
brand positioning 106
break-even point 128–31
broadcasting advertisements 179
budgeting 145–8, 156, 326
buildings and contents insurance 109
bullet points 230
business cards 179
business insurances 108–9
business interruption insurance 108, 109
Business Model Canvas 91
business money insurance 109
business name 105–8, 207
business plan 52, 88–100, 138

business revenue and profits, growing
   conversion rate 237, 239
   lifetime value, increase 238, 239
   number of leads 237, 239
   number of sales 237, 239
   profit margin 238, 239
   repurchase rate 238, 239
   value of sales 237, 239
business risks, identifying 306
business scorecard 155
business summary 52
business tax 51

capital allowances 117
capital and reserves 126
caps 138
cash 131–2, 158
cash flow 326
   management 241
cash on delivery 151
cash reserve 157
cash with order 151
cashflow budget 147
cashflow forecast 147
cashflows 146–7
change management 295
change, openness to 7
checklists 297
Clear, James 21
   Atomic Habits 69
client number, increasing 314–15
closure, sales 225–6
cloud computing 120, 121, 302
collaboration 294
collars 138
comfort zone 24
commitment 35, 37–8
communication 220, 279, 294, 302
   auditory 220
   kinaesthetic 220
   personalised 316
   skills 288
   style 286
   technologies 302

visual 220
with customers 48
with staff 47
with suppliers 47
Companies House 51, 54, 107
comparison guide 208
competition 47
competitive advantage 284
competitor analysis 76
complaint handling 284, 287
compliance risks 306
confidence, business 48
conflict avoidance 17, 19
consultative selling 320
contact calendar 202
contacts, re-connecting with 206
content marketing 320, 323
continuous improvement 294
contract hire 140
contract insurance 109
contract of employment 275
control and integration of employees 268
conversion rate 237, 239
copyright 111, 112
core values 56, 136, 169
corporation tax 51, 119
costs
   finance 117
   labour 303
   operating 134
   of sales 134
   of start-up 44–5
   of wrong selling 234
   up-front 303
Covey, Stephen: *7 Habits of Highly Effective People* 97
creativity 3, 4, 12
credibility document 212
credit cards 139
credit control 150–5
credit insurance 109
criticism, immunity to 16, 26, 327–8
culture of excellence 294
customer acquisition cost 134

customer experience 283–8
    consistent excellence through 289–91
    improving 291–3
customer feedback 292
customer knowledge 172
customer profile 188
customer relationship management (CRM)
    software 302
    system 174, 320
customer relationships 173
    building 288–9
    lifetime value 284
customer retention 284, 321
customer review meetings 198
customer satisfaction 55, 287
customer service 323
customer total spend 283
customer-centric experience 289–91
customers, contacts of 192
customers, understanding 322
CVs 259, 261, 262
cybersecurity 302

daily planning 29
dark web 112
data 79, 81
data analytics 303, 324
data-driven insights 24, 55
data protection 54, 111, 115
debt finance 139
debtor days 134, 154
debts 47
    recovering 111
decision making 12, 20, 56
    data-driven 324
delegate 28, 30
designs 112
determination 326
digital marketing 303, 320, 322
digital transformation 120–2
direct mail 178, 179, 191
disappointment 24–5
discipline 5

discounting 231, 247
Disney 6
distractions 27
diversification 320, 323
domestic insurance 108
door-to-door knocking 178, 206

EBITDA (earnings before interest, taxes, depreciation and amortisation) or 'free cash' 136
economic conditions 39
Eisenhower 'Priority' matrix 98
email 178, 302
    auto-response 174
    footer 203
    marketing 212–13, 320, 323
emotional demands 35
emotional intelligence 12
employee referrals 260
employee, defined 254
employees, investing in 323
employers' liability insurance 108, 109
employment documentation 275–6
employment law 110
ending balance 147
entrepreneur mindset 4–7
entrepreneur, definition 4
Entrepreneur's Circle, The 186
environmental risks 306
equipment investment 117
equity finance 139
ethics and values 327
events 179, 182
exhibitions 178, 179
exit options 10, 317–19
expectations, customer 288
expenditure list 94
expenses 156–7
expert hotline 200
expertise 286
expertise seminar 200

Facebook 196, 209, 260
face-to-face meetings 179

failure 71
    learning from 26
    reasons for 46-8
family support 42, 139, 327
FEAR (False Expectations Appearing Real) acronym 17
fear 48
    overcoming 17-20
    responses to 17-18
feedback 202, 286, 303-5
Ferrari 6
fight-or-flight response 17
finance lease 140
finance, raising 138-40
financial controls 47
financial health indicator 241
financial management 156-7
financial plan 156
financial records 140-2
financial risks 306
financial stability 40
fixed costs 136
fixed rates 138
flexibility 324
Focus 5
focus groups 74
food hygiene certificate 277
forecasting 145-8, 326
forms 297
franchise, buying 61-2, 111
free cash 131-2
free taster 205
friendliness 286
friends, support of 42, 139, 327
frontal lobe 12

Gantt chart 171
Gerber, Michael E.: *E-Myth, The* 82, 264
gift, promotional 203
GitHub Jobs 260
giveaways 190-1
Glassdoor 260
goals 55, 327
    business 38

failure to achieve 24
    personal 38
    planning 99, 100
    setting 40
    see also SMART goals
goods in transit 109
Google 173, 216, 293
Google Alerts 196
Google Analytics 81, 174, 197, 292
grant support 139
gross profit/margin 134, 136, 137, 241-2
growth
    business 241, 319-22
    readiness for 313-14
    strategies 322-4
growth opportunities
    defined 311-12
    types of 312
gut feeling 20

habit creation 20-3
habit stacking 21
health and safety 54, 117-18
    documentation, 275
    training 277
health and safety executive 118
helicopter view 86-7
Hersey, Paul 280
high pay-off activities (HPAs) 7, 13-14, 42, 102, 327
hire/lease purchase 140
HM Revenue & Customs (HMRC) 50, 51, 119, 120, 273, 274

impact statement 258
imposter syndrome 14-16
Indeed 260
industry conferences 260
industry job boards 260
information gathering 198
information technology (IT) 114-15
initial public offering (IPO) 318
innovation 4, 55
Instagram 260

instant messaging apps 302
insurance company 54
insurances 108–9
integrated business management systems 302
intellectual property 111–13
interpersonal interactions 12
interruption and distractions log 29, 103–5
interviews 74, 261
investment 241
invoice discounting and factoring 138, 139
isolation, feelings of 42

job description 80, 257, 279
job security 2
joint ventures 203–4
journal 27
journaling 19

Kaizen approach 294
Kennedy, Dan 16
key performance indicators (KPIs) 56, 58, 132, 149–50, 294, 321
key person insurance 108, 109
King, Martin Luther, Jr 58

labour cost 303
landing pages 199
lead funnels (or magnets) 174, 229
lead generation 172–5
leadership 328
  legacy of 270
  ripple effect of 269–70
  styles 81
leading questions 224
leads, number of 237, 239
learning 5, 40
legal considerations 106, 109–11
legal expenses 109
liabilities 126
  current (short-term) 126
  long-term 126

lifestyle plan 37–9
lifetime value 238, 239, 284, 314, 316
limited company 51, 54, 107, 273
LinkedIn 172, 173, 182, 188–9, 216, 259, 261
LinkedIn Groups 189
LinkedIn InMail 189, 205
LinkedIn Invitation 189
listening 223, 320
  active 174, 191–2
lists 202
loss leaders 247
loyalty 56, 283, 288, 316
loyalty programmes 316, 321
luck 48

machine learning technologies 120, 303
mail 179
Maister, David H., Charles H. Green and Robert M. Galford: *Trusted Advisor, The* 220
Making Tax Digital 120
manager, first-time 273–4
market conditions 40
market expansion 55, 312
market opportunity 39
market research 45–6, 52–3, 73–6
market risks 306
marketing 328–9
  activities to win more customers 187–214
  clarity 159–60
  exploring new markets 323
  foundations 161–3
  introduction 160–1
  one-to-one or to multiple 178
  stadium analogy 176
  strategy 163–8
  through storytelling 177
  tracking methods 214–15
marketing budget 184–5
  per customer 186–7
marketing mix 179

marketing plan 168–71
  activity plan 171
  brand and its offering 169–70
  marketing tactics 170
  objectives 168
  stages 171
  understand your audience and markets 168–9
maternity leave 275
McDonalds 199
mean value of your work 26
meditation 19, 27
mental health management 26–9
merchandising 179
mind map 52
mindfulness 19, 27
minimum viable product (MVP) 159
mission *see* vision and mission
mission, vision, values and purpose (MVVP) 271–2
mistakes 29
mood board 52
motivation 9–11, 39
motor insurance 108, 109
multiple marketing methods 178, 181
mystery shopping 74, 287

National Insurance 50, 51, 53, 119, 120
net cash flow 147
net number of days 151
net profit 136
networking 5, 179, 181, 182–3
  events 260
  group 193
Nike 6
No, saying 31, 56–7, 329
Non-Disclosure Agreements (NDAs) 112
north star metric 136

objections 224
objectives *see* goals and objectives
obstacles 79, 83
occipital lobe 12
odd value pricing 247

one-page plan 59–61
one-to-one meetings 182
online advertising 179, 181
online job boards and marketplaces 259–60
online presence 303
open questions 224, 227
opening balance 147
operating costs 134
operating lease 140
operational efficiency 312
operational excellence 55, 294
operational risks 306
operations and processes, optimising 320–1
organisational chart 80, 263
Osterwalder, Alexander 91
outsourcing 28, 30, 42
overheads 47

packaging 179
paraphrasing 224
Pareto Principle *see* 80/20 rule
parietal lobe 12
partnership 50–1
partnership agreement 110
part-time work 40
passion 39
patents 111, 112
pay rates 275
PAYE scheme 53
payment in advance 151
pay-per-click (PPC) advertising 175, 181, 194–5
payroll 275–6
peer-to-peer lending 139
penetration 247
pensions 275
people 79, 80–1
  management 279–80
people-pleasing 19
perception 20
perfectionism 34
  combatting 25–6

performance analysis 241
performance measurement 294
performance monitoring 321
performance reviews 279
person profile 80, 257
person specification 258
personal development 86
personal goals 38
personal income tax 51
personal readiness 40
personalities 329
personality profile assessments 262
physical demands 35
Pigneur, Yves 91
pilot testing 40
plan and stick to it 27
planning 24, 49, 65–9
  poor 48
podcasts 178, 195
Pomodoro technique 98
portable equipment 109
premises and location 110, 115–16
preparation 40
pre-sales 140
price constraints 247
price objections, overcoming 231–2
price setting 245–8
pricing
  basis of 243–5
  fixation on 248
  low 47
  as marketing issue 246–7
  strategy 241
print advertising 179
proactivity 5, 197–8
problem solving 12
process map 296
procrastination 62, 104
product development 45
product innovation 312
product liability 109
product line, expanding 323
product tests 74
professional indemnity 108, 109

professionalism 286
profit and loss account 127–8, 134
profit forecasts 146, 147
profit margins 238, 239, 242–3
project management software 302
project review 26
promotions 203, 247
property-related insurance 54
prospects
  list of 204–5
  paying for 175
protection of business idea 111–13
public liability 108, 109
public speaking, fear of 48–9
purpose 271

QR code 201
quality 329
quality management 294
questioning 74, 224

reality check time 50
reasons
  for business 8–9
  for starting business 15–17
  for starting now 39–40
  to wait 40
recruitment 42, 253–63
references 261, 262
referral bonus programme 260
referral certificates 192
referral contacts 173, 214
referral networking 48
regulations, industry 111
rejection
  avoidance of 17
  fear of 17
repurchase rate 238, 239
reputation 72, 306
research 40
resilience 4
resistance to change 21
resource allocation 312
resource availability 39

resource management and efficiency 302
resourcefulness 5
retainer agreements 315
return on investment (ROI) 55, 80, 187, 312, 329–30
revenue 134
revenue growth 55
reviews 293
RIDDOR 118
risk acceptance 307
risk assessment 275, 306–7
risk avoidance 307
risk management 306, 307, 312
risk matrix 306
risk mitigation 109, 307
risk reduction 307
risk tolerance 5
risk transfer 307

sale, defined 219–20
sale and leaseback 140
sales
   number of 237, 239
   value of 237, 239
sales call 228–30
sales opportunities 222–6
sales process 320, 323
scorecards 155
scoring system 280
scripts 297
search engine optimisation (SEO) 106, 320, 322
secondary research 76
self-assessment return 50, 51, 119
self-care 19, 235
self-compassion 20
self-doubt 19
self-preservation 14
selling
   at low margin 234
   to right client 235
   to wrong client 234
service innovation 312
service line, expanding 323

shareholder agreement 110
Shopfront 179
shortlist 261
sick pay 275
signage
   premises 213
   vehicle 200–1
Sinek, Simon 8
Situational Leadership Model 280
Six Sigma 294
skill gap 253
Skill vs Will Matrix 280
skills 40
skimming 247
Skype 302
Slack 302
sleep 331
SMART goals 55, 146
social media 112, 180, 189, 216, 260, 320
   advertising 179, 181, 292, 323
   see also under names
software 297
   financial 141, 275
   licences 111
sole trader 50
speaking engagements 211
split testing 195
sponsorship 179, 206–7
squeeze page 199
standard letters 297
standard operating procedures, creating 297
standardisation of processes 294
start with why theory 8
starting a business, steps in 49–54
   initial considerations 49–50
   planning your business 52
   positioning 52–3
   promotion 53
   what sort of business are you? 50–2
   whom to inform 53–4
stationery 179
statistics 74, 197
step change 58

step-by-step processes 297
stock turnover days 134
stock, loss of 109
storytelling 177, 195-6
strategic business model 90-4
   channels 92-3
   cost structure 94
   customer relationships 92
   customer segments 92
   external partners and internal resources 94
   key activities 93
   revenue streams/turnover 93
   value proposition 91-2
strategic partnerships 312, 320, 323
strategic planning 312
strategic risks 306
strategic thinking 86-7
Strategyzer 91, 96
stress, entrepreneurial, coping with 29-31
subconscious 11
subcontractor vs employee 267-8
subscription model 316
success drivers 87, 133
success, definition of 5, 10, 58
supply chain 113-14, 140, 295
support network 40
sustainability 241
SWOT analysis 53, 55, 83-6, 87
systems and processes 79, 82, 233, 266, 295-7, 330

taxation 3, 50, 51, 118-20
   employee benefits 120
   limited companies 119
   Pay-As-You-Earn (PAYE) 119-20
   self-employed/partnerships 119
   VAT 119
teams 271, 302, 330
   induction 276-7
   productivity 134
   structure 80
   see also employees
technology 208, 294, 301-3

telecommunications 287
telephoning 178, 179, 192-3
templates 297
temporal lobe 12
test marketing 74
testimonials 209-11
text message 209
time management 30, 38-9, 97-101, 102-5
time, value of 42-3, 122, 248-50
time/worth calculation 250
'to-do' list 102
total income 147
total outgoings 147
Total Quality Management (TQM) 294
traction 79, 81-2
Tracy, Brian: *Eat That Frog* 97
Trade Descriptions Act 111
trademarks 106, 108, 111, 112
trading terms and conditions 110
training and development 277-8, 287, 293, 294, 297
trauma, overcoming 17-20
trust 54, 56, 72, 109, 270
   building 220-1
Trust Creation Process 220
Trustpilot 173, 293
turnover 131, 132
   cash 132
   margin 132
   market share 132
   number of customers 132
   profit 132
   value 132

unique selling point (USP) 91, 95, 106
universities and colleges 261
unplugging 27
upselling 198-9, 315

value, giving 174
value for money 286
value proposition 95-7, 320
Value Proposition Canvas 96-7

values 271
variable rates 138
VAT 50, 51, 53, 141
verbal contract 110
video 178, 297
video conferencing platforms 302
video platforms 194
virtual presence tools 302
vision and mission 79, 80, 251, 271, 330
vision board 10, 38, 104
visionary thinking 4
voicemail 178
volunteering 201–2

Web pages 75, 179
webinars 178, 260
website 76, 173–4, 180, 291–2, 320
weekly planning 29
'What, Why and So' sales technique 227–8

WhatsApp 178
wish list 204
word of mouth 179, 284
work/life balance 37, 41–4, 273, 329, 331
workflows 297
working 'in' the business 264–6
working 'on' the business 264–6
working capital 46
working hours 41
worst-case scenarios 17

X (formally known as Twitter) 260

yoga 19
Young, Edward 104
YouTube 194

zest 331
Zoom 302